Crosscurrents / Modern Critiques / Third Series

Edited by Jerome Klinkowitz

Richard Kostelanetz

The New Poetries and Some Old

Southern Illinois University Press
<small>CARBONDALE AND EDWARDSVILLE</small>

Printed in the United States of America
Edited by Mara Lou Hawse
Designed by Design for Publishing, Inc.
Production supervised by Natalia Nadraga

94 93 92 91   4 3 2 1

Library of Congress Cataloging-in-Publicaton Data

Kostelanetz, Richard.
  The new poetries and some old / Richard Kostelanetz.
    p. cm.
  Includes index.
  1. American poetry—20th century—History and criticism.
2. Poetry. I. Title.
PS323.5.K59   1991
811'.509—dc20
ISBN 0-8093-1656-0   90-9886
                                                      CIP

Requests for permission to quote should be directed to: Richard
Kostelanetz, P.O. Box 444, Prince Street, New York, New York 10012-
0008

The paper used in this publication meets the minimum requirements of
American National Standard for Information Sciences — Permanence of
Paper for Printed Library Materials, ANSI Z39.48-1984. ∞

for Charles Doria

There is a poetry independent of an idea and which only acts in words, in a verbal music, in a succession of vowels and consonants.

—Honore Balzac, translated by Peter Mayer

Above all I think that the rhythmic aspect [of language] contains unimagined possibilities. Not only in music is rhythm the most elementary, directly physically grasping means for effect, which is the joy of recognizing something known before, the importance of repeating, which has a connection with the pulsation of breathing, the book, ejaculation. It is wrong that jazz bands have the monopoly of giving collective rhythmic ecstasy. The drama and poetry can also give it.

—Öyvind Fahlström, "Manifesto for Concrete Poetry" (1953)

But there is always an avant-garde in the sense that someone, somewhere is always trying to do something which adds to the possibilities for everybody, and that that large everybody will some day follow this somebody and use whatever innovations were made as part of their workaday craft.

—Dick Higgins, "Intermedia" (1984)

Anxiety is based on the desire to exclude or subordinate, to preserve the values of benefits of society for the group of right people who know the right answers.

—Northrop Frye, "Rear-View Mirror" (1978)

Criticism reminds every art, no matter what its claims to grandeur, that it is composed of mortal as well as immortal elements, and that it is not always clear which is which— reminding it that just that element which everyone thought guaranteed its immortality at the time of its making may turn out to be just the element that will make it look vulnerable and mortal to a future generation.

—Donald Kuspit, "The Subjective Aspect of Critical Evaluation"
(1985–86)

Richard Kostelanetz usually uses more words.

—Among a magazine's contributors' notes to a four-word poem,
New York Quarterly (1989)

Contents

Crosscurrents/
Modern Critiques/
Third Series

I N THE EARLY 1960s, when the Crosscurrents/Modern Critiques series was developed by Harry T. Moore, the contemporary period was still a controversial one for scholarship. Even today the elusive sense of the present dares critics to rise above mere impressionism and to approach their subject with the same rigors of discipline expected in more traditional areas of study. As the first two series of Crosscurrents books demonstrated, critiquing contemporary culture often means that the writer must be historian, philosopher, sociologist, and bibliographer as well as literary critic, for in many cases these essential preliminary tasks are yet undone.

To the challenges that faced the initial Crosscurrents project have been added those unique to the past two decades: the disruption of conventional techniques by the great surge in innovative writing in the American 1960s just when social and political conditions were being radically transformed, the new worldwide interest in the Magic Realism of South American novelists, the startling experiments of textual and aural poetry from Europe, the emergence of Third World authors, the rising cause of feminism in life and literature, and, most dramatically, the introduction of Continental theory into the previously staid world of Anglo-American literary scholarship. These transformations demand that many traditional treatments be rethought, and part of the new responsibility for Crosscurrents will be to provide such studies.

Contributions to Crosscurrents/Modern Critiques/Third Series will be distinguished by their fresh approaches to established topics and by their opening up of new territories for discourse. When a single author is studied, we hope to present the first book on his or her work or to explore a previously untreated aspect based on new research. Writers who have been critiqued well elsewhere will be studied in comparison with lesser-known figures, sometimes from other cultures, in an effort to broaden our base of understanding. Critical and theoretical works by leading novelists, poets, and dramatists will have a home in Crosscurrents/Modern Critiques/Third Series, as will sampler-introductions to the best in new Americanist criticism written abroad.

The excitement of contemporary studies is that all of its critical practitioners and most of their subjects are alive and working at the same time. One work influences another, bringing to the field a spirit of competition and cooperation that reaches an intensity rarely found in other disciplines. Above all, this third series of Crosscurrents/Modern Critiques will be collegial—a mutual interest in the present moment that can be shared by writer, subject, and reader alike.

Jerome Klinkowitz

Preface

I've had trouble with this myself, everybody telling me or implying
that I shouldn't really write the way I do. What do they want, that
I should write some other way I'm not interested in? Which is the
very thing that doesn't interest me in their prose & poetry &
makes it a long confused bore?—all arty & by inherited rule & no
surprises no new invention—corresponding inevitably to their own
dreary characters. . . .

> —Allen Ginsberg, "When the Mode of the Music Changes the
> Walls of the City Shake" (1961)

THIS IS THE sequel to an earlier book, *The Old Poetries
and the New* (University of Michigan Press, 1981), which
is similarly a collection of essays organized around a theme—
how current avant-gardes (and their precursors) diverge from
more familiar work. Thus, in the opening section, The Old
Poetries, were essays about Ezra Pound, John Ashbery, and
Allen Ginsberg, as well as post-World War II poetry in general;
in the later section were essays on John Cage, Dick Higgins,
Jerome Rothenberg, Emmett Williams, and E. E. Cummings
(emphasizing his most innovative works), as well as visual po-
etry and sound poetry.

The Old Poetries and the New was put into Donald Hall's Poets
on Poetry series to expand its scope beyond the university
poets featured before me. However, since far fewer copies of
my book were sold than any other volume in the series, Hall
and I agreed that it must have fallen *outside* the boundaries of
his project. In a recent promotional flier for the University of
Michigan Press's poetry books, it was omitted entirely, prompt-
ing me to ask whether my book was still in print with them. It

is available, I'm told, though seeing is believing. (Rumor has it that the comparative unsuccess of my book, along with Hall's generous commitment to representing avant-garde poets, prompted the founding of a Southern Illinois University Press series, "Poetics of the New," that has so far included the collected criticisms of Dick Higgins and Barrett Watten. So much for history.)

This new book collects essays not included there, most of them written in the decade since that book was put together; since the volumes are complementary, articulating a similar theme, the new title echoes the earlier one. However, there is a distinct difference in emphasis. Since the governing dichotomy of the earlier book is by now less unfamiliar, here newer poetries are discussed first. Both books conclude with my observations on my own work. Another difference between the two books comes from my going to Europe to work in 1981 for the first time in sixteen years and returning there annually ever since, thus making me more immediately aware of cultural differences between here and there.

What remains constant is my commitment to the esthetics of high modernism— innovation, abstraction, intelligence, and complexity in all the arts; for what I like in poetry usually resembles, in a fundamental way, what I like in music or painting. I remain devoted as well to the principles of intermedia and the concomitant expansion of the territory of art, both in general and in particular, all of which is, in my view, continuing. The first commitment accounts for why I've resisted "postmodernism" and related retrograde fads, including such current poetic aberrations as, say, rhymed verse. In poetry as well as other arts, my taste still inclines to the most extreme, the most audacious, the most innovative, the most idiosyncratic, especially when incorporated in formats previously unavailable to poetry. The second commitment—to expanding the field—accounts for why many of these essays deal with audio, video, and other new media for poetry. Given these two overarching principles, it is scarcely surprising that the subjects of my essays are so different from those featured in poetry magazines or other collections of criticism of recent poetry. It should not be forgotten that critical courage comes not only from taking an opinion different from the common run (see me on Joseph Brodsky) but also from selecting different subjects. Beyond that, I've tried to write genuine poetry *criticism* at a time when, to put it generously, most commentary about poetry came from people implicitly trying to do something else.

I noted long ago that what distinguishes conservative critics from those predisposed to the avant-garde is that the latter eventually get around to producing their own creative work and that this creative work at its best (and truest) reflects principles articulated in their criticism. Given my critical interest in intermedia, beginning with *The Theatre of Mixed Means* (1968), it follows that most of my poetry belongs to literary intermedia, initially visual poetry, then audio poetry, more recently video poetry and holopoetry, as my colleague Eduardo Kac calls our mutual poetic interest in language-based holography. However, the further I have moved into creative work, the less interested I have become in writing the kinds of "disinterested" arts history I did in the 1960s (culminating in my introduction to *Possibilities of Poetry* [Dell, 1970]). Since the 1970s, I've been more inclined to write theoretical essays, polemical position papers, often in an autobiographical mode. I've not resisted the opportunity to write about my own work, in part because I feel critically responsible for its initial reception but also because I've always admired artists such as Moholy-Nagy and John Cage, who understood their work better than their commentators.

I would like to think that the variety of original sources for these essays reflects a certain personal/professional integrity, to use a word that is not often heard in critical discussion nowadays; for I chose my own subjects and made my own decisions, rather than toeing one or another editorial line. The variety also accounts for differences in degree of explanation and cultural pitch, as well as those introductory repetitions that wouldn't be necessary if all the pieces were originally addressed to a single audience. Indeed, the fact that these essays have appeared so variously becomes a good reason for collecting them between a single set of covers. Every effort has been made to verify the spelling of all proper names; if any error or omission has occurred, it will be corrected in subsequent editions, providing that appropriate notification is submitted in writing to the author. Finally I am grateful to many colleagues, beginning with Jerome Klinkowitz, for supporting my critical work, sometimes against predictable opposition to it; to publishers for letting me reprint work initially done for them; to Mara Lou Hawse for copyediting the manuscript; to Charlotte Bonica for her criticisms; to Nisma Zaman, assisted by Desirée Ortiz, for the index; and to Kenney Withers, Curtis Clark, and their colleagues for contracting and producing it. May we celebrate together in Heaven.

Richard Kostelanetz, New York, New York, May 1990

Acknowledgments

INTERVIEWS AND ESSAYS contained in *The New Poetries and Some Old* previously appeared in the following journals, newspapers, magazines, and books:

American Book Review: "Claims by Poets? (1985)," "False and True: Criticism of Avant-Garde Writing (1986)," "Avant-Garde Poetry in America Now (1986)," "Literary Videotapes (1989)"
American Poetry Review: "Kenneth Burke at 92 (1990)," "John Berryman (1969)"
Black River Review: "Notes on 'Duets, Trios & Choruses' (1988)"
Bookmark—University of Missouri at Kansas City: "*Arenas, etc.:* An Introduction (1982)"
Boston Review: "Joseph Brodsky: 'I Keek It, I Vin It' (1987)"
Centennial Review: "On Anthologies (1987)"
Hackett Publishing Company: "Michael Joseph Phillips (1980)"
High Performance, Sound Choice, Theater Ex, Ice River: "Why Audio Theater Now (1986)" in different versions
Horn of Plenty: "S. Foster Damon, 1893–1971 (1968–90)"
Massachusettes Review: Earlier version of "John Berryman (1969)"
Michigan Quarterly Review: "Northrop Frye (1975)"
New England Review/Bread Loaf Quarterly: "Literary Holography (1990)"
New York Arts Journal, PN Review, Art and Artist, and *Chronicles:* "Unloaded Canons (1980, 1989)"
New York Quarterly and *Chiron Review:* "Notes on the Poetry Biz, 1985–89 (1990)"

New York Times: "Making Music from the Sound of Words (1977)"
New York Times Book Review: "Thomas Merton (1978)," "Ezra Pound: A Person of Arts (1981)"
Northwest Review: "Teaching and the Nonstandard Writer (1989)"
Perspectives of New Music: "Milton Babbitt's Text-Sound (1987)"
Pulpsmith and *Art & Artists:* "Herd of Independent Minds (1987)"
Re*dact: "The Republic of Letters (1984)"
Shantih: "The Literature of SoHo (1983)"
Talisman: "Video Writing (1987)"
Textile Bridge Press, Clarence Center, N.Y.: "Harry Polkinhorn's *Anaesthesia* (1985)"
The World & I: "Americans Make Audio Art in Germany (1989)"
Woodrose: "Interview (1983)"

The New Poetries

It is to divorce words from the enslavement of the prevalent clichés that all the violent torsions (Stein, Joyce) have occurred; violent in direct relation to the gravity and success of their enslavements.

—William Carlos Williams, *The Embodiment of Knowledge* (1974)

Any artist does not know that he is advance-guard, he must be told so or learn it from the reaction of the audience. *All* original composition—classical, standard, or advance-guard—occurs at the limits of the artist's knowledge, feeling and technique. Being a spontaneous act, it risks, supported by what one has already grown up to, something unknown. The action of all art accepts an inner problem and concentrates on a sensuous medium.

—Paul Goodman, *"Advance-Guard* Writing in America: 1900–1950" (1951)

Poetry starts with sound as a positive, rather than as differential or negative, value: sound as engineering meaning, its corpse—begotten, *gnosis,* knowledge. No ideas but as sound. Are there *purely* visual ideas? Sure, just as olfactory, or tactile. *Synaesthesia. Thought* as mediating among these, supra-ideational. To sound the language, make it resound. . . .

As against other writing practices, poetry explicitly holds open the possibility of producing, rather than reproducing, ideas. Beyond that, it may make this production of ideas audible—in measuring and placing, sounding and breaking; and visible—in page scoring and design.

—Charles Bernstein, "Living Tissue/Dead Ideas" (1984)

"Mixed media" . . . is a venerable term from art criticism, which covers works executed in more than one medium, such as oil color and guache. But by extension it is also appropriate to such forms as the opera, where the music, the libretto, and the mise-en-scène are quite separate: at no time is the opera goer in doubt as to whether he is seeing the mise-en-scène, the stage spectacle, hearing the music, etc. Many fine works are being done in mixed media: paintings which incorporate poems within their visual fields, for instance. But one knows which is which. In intermedia, on the other hand, the visual element (painting) is fused conceptually with the words.

—Dick Higgins, "Intermedia" (1984)

Avant-Garde Poetry in America Now (1986)

> Whenever there appears an art that is truly new and original, the
> men who denounce it first and loudest are artists. Obviously,
> because they are the most engaged. No critic, no outraged
> bourgeois, can match an artist's passion in repudiation.
> —Leo Steinberg, "Contemporary Art and
> the Plight of its Public" (1962)

THE SUREST DEFINITION I know of *avant-garde* is
"those who march ahead of the pack." In art the term
refers to work that suggests the future by making drastic
departures from not only the traditions of art but from the
currently predominant conventions. Such work is so different
it is thoroughly unacceptable to those comfortably in the main-
stream. Customarily they ignore it. If pressed to make a judg-
ment, they usually cite the most obvious aspects of departure
as sufficient reason for a perfunctory dismissal (and then usu-
ally ask the questioner for smug consent, in an implicit illustra-
tion of self- serving narrow-mindedness).

It is not for nothing that avant-garde work rarely appears
in *Poetry,* that it is always excluded from pseudo-definitive
anthologies, even one as recent as Helen Vendler's *The Har-
vard Book of Contemporary American Poetry* (1985). It cannot be
for nothing that practitioners of avant-garde poetry are never
awarded professional prizes and are not invited to teach "po-
etry workshops" in the M.F.A. programs. Were their work not
so different (and apparently so threatening), it would not
be so thoroughly excluded; this is an elementary (and fairly
objective) measure of its avant-garde value.

For the last quarter century, there have been in every American art two, divergent, avant-gardes. One would purify the materials of the medium—Ad Reinhardt and minimalism in painting, Elliott Carter and Milton Babbitt in music composition, primary structures in sculpture. The other avant-garde would mix the materials of one art with another—happenings in the visual arts, John Cage in music composition, Alwin Nikolais, among others, in dance. One useful term for this art that incorporates two (or more) arts is *Intermedia*.

In our poetry as well, work that is genuinely avant-garde has gone in divergent directions, one emphasizing language and the possibilities of it alone (and is thus often called "language-centered"), and the other mixing language with the media of visual art and music. Both these new strains of poetry were initially called "concrete," a label that once seemed so encompassingly applicable to new work that was so different from mainstream poetry, that regarded language as empirical matter, apart from symbolic and even syntactical considerations. However, even within the "concrete poetry" that appeared in print, one could clearly distinguish work in which language was visually enhanced from poems in which words were only isolated or fragmented. The former should be called "visual poetry" and as such distinguished from another intermedium—"sound poetry"—that mixes language with structures more typical of music and is, thus, usually not printed but heard.

The other avant-garde of American poetry has been concerned with purifying language—with using it sparely and abstractly, in isolation, often with fragments, all to discover what poetry is possible in structured language alone. Within this general direction belong aleatory poetry, asyntactic poetry, modular poems, and minimal poems, among others. This sort of avant-garde poetry is easier to do than intermedia, and has, perhaps for that reason, attracted more adherents. It is scarcely surprising that each avant-garde has developed its own magazines, in addition to its own critical-theoretical journals: first *L-A-N-G-U-A-G-E* and now *Poetics Journal* for the purists, and my own *Precisely* for literary intermedia.

Both avant-gardes departed radically from the kinds of poetry established in the American magazines and universities during the post-World War II decades—kinds of poetry that are still visible today, needless to say, even if their edge has dulled; both avant-gardes share certain esthetic assumptions about the impersonal use of language and the importance of mediumistic discovery. However, in the quarter-century that they have been alive, the two avant-gardes have moved apart from each other, each at its most parochial, scarcely acknowledging that the other exists. This is unfortunate, because the dismissive criticisms they (we) were trying hardest to refute (and still must work to refute) in these stagnant times come not from each other but from the entrenched remnants of the rear-guard.

The Literature of SoHo
(1983)

In many respects the literature of experimental Modernism which emerged in the last years of the nineteenth century and developed into the present one was an art of cities, especially of the polyglot cities, the cities which, for various historical reasons, had acquired high activity and great reputations as centers of intellectual and cultural exchange.
                    —Malcolm Bradbury, "The Cities of Modernism" (1976)

WRITERS OUTSIDE NEW York City customarily perceive it as a monolithic entity, a single city with a single literary world. However, just as New York itself incorporates many communities, so it has not one literary "scene" but several, each hardly in contact with the others; and the lines dividing the writers of the city are as much those of residence as of style. Within Manhattan alone, there are at least four distinct literary neighborhoods, which I conveniently call Upper East Side, Upper West Side, Village, and SoHo. It can be observed that each neighborhood has not only a particular social style but a unique literary style as well. Moreover, in each group are writers who feel profoundly "out of place" in neighborhoods other than their own.

For two decades now the most famous "literary watering hole" on the Upper East Side has been Elaine's, a restaurant on Second Avenue near Eighty-eighth Street; and the "writers" it reportedly attracts are largely journalists working for newspapers and slick magazines or the authors of best-sellers and/ or films, such as Gay Talese, George Plimpton, Bruce Jay

Friedman, David Halberstam, Woody Allen, and Nora Ephron, among others. These are the kinds of writers featured at the Ninety-second Street YMHA, which has become their neighborhood's principal literary platform. Elaine's is comparatively expensive (as is its imitator, Niccolo's), and so are the apartments on the Upper East Side.

The Upper West Side, by contrast, tends to house writers who also teach at universities or work for less slick cultural magazines. These writers usually have families (and are thus less inclined to patronize restaurants); and for the same amount of monthly rent as might be paid on the East Side, they can currently get, on Manhattan's West Side, an apartment twice as large. The West Side equivalent of Elaine's is Zabar's, which is, indicatively, not a restaurant but a gourmet food store. Most of the so-called New York Intellectuals live here, and so do the novelists Isaac Bashevis Singer, Joseph Heller, Elizabeth Hardwick, et al. (It should be understood that the term New York Intellectuals is a misnomer, as it does *not* refer to all intellectuals resident in New York but a particular clique that has opportunistically appropriated a general category exclusively for itself.)

The Village literary scene centers around St. Marks-in-the-Bowery Church, which has the oldest continuous poetry reading program in downtown New York. It is here that the so-called New York School of poets congregates; and though that epithet has been passé for the past decade, its followers survive. (This term too is a misnomer, needless to say perhaps, coined as it was to exploit a previous identical term for a certain group of painters. The earlier term was likewise a misnomer, artists emulating artists and art publicity art publicity, very much as art imitates art.) Village writers are largely poets and largely single. Their watering holes are the apartment parties that are improvised after poetry readings. In different ways, the doyens of this literary community are Allen

Ginsberg and John Ashbery; its younger stars include Anne Waldman and Ron Padgett, both of whom have at different times personally directed the St. Marks poetry programs.

New York City zoning ordinances have restricted residence in the industrial neighborhood South of Houston Street (and thus south of the Village) to "certified" artists who can justify the need for larger loft spaces. (In practice, slides, a resumé and references are presented to a city commission which can decide to grant certification in the form of a legal variance.) Traditionally, a writer has been unable to obtain the certification required to live in SoHo unless he or she were also a visual artist, a composer, or a playwright, or married to one. (I remember, in my own case, in 1974, that I had to make a special plea to prove that I did visual art *in addition to* the writing that was more familiar to the commission members.) Given this legal restriction on the kinds of writers who can live here, it is scarcely surprising that the literature of SoHo relates closely to current developments in the nonliterary arts. Not only are SoHo's writers more likely to incorporate the kinds of esthetic ideas more familiar in other arts, but they are more likely to work and publish (i.e., to make public) in other media as well. Its platforms are Franklin Furnace, which doubles as an exhibition gallery for printed materials, and the Kitchen, especially for literature in media other than the printed page.

It should be understood that in defining these neighborhood categories I am talking ultimately not about residence but about literary style—not only where you live but what kind of writing you choose to do and how you choose to conduct your literary life. Not everyone writing in New York City belongs to the literary scene in which he actually resides, and some have overlapping allegiances, while many writers have none.

It follows that not everyone writing in SoHo writes SoHo literature. In the several years that Lawrence Shainberg lived here he wrote conventional fiction and a commercial book about brain surgery. (It was his wife, a painter, who got him past the certification barrier.) Others, including myself, write SoHo literature some of the time and more conventional writing at other times. (This introduction is not SoHo literature, although my contributions to an anthology of it purportedly are.) Conversely, it follows that one need not live in SoHo proper to do SoHo writing. John Cage, in certain respects, the father of SoHo literature, has for the past three decades lived successively in exurban Rockland County, the West Village, and Chelsea.

The distinctive characteristic of SoHo literature is its close relation, in both style and society, to advanced developments in the other arts—the visual arts, the musical arts, choreography. That is to say that SoHo writing is concerned, like the other SoHo arts, with issues of abstraction and minimalism, of fragmentation, of alternative scale and coherence, of patterning and difficulty, of perceptual stretching, of unconventional signature, of the exploration of media other than one's initial mastery (which, for writers, would be the printed page). It follows that such writing is *not* about expressionism or about classicism or about "poetic feeling" or about realistic portrayals—it is *not* about all the styles and stances that are taught in the creative writing programs of America; it does not observe any of the other more commercial literary fashions. Both the art and literature of SoHo are concerned with discovering the radical possibilities of one's art, rather than the exploitation of familiar conventions. To put it differently, this is writing that approaches Art and still remains Literature.

It follows that many of its authors work in arts other than writing—Claes Oldenburg doing sculpture and, in the past, performance; Dick Higgins doing musical composition and performance, in addition to distinguished book publishing; John Cage and Jackson Mac Low doing music and performance; Alison Knowles and Rosemarie Castoro doing sculpture; myself doing audio, video, and holography; and so on.

Many of us do mixed media, such as a visual field of separate words and images, in addition to intermedia, such as designs in which word and image are entwined. Some also write criticism of the avant-garde arts.

Most of us have evolved plural professional situations, where we can do one art one day and another the next, as our spirits and schedules move us; and since it took me a while to get to this point where I can move easily from one to another, I am scarcely alone in objecting to the use of artistic categories to characterize people, rather than work. I personally create videotapes and films as well as writing, and I know at firsthand the technical as well as creative differences between video and film, say, as well as between both and writing. However, I resent such purported definitions as "writer" or "filmmaker," because they not only lie about my creative activity, they restrict it. I am not a "filmmaker" when I make films and a "writer" when I write. I am a human being involved in a variety of artistic situations. I do not change heads in going from one art to the other; I scarcely change clothes. Second, professional categories function to make disciplinary transgressions into a pseudo-event—a "poet's film" is no different in essence from anyone else's film, while the "artist's book" is, all current rationalizations to the contrary notwithstanding, still a book.

One way I have personally gauged the impact of the community is noticing how my own writing has changed since I moved here in 1974. It is true that I began doing visual poetry in 1967, the year after I moved from the Upper-Upper West Side (north of Columbia University) to the East Village (and thus began an earlier literary metamorphosis); however, while living in a small apartment, I could not make anything larger than 8½-by-11-inch sheets of paper. Once I moved to SoHo, however, in a residential loft that is by neighborhood standards comparatively small (and yet thrice the size of my East Village apartment), I could do silk-screened prints and drawings, and even have a place to hang them amidst my thousands of books. Then, talking with my neighbors made me think about working in media other than paper. By 1975, I had gotten into audiotape and videotape, by 1976 into film, by 1977 into photography, by 1978 into holography, and by 1980 into live theater. Much as I would like to claim full credit for this artistic adventure, I honestly doubt if any of it would have happened had I not moved to SoHo.

II

Choosing a place to live has been for the American artist a problem of the first order.
—Harold Rosenberg, "Tenth Street" (1954)

Outsiders find SoHo an incredible place, and indeed so much that we residents take for granted is really quite extraordinary and singular. Art here is not a recreation practiced in spare time by shy, apologetic people off in the corner of a community; rather, art is here the center of attention in an expanding, thriving one-industry town (located within New York). It is true that the small factories remain in SoHo, producing all sorts of industrial goods; but nearly everyone *resident* here is involved with art in some way—not only as creators but as art entrepreneurs, art handimen, or lovers of artists. Since the business of art involves most people residing here, no one in SoHo need apologize to anyone for working at art all day, or for neglecting bourgeois amenities. Everyone residing in my loft building knows that I arise late in the morning and like to go straight to my typewriter, and rarely do my neighbors disturb me during the day. That is a consideration extended out of respect (or fear) less for me than for the processes of what I do. Because so many people here work on their art all the time, one feels inspired to do so as well, less for competitive reasons than (at least for me) for a sense of appropriateness—that is what everyone does around here. One contributes as well to an esthetic exchange far more intense than any semblance existing anywhere else. When I spent a semester in Austin, Texas, "the place got to me," so to speak, which is to say that nothing I began in Austin got finished there. I found no immediate incentive to complete the kind of work that at home would almost finish itself, so natural and powerful here is the energy for artistic creation and completion.

The central merchandising difference between visual art and literature is that the latter is a wholesale business while the former is retail. That is, an art dealer takes from an artist works that are largely unique (one-of-a-kind) and sells them directly to customers whom he mostly knows. A book publisher, by contrast, takes a manuscript and produces it in an edition of several thousand copies that are distributed not directly to the ultimate customers but to bookstore managers who think they are familiar with the tastes of their regular customers. Therefore, in visual art, unlike literature, artists are often personally acquainted with their customers who indeed sometimes cultivate not only an artist's friendship but his or her advice on other purchases.

To me this central economic difference accounts for why both dealers and artists feel obliged to be personally charming to a degree that writers and book publishers would not. For the latter pair there are middlemen to insulate them from ever having immediate contact with the ultimate customers. Indeed, the publisher hires minions to package favorably not only the book but the author and the publishing house in their public relations, initially not to impress the customer, who has almost no chance of meeting a live author, but the intermediaries who review books and interview authors, which is to say the proprietors of the prominent channels of publicity.

Because art is a retail commodity, rather than wholesale, it is purchased in a different way. Book publishers advertise and solicit reviews not only to persuade customers but to persuade bookstore managers in stocking their stores and filling their windows. New York art dealers do not need advertisements to reach their customers (though they may make take an ad to appease the artist and then include an illustration of work[s] that provincial art dealers might think appropriate for their regular customers). Art dealers scarcely need reviews, because they are selling to individuals who generally buy for one of two other reasons: (1) they actually like the art and think they would enjoy possessing it; (2) they have been advised that it is good, important, and/or worthwhile by someone they trust. That adviser may be the art dealer, especially if the buyer has reason to be pleased with the dealer's previous recommendations; it may be another artist whom the buyer has cultivated. Only an art-buying bumpkin would follow the advice of a periodical reviewer, no matter if his or her notices appear in *Artforum* or *The New York Times*. In truth, published reviews are influential only if a functionary must justify his or her purchase with someone else—only if, say, a curator at a university museum must persuade his or her board of directors. Every time I see a Philip Pearlstein painting in a university museum, as often I do, I calculate that Hilton Kramer's reviews helped sell it.

Given the importance of word-of-mouth recommendations in the art world, it is inevitable that it develops institutions where opinions can be conveyed and measured. One is the art opening, especially at a major New York museum, where people do exchange words about art with one another, in spite of the oppressive crowds. The second is a less formal gathering that takes place in SoHo every Saturday afternoon from the beginning of fall to the end of spring. I call it "SoHo Saturday Afternoon." In essence, SoHo remains a manufacturing community for five daytimes of the week, and that business drips out into the streets in such forms as delivery trucks and Spanish-speaking workers. On Saturday, however, nearly all the factories are closed, while the galleries remain open. People from elsewhere feel that they can walk about without encountering the weekday discomfort of an industrial neighborhood. Friends greet one another and introduce old friends to new friends; and if someone particularly likes a current show, he or she will incidentally tell everyone he or she meets. If that artist is known and if the listener is someone who collects, then an impetus to purchase has been generated. If that artist is unknown, the beginnings of a collectible reputation are made.

Fundamentally, this word-of-mouth process has a certain integrity—more integrity, let's say, than the Saturday reviews in *The New York Times*. While someone may want to corrupt the process by recommending a friend or a lover, there is a limit upon how many people can be reached on Saturday afternoon; and should men and women in this secondary group not like the recommended artist or suspect the motives of their informant, they won't tell anyone else, thus halting the dissemination. On the other hand, if several people independently tell others who in turn tell others, then a reputation has been established on Saturday afternoon, and benefits for that artist will usually follow.

The point of this digression is to show how the literature of SoHo is the victim of a merchandising predicament. It is too unusual, too avant-garde, too difficult, ever to go through commercial channels. Rather, it is published in magazines of modest circulation or in editions of a thousand or less. Such books are then placed in stores such as Printed Matter whose proprietors are personally known to the author; and many buyers of such books are people whom the author has at one time or another met (and perhaps charmed). In process, this is a kind of retailing more characteristic of the visual arts, especially the distribution of limited editions (prints, say) than conventional book publishing. One reason why SoHo literature is so scarcely known is that neither *Publishers Weekly* nor the *New York Times Book Review* is prepared to acknowledge this kind of distribution (let alone this kind of writing). For all that advanced art and literature might resemble each other esthetically, they reach their audiences through radically different channels.

Even the best Soho literature is thus generally less familiar than other New York writing. Part of the problem is that much of it is the sort of work that literary arbiters dismiss as "not literature," which is purportedly beneath "bad writing." (In truth, such dismissals become one measure of its avant- garde distance from conventional writing.) Second, little of it enters the familiar channels of literary magazines and literary book publishing. Third, even when SoHo Literature appears in print, it is rarely reviewed. Fourth, much of it is produced by people whose professional energies are concentrated elsewhere and thus have neither the time nor inclination to hustle the literary world.

Given these contrasts, it is interesting to observe that both Richard Foreman and Robert Wilson "made it" as playwrights not through the turfs of off-Broadway or even off-off-Broadway but through SoHo, and perhaps the same could be said of Philip Glass and Steve Reich in the musical world—it was SoHo, not another cultural entity, that initially established their reputations. However, no poet or fictioneer has similarly "made it" through SoHo. One reason I've heard to account for this discrepancy is that people here do not read. However, this is not true, as rare is an artist's loft without a collection of books. It is more appropriate to say that in theater and music, unlike literature, major reputations can be founded in America today upon the nucleus of a small enthusiastic audience. However, as commercial book publishers increase their minimal sales figure from two thousand hardbacks of fifteen years ago to ten thousand hardbacks (or more), book publishing becomes more and more like Hollywood, with its boom-or-bust, "big money" mass merchandising mentality, which has no interest in "coterie" writing regardless of quality.

As for myself, I wouldn't live anywhere except New York and within New York City I would still rather live in SoHo. I have never been to Elaine's and go to a reading at St. Marks no more than once a year, while the Upper West Side, to be frank, gives me the creeps. In nearly twenty years as a full-time New York writer who reputedly "gets around," I have never met scores of prominent New York writers (especially Upper East and Upper West). More tellingly, I do not know anyone who knows them. Colleagues living outside New York, with their monolithic sense of this city, can hardly believe that. On the other hand, I think I have at one time or another met everyone writing in SoHo, and in certain ways have found their work not only different from what is being written elsewhere in New York now but in certain ways close to my own.

Making Music from the Sound of Words (1977)

True poetry is much closer in relation to the best of music, of painting, and of sculpture than to any part of literature which is not true poetry.

—Ezra Pound, *The Spirit of Romance* (1910)

THERE IS A new art around, which I call text-sound, as distinct from text-print and text-seen. In this new art, texts must be sounded and thus be heard to be "read," in contrast to those which must be printed and thus be only seen. The art is text-sound, rather than sound-text, to acknowledge the initial presence of a text, which is subjected to aural enhancements more typical of music, pitch excepted. To be precise, it is by nonmelodic musical techniques that words (or verbal sounds) are poetically charged with meanings that they would not otherwise have, but precisely in the absence of melody or intentional pitch does text-sound differ from song. A historical precursor in this vein is Kurt Schwitters' *Ursonate* (1922–32), which is partially available, with the author himself reading, on the German record *Phonetische Poesie;* a non-Western modern masterpiece is *Ketjak: The Ramayana Monkey Chant,* on Nonesuch. What is surely new is the art's consciousness of itself and its particular traditions. As this is a genuine intermedium, located between language arts and musical arts, its creators include individuals who initially established themselves as "writers," "poets," "composers," and "painters."

The first record-anthology of exclusively native work, *10 + 2 American Text Sound Pieces* (1975), contains previously unavailable pieces by Charles Amirkhanian, Beth Anderson,

Robert Ashley, John Cage, Clark Coolidge, Charles Dodge, John Giorno, Anthony Gnazzo, Brion Gysin, Liam O'Gallagher, and Aram Saroyan. The star here is Amirkhanian, who is also the record's producer and the author of its insert notes. By trade the "sound sensitivity information director" at KPFA, the Pacifica Foundation station in Berkeley, he has created text-sound pieces that employ a variety of electronic devices, such as overdubbing, delicate tape editing, looping, and stereoing. In "Just" (1972), the four words "rainbow," "chug," "bandit," and "bong" weave in and out of one another in patterns of rhythmical counterpoint. (Repeat the four words aloud and rapidly to yourself, and you'll get an inkling of what can be done.) Amirkhanian's second contribution to the record is "Heavy Aspirations" (1973) in which a lecture by the eminent musician/writer Nicolas Slonimsky is ingeniously taken apart and reassembled to emphasize characteristic phrases, preoccupations, and speech patterns. (A careful listener can also recognize, in distorted form, Slonimsky's passing reference to Amirkhanian's "Just.")

My major criticisms of *10 + 2* are that Amirkhanian has done better elsewhere, as in his masterpiece, "Seatbelt, Seatbelt" (1973), which is not yet available on record, alas; and then that nobody else on the record offers work that is quite as good as his. The Clark Coolidge piece is a silly tape scrambling that is untypical of this important poet's work; the John Cage selection is read not by Cage, who is his own best text-sound performer, but by someone else; both Brion Gysin and John Giorno have done better elsewhere. Robert Ashley's piece is a prose monologue, spoken rapidly in a flat, unemphatic manner, against a background of undefinable electronic sounds. The next work on the record, Beth Anderson's "Torero Piece" (1973), has roughly the same form.

The Gysin selection is only the sound track of a television program in which the author is writing words on a blackboard. The voice sounds terribly distant, implicitly reminding us of how television's microphones differ from radio's. (Worse, this Gysin contribution is inferior in every way to his acoustic masterpiece, "I Am That I Am," that is available on one of the John Giorno record-anthologies mentioned later.) My own favorites, aside from the Amirkhanian pieces, are the endless pieces that cleverly conclude each side of the disc (and exploit a technical capability unique to phonograph records)—Aram Saroyan's "Crickets," in which that single evocative word is repeated over and over again, like their sound on the summer evening (until one removes the player arm), and Anthony Gnazzo's "The Population Explosion," which says "bang" interminably.

A third limitation of *10 + 2* is that the record does not include the work of several important American text-sound practitioners. The first to get his work commercially issued was Steve Reich, with *It's Gonna Rain* (1965) and *Come Out* (1966); and these remain among the best text-sound art ever produced on these shores. For the first, Reich recorded a Pentecostal preacher declaiming a longer sentence that included "It's gonna rain." As Reich remembers it, "Later at home I started playing with tape loops of his voice and, by accident, discovered the process of letting two identical loops go gradually in and out of phase with each other." The first part of this piece realizes an incantatory intensity ("energy level") without equal in audio language art, as a single phrase is multiplied into a pulsing chorus of itself, and the phrase as a whole plays against a repeated bass of its parts. Since the record including *It's Gonna Rain* has not been available for several years, that Reich piece would have enhanced *10 + 2*.

A second major text-sound artist omitted from Amirkhanian's survey is W. Bliem Kern, whose single published tape is part of a boxed book, *Meditationsmeditationsmeditationsmeditations* (1973). On the cassette, Kern reads texts that are also in the book; but since his poems are scarcely conventional, neither are his readings. A visual poem entitled "Jealousy" contains the phrase "belief in the illusion of," which Kern rapidly repeats until it sounds like something else. (Say this phrase rapidly to yourself, and you'll get an idea where Kern's art goes.) Other Kern poems mix familiar words with unfamiliar, the former becoming semantic touchstones for the latter, as in "magweba":

> prom enu how ek anu
> time was psom
> enu how ek anu time was
> prom enu how ek anu
> time was

Kern also composes in an entirely fictitious language that he calls Ooloo. "Don't try to figure anything out," he once told an interviewer; "there is nothing to figure out." The best Kern pieces, in my judgment, are less these than his longer works, such as "Dream To Live," which are really closer to fiction or essays than to poetry. That last piece narrates in words, phrases, and phonemes the ending of a love affair. Kern is presently completing a "novel" that, like his first book, will be published as both a spine-bound book and a cassette.

John Giorno is one *10 + 2* contributor who is better represented elsewhere: on the record-anthologies (mostly of conventional poetry) that he has produced for his own company, Giorno Poetry Systems—*Dial-a-Poem* (1972), *Disconnected* (1974), *Biting Off the Tongue of a Corpse* (1975)—and on the two-record set, *John Giorno/William Burroughs* (1975). After hesitant beginnings with *Raspberry and Pornographic Poem* (1967), Giorno has become a masterful reader of his own texts, which are subject to an echo that aurally enhances his initial statement. As his control over electronic technique has become more sophisticated over the past decade, the best record of his work is indeed the last. His GPS anthologies have only a few text-sound works apiece on them—a brilliant Brion Gysin piece on the first, a Clark Coolidge on the second, and a John Cage on the third. By contrast, the sole periodical of recorded poetry, the *Black Box* cassettes, has used text-sound works even more sparsely—Jackson Mac Low on number 2 and Toby Lurie on number 4; that's all so far.

Charles Dodge is a curious case of a well-educated university composer who has developed an awesome technique for using a computer to generate semblances of comprehensible human voices. The best description of this technique appears, oddly, not on his own record, *Synthesized Speech Sounds* (1976), but in the Amirkhanian anthology. Essentially, Dodge records a human voice speaking a text, defines digitally the various components of this recording, uses the computer to reprogram the digital specifications that in turn are implanted on tape which, when run through a tape player, will reproduce "electronic" vocal sounds. Dodge can create synthetic females as well as synthetic males, except that they sound more like one another than anything human; and the background pitches sound more like one another than any instruments. Dodge draws his texts from the trendy poetry of Mark Strand, who can scarcely be thankful that his words are often obliterated beyond aural recognition. This computer-assisted text-sound procedure has, in my judgment, a long way to go.

Since no American company has issued one-person records or tapes of native text-sound artists, the initiative passed to a German firm, Edition S Press, formed by two young German scholars, Michael Koehler and Nicholas Einhorn. Edition S Press has released cassettes of John Cage quietly declaiming his verbal collage of Thoreau's writings about music, *Mureau;* Armand Schwerner reading the first seventeen sections of his brilliant long poem, *The Tablets;* Jerome Rothenberg performing his *Horse Songs of Frank Mitchell;* and Jackson Mac Low's eight-voice stereo realization of *The Black Tarantula Crossword Gathas.* European art galleries have issued three separate discs of Lawrence Weiner, a well-known "conceptual artist," reading his singular verbal style—in his best record with a woman repeating the same phrases in Dutch. No survey of one-person American text-sound would be complete without this author mentioning his own cassette, *Experimental Prose* (1976).

Among the other Americans who have done less distinguished text-sound work are Peter Harleman, who produces the record-periodical *Out Loud,* which is by now all but entirely devoted to his own work; Toby Lurie, whose *Word Music* (1971) and *Mirror Images* (1975) create an audio theater full of sentimental appeals and obvious effects; and Kenneth Gaburo, whose *Lingua II: Maledetto* (1967–68) opens with a softly hissing noise. I checked my record player, to make sure all was well, and then discovered on the album jacket a boxed footnote, set apart from the composer's garrulous self-description, which says that the opening "consists entirely of phonemes (S) and lasts 3 minutes." However, once Gaburo's group of garrulous gabblers gets going, one wishes for a return to the quiet, meditative hiss.

The major threat to the survival of American text-sound art is the current fact that so much first-rate work is unavailable. Some of the most promising performers have never been commercially recorded—A. F. Caldiero, Dick Higgins, Francis Schwartz—while others are available only with their inferior works. If the reader of this essay wanted to hear Amirkhanian's "Seatbelt, Seatbelt," for instance, the only current way to satisfy his curiosity would be to ask Amirkhanian himself for a copy; and if the artist replied that he was reluctant to go through the rigamarole of getting a master from a safe storage place and then lining up two machines for a dubbing, no one could blame him. Copying audiotapes is not yet as feasible or cheap as photocopying manuscripts. What is needed right now, of course, are more recordings, anthologies as well as one-person discs, of American text-sound art—especially of the very best work. Until these become available, it will remain, needlessly, a largely private pleasure.

Avant-Garde American
Artists Make Audio Art
in Germany (1989)

Poets should emphatically be brought into the wireless studio, for it is much more conceivable that they should be able to adapt a verbal work of art to the limits of the world of space, sound and music. The film demands the visual artist who has also a feeling for words, the wireless on the other hand needs a master of words who has also a feeling for modes of expression appropriate to the sensuous world.

—Rudolf Arnheim, *Radio: An Art of Sound* (1936)

EVER SINCE THE beginnings of our cultural history, advanced American artists have gone abroad to do work (and earn rewards) that could not happen at home; and what has long been true for advanced American art in general is now particularly true for audio art. The center for avant-garde American radio production has for the past decade been in Cologne, Germany, the home of Westdeutscher Rundfunk, the largest of the German stations. Of the Americans producing programs for WDR, as it is commonly called, nearly all initially earned their reputations in arts other than radio: the composers John Cage, Malcolm Goldstein, Sorrel Hays, Alvin Curran, Charles Amirkhanian, Tom Johnson, Pauline Oliveros, and Charlie Morrow; the poets Dick Higgins, Jackson Mac Low, and Jerome Rothenberg; and the visual artists Alison Knowles, George Brecht, Stephan von Huene, Faith Wilding, and Bill Fontana. Some of the extraordinary programs made by them are heard from time to time over public radio stations here. Some are available at your nearest Goethe House, where they are customarily kept in the library.

The principal patron for this beneficence has been Klaus Schöning, a staff producer for WDR's Hörspiel department since the 1960s. Hörspiel, pronounced "whore-shpeel," translates literally as ear-play; and within the bureaucracies of the huge German radio stations, such departments are distinct from "literature" and "feature." A comparable phrase here has been "radio drama," which has defined an acoustic art in which actors talk emphatically at one another, abetted by sound effects. One reason not to use that English term now is that the American artists working for Schöning have been doing something else; indeed, they use the term Hörspiel to define their own work, sometimes even dropping the umlaut and italics and thus making the word American.

Born in 1936, in part of East Prussia that is now eastern Poland, Schöning studied theater in West Berlin and Munich before going to work at WDR in the early 1960s. Becoming a staff producer in the Hörspiel department, he began twenty years ago to work with avant-garde German writers, sponsoring innovative programs that he called *Neues Hörspiel,* as they represented a departure not only from American kinds of radio theater, epitomized by the soap opera with its semblances of live theater, but from the more literary German radio play, customarily a dreamily evocative poetic text. Learning from the sound poets, Schöning realized that language could express in terms other than syntax; and from composers he learned that the musical organization of speech could be just as valid for radio as traditional theatrical sound. The key epithet in his esthetic became "acoustic."

Schöning first came to America in 1980. The turning point in his executive career, as he describes it, came two years before, when he commissioned John Cage to do *Roaratorio,* a magnificent hour-long mix of sounds with reference to James Joyce's *Finnegans Wake.* Working with John David Fullemann, an American sound designer now residing in Sweden, Cage composed an expansive collection of freshly gathered sounds from all the places mentioned in Joyce's book. Underneath the mix was the cantus firmus, so to speak, of Cage himself reading one of his own Writings Through *Finnegans Wake*. A masterpiece even in Cage's own *oeuvre*, *Roaratorio* won the coveted Karl-Sczuka-Prise of German radio. More recently, Cage's WDR tape became the score of a Merce Cunningham choreography performed at Brooklyn Academy of Music. The success of *Roaratorio* persuaded Schöning to see what else was happening here.

What he found on his maiden voyage to America was artists impressed by his success with Cage and thus prepared to accept his invitation to submit proposals and to do productions. One of the first to go was Alison Knowles, traditionally a sculptor, who composed a mix of associations on the word "bean." In 1982, her *Bohnensequenzen* (or bean-sequences) shared the Sczuka-Prise that Cage had won before. To Schöning, peer-juried prizes for his productions become the most convenient measure of success in a system that does not trust audience ratings; a second reason for his pride in prizes is, quite frankly, that he wants to produce classics that, as one measure of their acoustic excellence, will be broadcast again and again.

Unlike Knowles, the pianist/composer Sorrel Hays had worked elaborately with audiotape before meeting Schöning; her masterful composition *Southern Voices* (1980) had appeared here on a Folkways Record (under the name "Doris Hays"). WDR commissioned her to amplify a 1979 poem of hers into a multitrack composition in two languages; for unlike most of the other Yankees working at WDR, Hays actually speaks German, having studied music in Munich for two years. For *Something (To Do) Doing/Etwas Tun*, some parts were recorded here; most was recorded and mixed at a WDR studio that had audio processing gadgetry unavailable to her here.

The point of its acoustic busyness is, to Hays, "based on Gertrude Stein's comment that the materialism of Americans lies not in possessions but in constant activity."

A more recent work of hers, *Liebe im All/Love in Space* (1987), echoes both rock opera and vaudeville, to quote Hays again, "with two adults and four children in speaking roles, punk rock instrumental and vocal music, electronic score, sound effects and pop love songs from the fifties mixed with German love songs." Hays's pieces typically mix passages of speech and sound, along with snatches of her own music, so that they fade in and out of one another, offering a rich and various verbal-musical (i.e., acoustic) texture. Hays' proposal for *Love in Space/ Liebe im All* won a WDR "Acustica" competition to get itself produced; once done, it became WDR's nomination for the Prix Futura Berlin.

Sometimes these Americans would send in advance English manuscripts that could be translated into German. The most elaborate was Dick Higgins's *Scenes Forgotten and Otherwise Remembered*, a forty-nine-page text about Merovingian history in the sixth century. More literary than what other Americans have done, it was translated into German by the eminent translator Klaus Reichert and produced as *Vergessene Szenen* (1985). Jackson Mac Low's *Thanks/Danke* (1983) is an amusing radio play about making a radio play, with him and Anne Tardos speaking in both languages.

Most of Schöning's Americans come to Cologne to produce their work, not just because the studios there are better than those in any American radio station, public or private, but because in the new Hörspiel, unlike the old, the author customarily assumes responsibility for producing his or her text. As Professor Everett Frost succinctly put it, "The writer who hands over a script to a dramaturg and a producer/director is being replaced by a Hörspielmacher, the sound equivalent of a filmmaker or video artist."

Schöning and his WDR colleagues have also sponsored a

"Metropolis" series of extended audio compositions about the great cities of the world. These are less audio portraits in the documentary sense than compositions designed to reveal the acoustic uniqueness of each place. The pioneering French electronic composer Pierre Henry did Paris; Charles Amirkhanian, the music director of Berkeley's Pacifica station, was hired to do San Francisco; this writer composed *New York City;* the New York composer Charlie Morrow did Copenhagen, and the expatriate American Alvin Curran did Rome. All of these pieces were presented under Schöning's aegis in Documenta 8, the international art exhibition held last year in Kassel. Others were presented in "loudspeaker concerts," as he calls them, at the Frankfurt opera house and in a Cologne art museum.

The broadcast of these WDR works over our public stations is part of an international exchange that unites European broadcasting. *Roaratorio* was also broadcast in Sweden, Australia, Canada, and France; and many other compositions by Americans have pursued a similar multinational path. Though WDR owns its commissions, all fees received by it are customarily forwarded to the authors. When a work is rebroadcast over WDR, its author is paid again in full. People with experience at collecting fees around the world testify that WDR is remarkably scrupulous about paying its bills. (In America, by contrast, public stations customarily pay nothing, or next to nothing, for independent productions. Programs comparable to those described here are instead produced with funds obtained elsewhere.)

The author and editor of numerous books of and about Hörspiel, Schöning has also sponsored a series of extended critical features for radio about "Hörspiel U.S.A"—one about American sound poetry, two about classic radio comedy and newer comedy records, others about Glenn Gould's radio art, Orson Welles, and even Tony Schwartz, the last being by common consent the most serious American producer of radio commercials. On his own, Schöning has produced a 150-minute scholarly introduction to American Hörspiel, from its beginnings in the 1920s to 1986, that has been broadcast not only over his own station but over other German stations. Not even in America can we hear as much critical analysis of our own radio art as listeners in the Ruhr industrial valley!

All this interest reflects not only Schöning's personal initiative but the fact that Germans value radio far more than we; to them, radio is culture. In Germany, there are annual prizes for radio plays, the most prestigious being the *Hörspielpreis der Kriegsblinden* (or war-blind). Hörspiel texts are also collected into textbooks that are taught in the universities and gymnasia. German schoolkids will talk about what they heard last night, much as young Americans used to talk about Jean Shepherd's or Alan Freed's latest audacity in the 1950s. Anthologies of contemporary radio plays are frequently published there (whereas none have appeared here in several decades). A scholarly literature exists; critical debates persist. There is even a prodigious 1959 encyclopedia, now outdated, with the unfortunate title of *Hörspielfuhrer,* in which only one American work is represented, Archibald MacLeish's *Fall of the City* (1938); for the European assumption is that the kind of high literary radio drama memorialized in that encyclopedia's pages did not happen in America—that from the standard of critical quality, America was a radio desert.

The initial idea of Schöning's own weekly program, Hörspielstudio, which occupies the prime time of every Wednesday night from 9:00 to 10:30 p.m., was to broadcast the best work from around the world. Through the seventies, it featured the programs from continental Europe; now most Hörspielstudio programs come from Americans. "The potential of acoustic artists is more evident in this country than any other, including Germany," he explained during a recent visit here. "Americans are not radio makers first but performers, and they imported a performance quality that is absolutely professional acoustically and yet less academic than European, less bound to historical considerations. I discovered the Neues Hörspiel in another continent. The word Hörspiel has a new meaning in Germany because of American influence." It is not for nothing that his colleagues at WDR call Schöning "the American department."

The truth is that even in these days of arts councils and competitions supposedly mandated to fund indigenous excellence, the very best work is often done abroad, sometimes supported by foreign governments and their institutions, discovering more American genius than we know here, showing us what can be done, not only in the creation of American art but in its dissemination. The quantity of American art produced at WDR is as impressive as the acoustic quality. The notion may offend our patriotic sentiments (and expose the inadequacies of our "cultural endowments"), but to hear advanced American audio art we should have a cable or satellite dish connecting us to Cologne.

Milton Babbitt's
Text-Sound Art (1987)

I had always been fascinated by the relationship of voice to sound, the voice as instrument, the voice as affected by vowel sounds, consonant sounds, modes of production.
—Milton Babbitt, in an interview (1986)

TO MY TASTES, the best Milton Babbitt is his compositions for the alleged Mark II Synthesizer—I say "alleged," because, as no other composer publicly acknowledges using it, there is reason to doubt its existence. Nevertheless, within that general etiology, I've always treasured his three pieces for texts and synthesized accompaniment: *Vision and Prayer* (1961), *Philomel* (1964), and *Phonemena* (1974), regarding each as an advance over its predecessor.

For the earliest, Babbitt took a twelve-stanza emblematic poem by Dylan Thomas. The first six stanzas are diamond shaped, having lines with only one syllable at their top, and then increasing by one syllable for each line to a maximum of nine syllables at their midsection before returning to one syllable at the bottom; and the last six have the opposite hourglass form of nine syllables on top decreasing to one in the middle before returning to nine at the bottom.

To understand what was done to this rigorously structured text, it is best to quote Babbitt's masterful, inimitable description (epitomizing as it does Robert Frost's suggestion that true poetry is what cannot be translated) from his notes to CRI album SD 268:

The temporal, sonic and pattern characteristics of this poetic struc-
ture, as well as certain interpretations of these properties in strictly
musical terms, were initial determinants of both musical details and
the large-scale disposition of the compositional sections. The cumula-
tive musical progression from these details to the sections, and to the
totality of which these sections are members, is achieved by trichordal
and hexachordal derivation, harmonic succession through aggre-
gates—within which the polyphony and the counterpoint are shaped
by the properties of the work's third-order combinatorial set, and by
the increased dimensionality—the refinements with and the com-
poundings of primary dimensions—easily and precisely afforded by
the electronic medium.

Theory notwithstanding, his setting of the Dylan Thomas text
is filled with those rapid articulations, scrupulously nonrepeti-
tive, that I've always found superlative in Babbitt's music.
There is also some gorgeous composing for language, espe-
cially in the second hourglass stanza; and some ingenious
musical clarification of the poetry's ambiguities.

What Babbitt has done is rescue one of Thomas's more
obscure poems, an atypical poem Thomas did not record him-
self, avoiding the problem of needing to transcend the poet's
own aural "setting." (Indeed, it was courageous of Babbitt
to tackle Thomas who, among all modern poets except Carl
Sandburg, was the best at reciting his own poetry, whose recit-
als gave his lines the sound that most of us tend to hear.)
Nonetheless, I should add that to my ears the second half
of Thomas's poem is more articulate, simply because of its
hourglass form—language progressing from more words to
less to more is more comprehensible than the reverse. Also,
those of us familiar with this work have become so accustomed
to Bethany Beardslee's performance that I question whether
anyone else will ever sing this as persuasively. (In the course
of researching this appreciation I learned in passing that (1)
there was an earlier version for piano and voice; and (2) per-
mission to use the poem was obtained directly from Thomas

himself, around 1952, at Connolly's Bar, Third Avenue and Twenty-third Street, in the presence of the poet John Berryman, who later had to vouch for Thomas's promise.)

Philomel has a looser text, free verse composed especially for Babbitt by John Hollander, an American poet who is also an accomplished scholar; and this piece advances beyond its predecessor in electronically transforming the human voice (Beardsley's) into an entity that sings apart from the live soloist, and also in synthesizing spectacular speech choruses that would be impossible in live performance. (My favorites are the faint choral echoes that sound almost like electronic imprinting.) Again, there is a difference between words that are sung and words only spoken, but in this piece Babbitt introduces fluctuations between semantic speech and nonsemantic, or between comprehensible words and semantically indefinite vocables.

The problem here is the text. One distinguishing mark of Babbitt's settings of poetry is that here, unlike too much other contemporary music in this mode, his words can be understood. Nonetheless, my ears are scarcely alone in finding the repeated refrain of *Philomel's* third part a bit thuddish: "Thrashing, through the woods of Thrace." And my sensory apparatus succumbs to such heavy rhymes as:

> Emptied, unfeeling and unfulfilled
> By trees here where no birds have trilled—
> Feeling killed
> Philomel stilled
> Her honey unfulfilled.

To make the experience more cumbersome these rhymes are sung once live and then, for the last three lines, repeated on tape!

Some of the loveliest writing for voice and synthesized elec-

tronic accompaniment occurs in the middle of the third and
last section, around such lines as:

> I ache in change
> Though once I grew
> At a slower pace.
> And now I range

All of this is sublime until we hear again "thrashing," etc. And
a few lines later, the same thing happens—a beautiful setting
sabotaged by a verbal clinker. Can I be alone in wondering
why there should be so many rhymes and so much verbal
echo in serial music that otherwise eschews repetition? A final
problem is that the recorded version isn't always as clear as a
live performance in letting the listener know which lines are
sung live and which (other than the choruses) are prerecorded.

For *Phonemena* (not "Phenomena," which are something
else), Babbitt decided not to use a poet's text but to compose
his own, entirely of basic speech units, phonemes, made by
combining twelve vowel-based sounds with twenty-four dis-
crete consonants, thereby making a kind of sound poem, or
text-sound. Let me quote from the first sixty-two bars:

DĒ SHĒ JĒ TĒ SHA LE RA ZHUH ĀNG SŌ THAW VE THĀ Ē
    VI SU FŌ VŪ VU
FU ZUH CHŪ SUH GU JĀ KŪ SHU GUH JA
CHAH LE Ō HĀ MA LAW GŌ LE MAH DĂ THAH SHĒ
LŌ ZHU SU JAW TŌ HAH DĒ SHE
WĀ E TŌ SHĒ MI ZA BŌ RU
YŪ SHU RU I SHA MĀ YU ZAW
THA GAW FE GĂ VA THA FĒ
THĒ AH VŪ BU WI DAW THŪ JU THU LŪ CHU HU THŪJ
PE MAH Ē VI CHĒ WĒ E GĂ HI LE Ā RŌ
VAW L YAH Ō ZŌ AW YŌ BAH SHŌ PŌ,
LUH SAW PA SAH RA ZE RA ZHA
SHA YU KU SHU TU SHU GU ZO PO THI

MAW BĒ,
VU JU Ū, HU JU TĀ, SU
U VŪ, WŪ, MU RŪ, ZHUH KUH
WE NGU RU BĀ, SHUH LE THE RĀ, LE SHĀ, LAW LE
GA THI HE SE DI RAH ZHA TI DĒ AH FI DĒ WĒ
GA KAH MAW PŌ WE RŪ
MĀ NAH RA LU CHU LU NU ZŪ
LŪ GAW MA LE VŌ NU ZHE JŌ HU CHA DĒ THAH JAH
YĒ FU SŌ SHU DAW RI BŌ A PI VĒ
PE SHE VĀ KUR Ē Z

Taken by itself, this is magical language, one of the pioneering poems of the age. Not only does it reflect in vocables one of the great ideas of modern art (seriality) but it projects that idea in linguistic materials, semantics and syntax be damned. This is real radical poetry, pure poetry that today's "language-centered poets," as they are called, would give almost anything to have written two stanzas of.

To begin to explain what is done to this text musically, I need to quote Babbitt again, who told me that, while "neither vowels nor consonants are serialized in any independent sense, the vowels function as instruments projecting lines in the total pitch organization as it moves through the aggregates and the consonants project the rhythmic structure," which is to say that there is a continuous relationship between the textual choices and musical structure. A further connection, I've been reliably informed, is that a particular vowel, if followed through the piece, will touch upon every class in a pitch series. The principal achievement is a text that, even though it is less accessible than those used in the earlier text-sound pieces, is every bit as *busy*, deliciously busy, as Babbitt's music. While I admire the musical setting, and the virtuoso performances of Lynn Webber on record and Judith Bettina live, I would personally like, as an enthusiast for sound poetry, to hear the text simply declaimed, spoken with comparable virtuosity and speed, to discover whether its structure would be audible on verbals alone.

A further odd truth is that the only other composer today to make excellent text-sound from phonemes is John Cage, with whom Babbitt's name has often been paired, and more often opposed, for over two decades now! I should add that I've known Babbitt and his ideas long enough to know that I generally hear something other than what he wants me to hear, something that reflects his designs, to be sure, but in terms other than he had in mind.

Michael Joseph Phillips
(1980)

MICHAEL JOSEPH PHILLIPS is one of the most audacious poets in the English language, mostly because he risks appearing not only simple (and, thus, in a poetic heresy, comprehensible) but simple-minded as well. In his intentionally limited vocabulary and his penchant for exact repetition is a radical repudiation of two traditional values of English poetry; for whereas even Gertrude Stein claimed that nothing she wrote was ever repeated precisely, Phillips often repeats and repeats exactly. The most successful of his poems in this mode is, in my opinion, "On Claudia Cardinale," in which the phrase "I have never seen so much so well put-together" is repeated in a staggered visual form that generates an erotic complement. Obsessed by women, Phillips is less an erotic poet than a voyeuristic one. As a man of taste, he apostrophizes only the most beautiful public women of his time—Loren, Lollobrigida, Cardinale, Tiegs.

From the opening page of his *Selected Poems* Phillips announces he is doing something special, and in this respect—in the desire to create from his professional beginnings an individual style—he differs from 99 percent of the M.F.A. poets in America. In this age of so much mediocre, utterly

On Claudia Cardinale

I have never seen so much so well put-together. I have
never seen so much so well put-together. I have never
seen so much so well put-together. I have never seen
so much so well put-together. I have never seen so
much so well put-together. I have never seen so
so well put-together. I have never seen so much so well
put-together. I have never seen so much so well put-
together. I have never seen so much so well put-together.
I have never seen so much so well put-together. I have
never seen so much so well put-together. I have never
seen so much so well put-together. I have never seen
so much so well put-together. I have never seen so
much so well put-together. I have never seen so much
so well put-together. I have never seen so much so well
put-together. I have never seen so much so well put-
together. I have never seen so much so well put-together.
I have never seen so much so well put-together. I have
never seen so much so well put-together. I have never
seen so much so well put-together. I have never seen
so much so well put-together. I have never seen so
much so well put-together. I have never seen so much
so well put-together. I have never seen so much so well
put-together. I have never seen so much so well put-
together. I have never seen so much so well put-together.
I have never seen so much so well put-together. I have
never seen so much so well put-together. I have never
seen so much so well put-together. I have never seen so
so much so well put-together. I have never seen so
much so well put-together. I have never seen so much
so well put-together. I have never seen so much so well
put-together. I have never seen so much so well put-
together. I have never seen so much so well put-together.
I have never seen so much so well put-together. I have
never seen so much so well put-together. I have never
seen so much so well put-together. I have never seen
so much so well put-together. I have never seen so
much so well put-together. I have never seen so much
so well put-together. I have never seen so much so well
put-together. I have never seen so much so well put-
together. I have never seen so much so well put-together.
I have never seen so much so well put-together. I have
never seen so much so well put-together. I have never
seen so much so well put-together. I have never seen
so much so well put-together. I have never seen so
much so well put-together. I have never seen so much
so well put-together. I have never seen so much so well
put-together. I have never seen so much so well put-
together. I have never seen so much so well put-together.

interchangeable poetry, he should be taken seriously initially for his courageous assertion of a highly characteristic signature.

For all of the superficial appearances of simplicity, Phillips is clearly a literate gent with a doctorate on Edwin Muir, a love of sonnets and stylistic debts to the poems of E. E. Cummings and José Garcia Villa, both of whom also specialized in poems less than a page in length. Along with others, Phillips refutes the common piety of United States literary criticism that "nothing came from Cummings."

It is indicative that the only other American poet who has risked such poetic minimalism—Aram Saroyan—gave it up to write fairly conventional, commercial prose. On the other hand, one price that Phillips pays for his continued integrity is that his work never appears in the prominent American poetry journals, it is scarcely anthologized, his books are rarely reviewed, and literary awards and professorships have never been his; but since he has been publishing for two decades, these ugly effects become merely signs of his importance.

My own favorite Phillips poem—the real knockout—is the visual poem beginning "Tall Black Hair." I reprinted it in the anthology *Imaged Words & Worded Images* (1970) and am pleased to discover my taste of a decade ago confirmed. A second gem, "Life Cycle," ranks among the best three-word poems in the language. Both of these Phillips poems, at least, belong in every putatively comprehensive anthology of contemporary American poetry.

I have enjoyed his books and booklets in the past—especially the silk-screened *8 Page Poems* (1971) and *Kinetics and Concretes* (1971)—and thus congratulate both him and his publisher for bringing out the large volume, *Selected Love Poems* (1980), that I hope will win for Phillips the readers (and fans) his audacious work deserves.

Michael Joseph Phillips

WOMAN POEM

```
                    Tall
   This hair,       black        hair, This
        is          O           is
        o          you          o
        so         are          so
                    ''
                   much
                   beauty
                    ''
                    O
                   this
                   part
          (is     wonderful    is)

   round,                        round,
        is         and            is
   warm,                        warm,


                   white

                    Oh

                   sOFt

     and                          and
                   ccc
   curves           u           curves
                    r
     and            v            and
o                   !                    o!




     0?                          0




     oh-                        oh!
```

Harry Polkinhorn's
Anaesthesia (1985)

A NYONE WITH A good heart and a fifth-grade educa-
tion can write an antiwar poem. Any experienced poet
with a sense of an audience can read an antiwar poem that will
summon an audience's applause. However, to write such a
poem in unfamiliar ways, with unobvious turns, takes great
intelligence, as well as confident courage; and since these last
two qualities are quite rare, especially in tandem, Harry Pol-
kinhorn's *Anaesthesia* deserves everyone's attention.

Whereas most poetry is based upon sentences, albeit sepa-
rated into "poetic" lines, Polkinhorn's unit is phrases; and
his best passages are incomplete sentences strung together.
Introducing *Anaesthesia*, I would like to advise readers of its
pages to appreciate passages that begin with each of these
phrases:

officially condemned

but a simple little smile

no way out, the message of clear shrewd inversions

as for you loaves and fishes

asphodel

willing eat gas dirt skin last their action

These examples, as well as the whole poem, should indicate
that Polkinhorn has read enough to know what kinds of po-
etry, especially what kinds of antiwar poetry, need no longer
be done; he has chosen to do something else. It is not for
nothing that he already ranks among the best critics of avant-
garde writing, especially in intermedial forms. Indicatively,
his title is richly resonant (as titles should be, but rarely are).

Literary Videotapes
(1987)

In the face of the ubiquity of machines, the value of a machine made of words is now of another order than in the period of modernism that generated the prototypes of [W. C.] Williams, [Viktor] Shklovsky, Duchamp and Man Ray.
> —Barrett Watten, "The World in the Work" (1985)

VIDEO BEGAN AS an offspring of television, itself the product of the marriage of radio and film; and just as the first television shows were extensions of radio, so videotapes were initially extensions of television and then film, all of them at their best providing visual-kinetic-acoustic images unknown before. In time came artists' video, and music video, and dance video. Now we have literary video, which is to say videotapes based upon writers and writing; for language and literary forms can be as feasible for video as music or art or sport or anything else. Since this is an emerging genre, most of the tapes come from small companies; some are best ordered from the artists themselves.

There appear to be several kinds of literary videotapes: (1) a recording of a poetry reading or other kinds of literary recital; (2) an interview with a writer, ideally abetted by excerpts, declaimed or dramatized, from his or her work; (3) a portrait without an interviewer, in which the writer communicates directly with the camera; (4) dramatizations of classic stories; and (5) imaginative literary work produced directly for video.

For the first sort of literary video, documentations of literary recitals, the largest supplier is the American Poetry Archive at

San Francisco State University (1600 Holloway, San Francisco, CA 94132). Its 130-page catalog lists scores of videotapes, available in both VHS and Beta, as well as the more professional ¾-inch format, mostly one hour long, most of them shot with a single camera at a standard diagonal angle, during readings at the San Francisco Poetry Center. Unlike other tapes discussed here, these are not sold; but they can be rented for noncommercial use for fifteen to twenty dollars apiece. This catalog offers conservative poets, academic poets, beat poets, minimal poets—almost everyone! Of the tapes screened for this review, the best featured the poets Clark Coolidge, Jackson Mac Low, Robert Peters (who opens by reading not his poems but his witty polemical remarks about the poetry scene), and Bay Area *Poets of the Forties*.

In this catalog are also readings by several poets who write in languages other than English, among them Yehuda Amachai and Czelaw Milosz, reading their works in their original languages (in those cases, Hebrew and Polish, respectively) and in English translations. A final section of the Poetry Archive catalog offers the outtakes, or footage not used, from another kind of literary videotape—a pioneering series of black and white portraits produced two decades ago for National Educational Television. Among the "younger" poets featured at the time were Allen Ginsberg, John Ashbery, Kenneth Koch, Gary Snyder, and Louis Zukofsky. The last is especially valuable for revealing the immense intelligence of a neglected writer whose hermetic work is, alas, no better appreciated after his death than it was before, while the Ginsberg footage, shot mostly with Neal Cassady beside him, is best at revealing their peculiar friendship. Nonetheless, in part because these outtakes are by current standards undistinguished as video, scarcely exploring the possibilities of the visual-verbal medium, they are best characterized as audiotapes with pictures.

A more contemporary development is the imaginative filming of a literary recital, as the prolific videomaker Doris Chase has done with several tapes that tend to be too long for their materials and visually too limited for their lengths. An exception to this general estimate, and Chase's best, is Claudia Bruce's solo performance of the playwright Linda Mussmann's knotty text *Window* (1981). In one especially beautiful passage, Chase has Bruce's face fill the screen as she recites nonsyntactic language, while wide horizontal bands sweep the screen from top to bottom. Beginning with "to wait" and ending "Mary, Mary," this monologue ranks among the greatest passages in all video art. All these tapes are part of Chase's concepts series, featuring artists in several fields, and are available for rental or purchase, in whole or part (Women Make Movies, 225 Lafayette Street, New York, NY 10012).

Ron Mann's *Poetry in Motion* (1982) began as a film, funded partially by the Canada Council, about poets' performing; and after a movie house tour, the film became available on videotape (Voyager Press, 1351 Pacific Coast Highway, Santa Monica, CA 90401). It differs from the tapes reviewed so far by including a large number of poets (Allen Ginsberg, Gary Snyder, John Giorno, Ed Sanders, Amiri Baraka, among a dozen others), and also in the director's impatience, as he swiftly moves from one poet to another, occasionally pausing for interviews. As the emphasis is upon performance, the film includes a couple of nonpoets (Tom Waits and Ted Milton) and semipoets (Jayne Cortez and Ntozake Shange) declaiming with musical accompaniments that distract from their poetry, rather than enhance it. Nonetheless, as a video anthology of contemporary poetic performance, *Poetry in Motion* is probably a milestone.

A trio of yet more imaginative video renditions of poetry performances appear in the short tapes that Rose Lesniak produced in 1984 for her Manhattan Poetry Video Project. "Father Death Blues" has Allen Ginsberg continually reciting one of his best recent poems, a memorial to his father, as he wanders through Ellis Island, inhabited by people with stark white smocks, and then around New York City. With its quick cuts from scene to scene, as well as its musical background, this tape is visibly indebted to rock videos, except that its star, Ginsberg, does not dance or prance or indeed flirt much with the camera. It is also the best of the bunch. In another tape, "Uh Oh Plutonium," the poet Anne Waldman does dance, along with a back-up group; but the apocalyptic imagery accompanying her recording is too familiar and obvious. A third Lesniak tape, "Rapp It Up," has Bob Holman, a bespectacled poet influenced by rap records, doing a prosy rap about the nature of rap, accompanied by the percussionist Vito Ricci; notwithstanding the charm of such an informal setting for a poetry reading, Holman's performance on videotape pales by comparison to his superhip models. All three Lesniak pieces are available on a single cassette (Out There Productions, 126 West Twenty-seventh Street, New York, NY 10011).

To speak of Eric Bogosian as "a writer" may be wrong, because he hasn't published much. He is essentially a monologist who rose out of the SoHo "performance" scene, writing his own material which he declaims adeptly, especially in mimicing many voices. His videotape *Fun House* (Metropolitan Pictures—EZTV Cassettes, 8547 Santa Monica Boulevard, West Hollywood, CA 90069) shoots his one-man show as it was given before a live audience at the Matrix Theater in Los Angeles. Since Bogosian is an accomplished performer, his capacity for theatrical projection, as well as clear articulation, makes most poetry-reading poets seem amateur and puny. Bogosian's show opens in darkness, which is, alas, more effective in live theater than on videotape; and the bulbous microphone he carries around with him looks far bigger on a television screen than it would on stage. Then, since the cameras must keep their distance in taping a live performance, this tape misses the intimate close-up that distinguishes video from film; and given the theatrical circumstance, there is little opportunity to play with lighting or camera angles. Since Bogosian's sound is better than his pictures, his show would have survived better on audiotape, at, needless to say, considerably less price.

The extended literary interview is something that British television does far better than American, and so it is no surprise that a series of such videotapes comes from London Weekend Television (distributed here by Home Vision). One attraction of this series, titled "Profile of a Writer," is that the hour-long interview is interrupted by dramatized excerpts from the writer's works. The three I saw were all hosted by the British writer Melvyn Bragg, a self-effacing inquisitor who gives the impression he has been doing this sort of thing far too long. Thus, in the samples reviewed here, David Mamet takes command of the situation with his provocative comments, while Alberto Moravia, though a superior writer, is, by contrast, too disengaged, not only from the interviewer, but from the camera, which shoots him from a longer distance. Also, perhaps because Mamet writes plays, the excerpts from his work are far stronger. In between was Joseph Heller, whose relationship to the British crew seems askew. His sentimentalizing of the Coney Island in which he grew up smacks of a put-on concocted to mock the British image of the place.

Other producers abolish the interviewer, speculating, not unreasonably, that the author can address the camera by himself. From Paradigm Video (6205 Guilford, Canton, MI 48187) come two cardboard boxes containing not only videotapes but books by the featured poets—Max Ellison and Donald Hall. The former is a seventy-year-old rustic, previously unknown to me, who lives in a single-room cabin that lacks electricity and running water. A self-contained soul, he talks mostly to his belly button. A previous reviewer judged, "Children will find the folksy Ellison irresistible, oral interpreters will find him inspirational." Though that may well be, this urban adult found him as limited as his poetry.

Donald Hall, by contrast, is a far more substantial figure, a genuine man of letters who has written a large amount of literary commentary and edited many anthologies in addition to writing poetry. About a dozen years ago, he gave up his tenured position at the University of Michigan to return to his grandfather's house in southern New Hampshire. In "Donald Hall at Eagle Pond Farm," he reads his best poems between commenting, directly into the camera, on his sympathetic relationship to his rustic situation. This performance makes Hall a far simpler figure than he really is; for while this imitation of Robert Frost's disingenuous act may be palatable to the "Grades 6-12" for which this tape was designed, it has more difficulty passing any adult familiar with Hall, his book-filled house, and his service to contemporary poetry. Not surprisingly, these boxes are priced at over a hundred dollars apiece and are thus probably meant for single-purchase by educational institutions.

James Jones: Reveille To Taps (1985) began as a fifty-seven-minute feature produced for NET by Sangamon State University, which subsequently released a videotape (Springfield, IL 62708). A very conventional profile, produced with grants from the both the National Endowment for the Humanities and the Illinois Arts Council (two stamps of mediocrity), this film traces the late novelist's life from its beginnings in rural Illinois through the writing of his best- selling "From Here to Eternity" to his expatriation in Paris and subsequent return to the United States. It has historic footage and photographs, interviews with his family and colleagues, and a marvelous conclusion of Jones's gravestone, while the sound track reproduces a tape of him reading the "reveille to taps" passage of his most famous novel. The trouble is that such conventional techniques, coupled with too many statements of the common sort that one writer might make to promote a colleague, will not succeed in establishing new interest, or winning new readers, for this marginal writer's work.

A more elaborate portrait is John Antonelli's *Kerouac* (1985), which had a brief life as a seventy-three-minute feature film. Since his subject too is dead, the director combines historical footage of Kerouac's appearances on, say, the Steve Allen Show with more recent interviews with his friends (Allen Ginsberg, Joyce Johnson, Father Spike Morrisette), all of which might have been enough; but Antonelli decided to add dramatizations of episodes from Kerouac's life, most of them featuring the actor Jack Coulter as his subject with background narration by Peter Coyote. Some critics did not like this additional dimension, but I do. This is a good film, though one senses a better one could be made about its subject (Active Home Video, 9300 Pico Boulevard, Los Angeles, CA 90035).

Howard Bookner's *Burroughs* (1983) likewise began as a film, produced without grants, before it appeared on an eighty-seven-minute videotape (Giorno Video Pak, 222 Bowery, New York, NY 10012); and though William Burroughs may not be as great a writer as Kerouac, this is a far more successful visual-verbal portrait. The writing is featured along with the man, and both are approached in a variety of illuminating ways: not only performances by Burroughs himself at occasions both private and public, interviews with both the subject and his friends, but sequences portraying Burroughs in such unusual situations as the street where he grew up in St. Louis and inside his home orgone box, spectacular dramatizations of choice scenes from his novels, and even a highly imaginative demonstration of his experimental cut-up compositional techniques. *Burroughs* is a thorough portrait of both image and texts, about as complete as a book biography might be, even confronting the difficult issues of Burroughs's homosexuality, his accidental murder of his wife, and his late son's self-destructiveness. There are, nonetheless, a few false notes, as in the interview with Burroughs's brother (who piously objects to filthy language) and the easy rationalizations of human waste. Still, if the

James Jones profile might serve as a model of how such things are conventionally done, *Burroughs* is full of suggestions of how else literary portraiture might be produced.

About the video dramatizations of literary classics, there is little good to say about those I have seen. In their simplicity, coupled with the shameless infidelity to the complexity of the original, they remind me mostly of "classic comics," especially when they are produced initially for video, rather than film, regardless of whether they are made in Britain or here. Didn't the critic John Simon advise us long ago: "Governing the dramatization of novels: If it is worth doing, it can't be done; if it can be done, [the original] wasn't worth doing."

An exception is Doris Chase's *Electra Tries to Speak* (1982), an interpretation of the Greek tragedy that focuses on a monologue spoken by Sondra Siegal. Coming to video from the avant-garde community, Chase prefers to use a hand-held camera and to move with her subject in ways that filmmakers cannot. Working as she does with modest budgets and insufficient lighting (that, especially when we see it on cable television, becomes the telltale visual sign of amateurism), she offers an esthetic authenticity that some viewers find more attractive than others. Her tape has the further virtue of image processing indigenous to video, of visuals that are not only beautiful and thematically appropriate but would be inconceivable in film with its large screens. To use a distinction basic to photography criticism, Chase in her treatment of a literary text has gotten beyond matching into making, but there's still a lot more making to be done.

The Pressures of the Text (1983), by Peter Rose and Jessie Lewis, is a genuine literary work made especially for video. Reflecting its title, with its allusion to Roland Barthes, it opens with a professorial young man speaking what initially sounds like pompous but credible academic jargon. Before long, this monologue slides into highfalutin doubletalk, spoken in various national accents, in a virtuoso performance by Rose himself. In the upper right-hand corner of the screen appears a woman making semblances of sign language, but it soon becomes clear that her moves are similarly nonsensical. In a second section is an off-camera narrator, speaking English that is mostly comprehensible, while on screen appear subtitles, initially in the semblance of western languages, until they visually disintegrate into squiggly imitations of oriental calligraphy and then merely shapes. All these visual-verbal plays with sense and nonsense are very funny, in sophisticated ways, intellectually as well as visually. For esthetic money, *The Pressures of the Text* is the best buy (4372 Fleming Street, Manayunk, Philadelphia, PA 19128).

What is otherwise scarce in the tapes surveyed here is video imagination in dealing with literature, a video imagination comparable to what we find in the best music video, which is to say a vision of what can be done with words, with literary language, in video alone, that would be as different from an author reading or talking about his work as a music video is different from a concert recital. It's not impossible.

Kenneth Burke at 92 (1990)

For me, his life is a design, gives me satisfaction, always from the viewpoint of an interest in writing. He is one of the rarest things in America: He lives there, he is married, has a family, a house, lives directly by writing without having much sold out.

—William Carlos Williams, "Kenneth Burke" (1929)

I N MAY 1975, the American Academy and National Institute of Arts and Letters had their annual simultaneous meeting in which new members were inducted and standing awards disbursed. I remember that the same level of polite applause followed every announcement until a swell of handclapping greeted an elderly, compactly built, short man whose name, while scarcely known to the general public, has long commanded the highest respect in the literary trade. Kenneth Burke is a writer whom other writers enormously respect; the Distinguished Service Medal he received that day was cast in gold.

There has not been anyone quite like him in American literature since Ralph Waldo Emerson; and Burke's activity, like Emerson's, falls into several categories and yet transcends any of them in its total scope. Burke has published one novel, *Towards a Better Life* (1932; augmented edition, 1966); a book of short stories, *The Complete White Oxen* (1924; augmented edition, 1968); and enough poetry to fill a thick *Collected Poems 1915–1967* (1968) and then some. He also did an early translation of Thomas Mann's "Death in Venice" that some people prefer to those more recently available. There are three big books ostensibly of literary criticism, *Counter-Statement* (1931), *The Philosophy of Literary Form* (1941), *Language as Symbolic*

Action (1966), and then six more titles that are about something else—sociology a bit, pedagogy a bit less, "theorizing" a bit more: *Permanence and Change* (1935), *Attitudes Toward History* (1937), *A Grammar of Motives* (1945), *A Rhetoric of Motives* (1950), *A Rhetoric of Religion: Studies in Logology* (1961), and *Dramatism and Development* (1972). These last books are so diffuse, so leavened, so unsystematic that they are not "philosophy" in any formal sense but something else—something thoroughly idiosyncratic: Burkology perhaps.

Born Kenneth Duva Burke in Pittsburgh, on 5 May 1897, he went to public high school (where one classmate was the late literary critic Malcolm Cowley) and then to Ohio State for a semester. Since his father had meanwhile taken a job in Hoboken, New Jersey, young Kenneth went to live with his parents in nearby Weehawken, commuting by ferry and subway to Columbia for another year, before dropping out of college completely, not because he disliked it but because academic rigamarole kept him from taking the advanced courses he wanted. Instead, he went to live in Greenwich Village, in a house that was filled with young artists and writers, the painter Stuart Davis and the novelist Djuna Barnes among them; and within a few years, his poems and essays were appearing regularly in literary journals.

Married in 1919, he had his first child in 1922, the year he moved to a farm on Amity Road in Andover, New Jersey, and he has lived there ever since. Initially he commuted by bicycle, train, ferry, and trolley to New York City and its literary scene, working for spells as an editorial assistant at *The Dial,* the most consequential literary magazine of the period, and then for a full year ghostwriting a book on drug addiction for the Rockefeller Foundation. Malcolm Cowley remembers his friend having "his janitor's mop of blue-black hair":

> He can outquibble and out cavil
> laugh at himself, then speak once more

of logic pure and medieval;
but that night will lie awake
to argue with his personal devil.

The last line refers to the chronic insomnia that has plagued
Burke for his entire life. Other contemporaries, such as the
writer Gorham Munson, remember Burke as visibly muscular
in the arms and wrists.

His 1930s were considerably tougher. He divorced his first
wife, Lily Batterham, the mother of his three daughters, and
then married her younger sister, Elizabeth ("Libbie"), moving
into the next farmhouse down Amity Road and fathering a
second family of two sons. He taught occasional semesters at
the New School and at the University of Chicago, wrote music
criticism for *The Nation*, participated anxiously at a Communist
writers congress, published his first books of literary criticism
and collected a Guggenheim. Nonetheless, the critic Stanley
Edgar Hyman once told me that when he first met Burke,
around 1937, "he was in bad shape," mostly from excessive
drinking.

Unlike his buddy Cowley, among other writers of his "lost
generation," young Burke never went to Europe. He remem-
bers that he had planned to go since the middle 1920s but
always a crisis got in the way. "A kid was born, or something
around here had to be fixed. Suddenly I discovered that every-
one was coming back here," which is to say that World War II
had begun. Not until 1969, after his second wife's death, did
Burke finally get to Europe, visiting Italy and France, mostly
to give lectures and participate in conferences. This absence
may explain why so little of his writing has been translated
into other languages or why so few European intellectuals
know his name. A second reason is that in his styles of thinking
and writing Burke has always been egregiously American.

Not until 1943, at the age of forty-six, did he get his first
academic job, teaching English alternate weeks at Bennington

College, where he stayed until 1961. An alumna from the early 1950s remembers, "He was the most perfect example of an absent-minded genius, so involved in what he was thinking that there was no awareness of audience. He would lean back against the blackboard, eyes glaring off into space. He would talk and talk and talk, free-associating, making great leaps that had connections in his head but were far above the comprehension of his audience. He did not play to anybody; he enjoyed himself immensely. Bells would ring, students would pack up their books, and he would still be talking. There was no awareness that they had left." Since retiring from Bennington he has spent many spells as a university visitor—at Harvard, Penn State, Wesleyan, the University of California at Santa Barbara, among other places. Nonetheless, once his commitments elsewhere are done, he always returns to his beloved Andover farmhouse.

Though Burke lives alone, even now, his home has often been full of people. Four of his five children lived in New York City, and they have visited often, usually with their own children. Eleanor Burke Leacock Haughton was, until her death in 1988, a professor of anthropology at CUNY and the mother of four children, who themselves now have children (who are thus Burke's great-grandchildren). Elspeth Burke Chapin Hart had six boys, including the late pop singer Harry Chapin, who in turn had several children of his own. France Burke is a poet; K. Michael Burke, a painter. The fifth sibling, Anthony Burke, is a professor of astrophysics at the University of Victoria in British Columbia. To this tight clan, Kenneth Burke, once an only child, is the patriarch. When I once asked Burke how many grandchildren and great-grandchilden he had, he said he did not know and then, as a joke on himself, recalled meeting on his property an unfamiliar young woman who, when asked who she might be, introduced herself as his granddaughter!

It was just after New Year's 1981 that I first went to visit Burke in Andover, which is a small town in New Jersey's northernmost county. "Rustic" is scarcely the word for his compound of renovated barns, small farmhouses, garages, and outhouses. Electricity and telephones did not come here until the late 1950s, and running water came just to his own house a decade later, during his second wife Libbie's terminal illness. Central heating has not yet reached the property. Until he got electric heaters, Burke regularly chopped his own wood (that accounted for his muscles). He is probably the last major American writer to have read mostly by kerosene light.

KB, as he is known to all, greeted me with a ready smile, his booming, folksy, distinctly American voice inviting me into his kitchen, which is the warmest room in the house. With piles of books and papers all over the other ground-floor rooms, this is clearly the home, within a farmhouse, of a literary bachelor. "Everything gets lost about this goddamn place ten minutes after I get it," he told me. "If you can't find something right away, it is ridiculous to look for it." Bookcases fill most of the walls. At one end of the space is a manual typewriter; at another end is a piano with handwritten scores of melodies that had recently been coming into Burke's head. On the mantelpiece is a certificate from the American Academy of Arts and Letters. The medal itself is in a vault. "It's gold, you know," he reminded me.

His hair has thinned considerably in recent years, and what remains is stark white. Around his mouth is a trim vandyke beard. The day we met he wore farm clothes—corduroys, a gray sweater over a flannel shirt that was open at the neck, a jacket with pens in the handkerchief pocket, and sensible walking shoes. To go outside in the snow, he merely donned an overcoat and cap—no gloves or earmuffs for him. He spoke in vigorous bursts, punctuated by pauses for breath, in a slangy style that I would characterize as "informal American." He liked to talk, to tell stories and jokes, and to laugh heartily at his own humor. Often brilliant by the sentence, he could become more confusing over longer units.

As usual, he had been working on his manuscripts, arising at dawn and working through the afternoon, cooking his own meals and then doing household chores, and watching television in the evening. At the time he spoke of having four books in progress—one on Shakespeare, another on devices, a third based on lectures he gave recently at SUNY-Buffalo, and "A Symbolic of Motives" that would complete the trilogy begun with *A Grammar*. None of these have appeared, because, then as now, he is more interested in working on his manuscripts than going through the nuisance of publishing them. "Since Libbie cleared out," he wrote Cowley in 1975, "I have quit putting out my books. For two reasons: The second is that she helped so much by having been a secretary; the first is that she helped so much by my being so crazy about her, I was driven to prove, prove, prove, only roundabout to the shitten world, because so directly every day and night to *her* I was appealing." Nonetheless, he releases essays and occasional poems to the American cultural magazines that have always been his principal forum. Nearly all of his nonfiction books are not sustained expositions but collections of previously published essays. None of Burke's books is necessarily more important or central to his critical enterprise than the others. (In both these last respects, the modern critic he most resembles is Edmund Wilson, who is otherwise thoroughly different from Burke.)

In 1988 appeared *The Selected Correspondence of Kenneth Burke and Malcolm Cowley*, a 448-page volume edited by Paul Jay, a professor at Loyola University in Chicago. Since the two writers first met when they were respectively four and three years old, they would regard each other as surrogate brothers. As Cowley writes, "You remember the story told, I think it was by your mother, about the first time we met—I was three and you were four; I walked around your parlor touching things, and you walked after me saying, Don't touch. Mustn't." Of different temperaments, with Cowley very much a Sancho Panza to Burke's Quixote, they could also be critical of each other's latest activities. (Cowley once shrewdly commented that Burke tended to be *logical* while his own critical predisposition was *chronological*.) With letters written between 1915 and 1981 (though Cowley lived into 1989), the book is quite unlike anything else in the history of American literature. It reminds us how difficult independent literary careers can be and then of what an angry independent figure Burke always was, "doing battle on several fronts," as he put it.

When I returned to his Andover compound, on an early afternoon in midsummer 1989, the lesser houses were now surrounded by summertime toys. Four generations of descendants had been coming on the weekends, a few staying during the week. KB had just finished his standard homemade lunch of sardines, pure peanut butter ("no salt"), red onions, and sprouts, all bundled between toasted slices of 100 percent whole wheat bread. As he had developed a bent frame, he needed a cane to walk. Now he was more inclined to let his drink sit, declaring, "I'm no alcoholic; I don't need to give up drinking." (I've always imagined a beaming KB appearing in a hard liquor print advertisement with his glass in hand, declaring, "I've been drinking this stuff for seventy-five years, and I've written twelve books; I'm a member of the American Academy of Arts and Letters and the American Academy of Arts and Sciences, etc.")

He frequently recalled the premature deaths of his eldest daughter, the anthropologist, who had died the year before during a field trip in the South Pacific, and of his grandson, the balladeer Harry Chapin, who died in an auto accident in 1983. At a Century Club memorial for Cowley, in the spring of 1989, Burke broke down in the middle of his speech. A true survivor of the generation that included Faulkner and

Hemingway, Burke remains the last major American writer to be born in the nineteenth century.

He had spent the morning, as he usually does, thinking and then writing about his thinking at his manual typewriter; for even in his nineties, Burke awakes ready to work. Though inserting his hearing aid, he tended to neglect my specific questions, preferring instead to talk about his thinking. His principal current interest is constitutions, about which he typed by his own hand the following outline for me:

> Non-human tribes, lacking human ways with words, are thus
>   by Nature so constituted
>
> that they cohabit, and raise their young
>
> in sufficient numbers to survive and in turn propagate
>
> without recourse to verbal usages.

The Founding Fathers who framed our Constitution, a masterpiece of verbal prowess, had (like their elders and contemporaries) arrived at a time when their Technology was so developed in Europe that it both induced and enabled them in increasing numbers to sail the Atlantic and to transport slaves from Africa, thereby settling a whole, to them, new continent in ways that constituted the human transformation of a Wilderness into Colonies that became tax-paying real estate. As the same technology developed further, the institution of outright slavery was abolished, to be replaced by what the framers of a rival Constitution, "The Communist Manifesto," called, for workers hired in our market economy, "wage slavery." But a friendlier look at our Constitution leads to such considerations as: Though but *one* document, it gave us in actuality TWO. There gradually developed in the TECHNOLOGICAL kind, fittingly defining itself by a mode of Artificial Intelligence, the "G.N.P., Gross National Product," comparing annually the total of goods and services turned out by the citizenry as a whole while the Constitution as a POLITICAL instrument pluralistically makes possible the organization of factions which compete by rhetorical devices of persuasion, dissuasion, deflection, deception designed to raise people's hopes, rightly or wrongly, that the policies pronounced in a given campaign platform will bring more profit than any competing policies could to the nation in general and the members of the immediate audience in particular.

Either you get it or you don't; I cannot help just now.

Surrounded by books and clippings, most of them heavily annotated in minuscule handwriting (which he reads without glasses!), he was also writing retrospective papers for the 1990 meeting of the Kenneth Burke Society, at New Harmony, Indiana, in early May, around the time of his ninety-third birthday. I noticed that his own house had a lot more technology than before, thanks in part to his son Anthony who nowadays spends his entire summers there (just as KB spends his winters with Anthony in Vancouver): not only a color television hooked by cable into New York City programming, but a photocopier, a small electronic keyboard, and hearing aids. After resisting technology for so long, Burke was finally living in a pastoral semblance of the late twentieth century.

II

He is a critic for the adventurous; you take from him what you can get and only later realize how much it was.
—Robert Martin Adams, *New York Review of Books* (1966)

One reason why Burke's name isn't better known is that his books are as uncompromising as his life and speech. There is no way that anyone, even the most aggressive publisher, can sell them (or him) to a large audience. His books are disorganized; they are filled with unfamiliar words at times of his own invention (e.g., "dramatism," "logology," "socioanagogic"). They abound with explanations that do not explain, elucidations that scarcely illuminate, clarifications that do not clarify. His use of evidence is at times capricious. His characteristic

structural device is the digression. As Howard Nemerov put
it, "His mind cannot stop exploding."

Some of his sentences are brilliant, if not aphoristic: litera-
ture is "equipment for living." "Nothing can more effectively
set people at odds than the demand that they think alike."
"Form in literature is the arousing and fulfillment of desires."
His metaphors are outrageous—who else in an essay about
John Keats and his Grecian urn would compare a literary
critic to "a radio commentator broadcasting a blow-by-blow
description of a prize-fight," or the Teutonic prose of Kant
and Hegel to "the shifting of cars in a freight yard"? Burke
loves to refer familiarly to earlier works of his, if not quote
from them at length, less out of egomania than out of impa-
tience to get into his next urgent point.

In part because of his incomplete education, his mind lacks
the definite cast that customarily defines a professional as, say,
"a trained sociologist" or "a lawyer." As a result, he is likely to
use the schemes of any one of several disciplines to explain
phenomena in yet another area. Temperamentally a free
spirit, he is capable of such wayward shunts as, in an essay on
Shakespeare's *Julius Caesar*, composing for Mark Anthony a
speech explaining the play. Since he chooses his subjects as
well, he is intellectually unpredictable even to those who think
they know him well. In truth, Burke's eccentric style is pro-
foundly American; no European thinker could perform like
this, even if he tried. (The poet Arthur Vogelsang tells of
taking in graduate school a modern literary criticism in which
students were required to imitate explicitly one or another
master, except Burke whose stylistic variousness makes him
inimitable.) Wayne Booth, a University of Chicago professor
who has been one of Burke's closest readers, warns that he
"invents problems that are essentially beyond solution and
then claims to solve them by using principles that can be
assumed only as part of his invention. His whole enterprise
is impossibly, shockingly ambitious; yet it finally frustrates

intellectual ambition by undermining all solutions." Burke's customary comment about any analysis by others is that they "didn't go far enough."

In truth, his ideas cannot be completely summarized in an article; a monograph is scarcely spacious enough. No abstract can substitute for the experience of reading the Burkean text itself; in that sense, his work is closer than most expository writing to the art of poetry. For now, it is best to identify certain themes. One is that a work of art is an organic collection of "strategies" or rhetorical devices that "aim" to affect readers in certain discernible ways, so that the first task for literary criticism is identifying "a generating principle, in terms of which you can account for all the work's most important developments." To put it differently, the job of interpretation begins not with searches for hidden meanings but principles or sympathies embedded in the structure.

A second theme is that narrative usually functions as a "symbolic action" for a mythic base; in literature, the principal ritual ("the arousing and fulfilling of an audience's expectations") portrays various forms of rebirth. A third related idea is that in creating a literary work the writer suffers a ritual of personal purification through the articulation of subconscious conflicts. When he or she succeeds artistically, the work relates to her or his life by offering model strategies for "encompassing situations." Thus, on the one hand, the analysis of a writer's language can be understood as revealing his deepest psychology; on the other, Burke echoes the Aristotelian idea of poetry as cathartic to its audience, the work thus requiring the "completion" or fulfillment of the expectation it creates.

Analysis of "symbolic action," that characteristic Burkean epithet, thus involves the study of the relation of the work both to its author and to its readers, for Burke has developed an original way of regarding literary works as reflecting and providing strategies for life. Another Burkean theme is that the critical tools developed in literary analysis can also be applied to nonliterary expository texts to reveal their imaginative, "dramatistic" organization. As Stanley Edgar Hyman put it, "Anyone reading them for the first time has the sudden sense of a newly discovered country in his own backyard."

As a critic of literature, Burke believes that it is better to trust the tale than the teller, and in the following passage is a glimpse of his analytic style:

> By charting clusters, we get out clues to the important ingredients subsumed in "symbolic mergers." We reveal, beneath an author's "official front," the level at which a lie is impossible. If a man's virtuous characters are dull, and his wicked characters are done vigorously, his *art* has voted for the wicked ones, regardless of his "official front." If a man talks of *glory* but employs the imagery of *desolation,* his *true subject* is desolation.

Thus, it is the ultimate aim of Burkean literary criticism to prepare readers' minds better to understand imaginative literature.

The keystones in his literary criticism are extended essays, many of them over ten thousand words in length, on such classic subjects as Shakespeare's plays, Goethe's *Faust,* Coleridge's "Kubla Khan," and Keats's "Ode on a Grecian Urn," as well as St. Augustine's *Confessions* and Hitler's *Mein Kampf.* It is in these essays that he demonstrates his capacity for spectacularly attentive and systematic reading of a verbal text—for going farther, much farther, than anyone else. When I asked him how this was done, he produced his copy of a book he had once reviewed, Harold Bloom's extended critical essay on Wallace Stevens. On every page are perhaps twenty inked annotations. Key words are underlined, vertical lines trace connections. On the blank pages in the back of the book and even on the fly leaves are more extensive notes, some of them referring to the book in general and others to particular passages. This is the kind of professional artifact that could be on permanent display in any criticism factory.

One quality these major essays have is the use of several sorts of critical tools, most of them drawn from intellectual domains outside literature; for in the practice of literary criticism, Burke has exemplified the principle of "all there is to use"—all the analytic equipment that is available. These essays are also so dense and suggestive with insights and hypotheses, as well as digressions and speculations, that they, unlike most literary criticism, can be profitably reread time and time again with increasing comprehension. As early as 1941, W. H. Auden identified Burke as "unquestionably the most brilliant and suggestive critic now writing in America." In *Modern Literary Criticism* (1977), a huge person-by-person survey, Elmer Borklund credits Burke with "a body of work which in sheer size and complexity is unmatched by the efforts of any critic since Coleridge," which is to say that for quality, variety, quantity, and originality Burke has no equal.

Because of his emphasis upon reading a literary text in a complex and thorough way, Burke was regarded as a principal figure of the so-called New Criticism that seemed so dominant in the 1950s, while his interest in psychology made him an exemplary Freudian critic as well. Nonetheless, his long-standing concern with the encompassing structural elements in literature relates him to today's fashions in sophisticated literary criticism. One reason why Burke has survived professionally is that current fads and interests keep abreast of him. Several years ago, Harold Bloom, the Yale literary theorist and critic, told me, "Kenneth Burke seems to me the strongest living representative of the American critical tradition. My own criticism, since it changed in about 1967 or so, owes more to Burke than to any other figure. Burke, rather than Foucault or Derrida, provides for central American critics their inevitable ideas of the Negative and its uses." Though never fashionable, Burke has not been out of fashion either.

The best guide to Burke's literary thinking remains the penultimate chapter of Stanley Edgar Hyman's *The Armed*

Vision (1949); the most useful introduction to Burkology are the two paperback anthologies that Hyman coedited with Barbara Karmiller, *Perspective by Incongruity* (1964) and *Terms for Order* (1964). The best summary of "dramatism," or Burkean sociology, is Burke's own contribution to the *International Encyclopedia of the Social Sciences* (1967). The closest semblance of an intellectual biography is Armin Paul Frank's *Kenneth Burke* (1969). He is the hero of Frank Lentricchia's *Criticism and Social Change* (1983). Among the more recent critical books are Robert L. Heath's *Realism and Relativism: A Perspective on Kenneth Burke* (1986), Samuel B. Southwell's *Kenneth Burke and Martin Heidegger* (1988), and Greig E. Henderson's *Kenneth Burke: Literature and Language as Symbolic Action* (1988). Both *The Legacy of Kenneth Burke* (1989) and *Representing Kenneth Burke* (1983) are polymathic anthologies of extended criticism that supplement *Critical Responses to Kenneth Burke* (1967), which mixes long essays with short reviews. Now that a society has formed around his name, the business of Burke scholarship is likely to grow.

Perhaps the surest index of the variousness and richness of Burke's writing is the richness and variousness of the works that they have clearly influenced—not only literary criticism but sociology as well, for sociologists, like literary critics, have found in his books fertile ideas that could be developed and formalized into well-known theories. Burke's analytical method of "perspective by incongruity" has visibly informed Erving Goffman's books, beginning with *The Presentation of the Self in Everyday Life* (1959), while Hugh Dalziel Duncan wrote several books, including *Communication and Social Order* (1962), on the Burkean theme that art is the base of all communication (in contrast to Durkheim, among others, who defined religion as the base). Burke is also cited at the beginning of Robert K. Merton's work on the bureaucratic personality, in C. Wright Mills's essay on the vocabulary of motives, by Harold Garfinkel in his essay on degradation ceremonies, and in Joseph Gusfield's brilliant examination of "drinking-driving," *The Culture of Public Problems* (1981). (Indeed, Gusfield further acknowledged his debt to Burke by editing and extensively introducing *On Symbols and Society* [1989], an anthology of those KB writings relevant to the social sciences.) Anyone who has read a lot of commentary about Burke, as I have recently done, will notice how his protégés draw from different books (confirming my earlier point that none is necessarily central) and then will be awed by the simple *range of remarks* made about him. You could think that several intellectuals must have published under the same name.

Burke is also the major influence behind Stanley Edgar Hyman's *The Tangled Bank* (1961), which is a brilliant and monumental analysis of the artistic strategies in the writings of Karl Marx, James G. Frazer, Sigmund Freud, and Charles Darwin. Burke's notion of the myth of purpose, passion, pain, and perception, as well as of narrative rebirth, inform his friend Ralph Ellison's classic novel, *Invisible Man* (1951). "Kenneth's analysis of how language operates in society has been very important to me," Ellison told me a while back. "He remains one of the most useful authors for the writer, or for anyone interested in how language shapes, directs and achieves human motives." These examples hardly expire an exhaustive catalog, for there is no one else for whom the epithet *seminal* is more appropriate. Nonetheless, precisely because Burke's writings cannot be reduced to a few accessible doctrines, there has never been a school, let alone a class, of Burkites.

III

Poetry is made of (just) words, like the anatomy books, the books of philosophy—only it is words used with a broader sweep of

understanding, a better knowledge of their capabilities, a greater accuracy—words raised to [their] highest power.
    —William Carlos Williams, *The Embodiment of Knowledge* (1974)

It should not be forgotten that Burke has always been a poet, whose last *Collected Poems* (1968) included works from 1915 to 1967. No one else's collected poems are like these, including as they do an "imitation spiritual" with a musical score and nursery rhymes amid the free verse lyrics. Since the mark of his poetry is stylistic variousness, it is scarcely surprising that his *Collected Poems* also include some marvelously complicated visual poetry (called "Flowerishes") in which aphoristic remarks in various typefaces are set at several angles, meaning that the individual poems have neither top nor bottom nor center, thus realizing Charles Olson's ideal of the page as a poetic field with far more sophistication.

There is also a special text I would now classify as a conceptual poem, even though Burke himself would not use that term. If what we call conceptual art conveys artistic experience through descriptive prose statements, Burke's "Project for a Poem on [FD] Roosevelt" is a suggestive prose outline that succeeds, poetically, on its own terms. Following roman numeral II Burke begins:

Critical interlude. His attack of paralysis. The resultant *physical necessity* of patience, since his cure cannot be hurried. Sense of *limitations* (how to work within limitations). Training in *vagueness*, resulting from the long interim (psychologically imposing) wherein there is a distinct breach between attitude and act. [Etc.]

There is nothing quite like this in American poetry and, need it be said, for variety and originality (but not quantity or quality) no poet quite like him.

Burke may not be writing his memoirs, but anyone who has seen him recently knows that he can look back proudly on

Flowerishes
Flowerishes

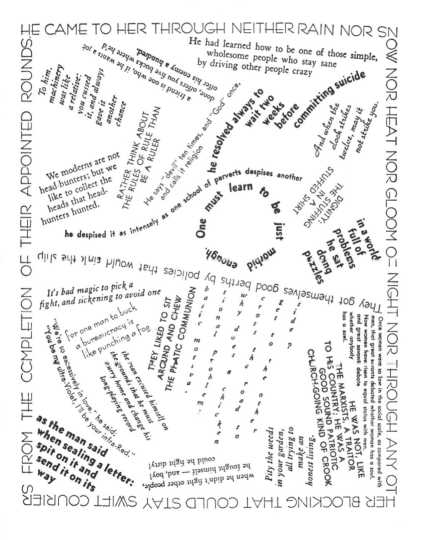

HE CAME TO HER THROUGH NEITHER RAIN NOR SNOW NOR HEAT NOR GLOOM OF NIGHT NOR THROUGH ANY OTHER BLOCKING THAT COULD STAY SWIFT COURIERS FROM THE COMPLETION OF THEIR APPOINTED ROUNDS.

He had learned how to be one of those simple, wholesome people who stay sane by driving other people crazy

To him, machinery was like a relative: you cussed it, and always gave it another chance

a friend is one who, if he wants a job done, offers you five bucks where he'd offer his enemy a hundred

he resolved always to wait two weeks before committing suicide

And when the clock strikes twelve, may it not strike you.

We moderns are not head-hunters; but we like to collect the heads that head-hunters hunted.

RATHER THINK ABOUT THE RULES OF RULE THAN BE A RULER

He says "devil" ten times, and "God" once, and calls it religion

One school of perverts despises another

DIGNITY: THE STUFFING IN A STUFFED SHIRT

One must learn to be just morbid enough.

he despised it as intensely as

in a world full of problems he sat doing puzzles

They got themselves good berths by policies that would sink the ship

It's bad magic to pick a fight, and sickening to avoid one

for one man to buck a bureaucracy is like punching a fog

THEY LIKED TO SIT AROUND AND CHEW THE PHATIC COMMUNION

The man excused himself on the grounds that he must hurry home and change his long-playing record

"We're so excessively in love," he said: "You be my ultra-Violet; I'll be your infra-Red."

as the man said when sealing a letter: spit on it and send it on its way

basic motivational problems: why did she get to the other side? chicken

when he didn't fight other people, he fought himself — and, boy! could he fight dirty!

Pity the weeds in your garden, all trying to make an honest living

Once women were so low in the social scale, as compared with men, that great servants debated whether women has a soul. Now women have risen to equal status with men, and great savants debate whether anybody has a soul.

HE WAS NOT, LIKE THE MARXISTS, A TRAITOR TO HIS COUNTRY; HE WAS A GOOD SOUND PATRIOTIC CHURCH-GOING KIND OF CROOK three-quarters of a century of writing, publishing mostly in literary magazines (that remain the cornerstone of our culture), of lecturing to scores of audiences, of earning a top-rank reputation without an agent or slick magazines or commercial publishers' publicists, of living a literary life with unfailing integrity. Just as he has no followers, so there are no genuine successors. Those who know about Burke can account for why, on that symbolic afternoon at the American Academy, he earned more applause than anyone else.

Some Old

Let me be specific as to what I mean by "official verse culture"—I am referring to the poetry publishing and reviewing practices of *The New York Times, The Nation, American Poetry Review, The New York Review of Books, The New Yorker, Poetry* (Chicago), *Antaeus, Parnassus,* Atheneum Press, all the major trade publishers, the poetry series of almost all the major university presses. . . . Add to this the ideologically motivated selection of the vast majority of poets teaching in university writing and literature programs and of poets taught in such programs as well as the interlocking accreditation of these selections through prizes and awards judged by these same individuals. Finally, there are the self-appointed keepers of the gate who actively put forward biased, narrowly focussed and frequently shrill and contentious accounts of American poetry, while claiming, like all disinformation propaganda, to be giving historical or nonpartisan views. In this category, the American Academy of Poetry and such books as *The Harvard Guide to Contemporary American Writing* stand out.
　　　　　　—Charles Bernstein, "The Academy in Peril" (1983)

The version of professionalization of poets at my institution is the dominant one of the American MFA industry: careful crafting (vowel-consonant music) of personal experience, the establishment of an authentic voice, the University of Iowa as the primary agency of certification (both poets on the faculty hold degrees from Iowa, the vast majority of poets who have read on our campus or have held the rotating endowed chair in creative writing have either taught at Iowa or graduated from there or both), a concentration on the lyric, etc. When I included Charles Bernstein in my symposium [titled "What Is a Poet?"], the poets at my school belittled Charles's work and urged some students to leave while he was speaking.
　　　　　　—Hank Lazar, in *Ottotole* (1989)

S. Foster Damon, 1893–1971
(1968–90)

> Many times he appeared at my door with a green baize bag full of books. He would open the bag, select a book and read aloud a passage that had struck his fancy; then we would talk about the usually forgotten or disparaged author.
> —Malcolm Cowley, "The New England Voice" (1978)

O F THE CONSEQUENTIAL teachers I had at Brown University at the beginning of the sixties, none taught me as variously as S. Foster Damon; so that even years later it is hard to select discrete dimensions from a web of influences. Let me begin by objecting to the fact that so much of the celebration of his career honors his path-breaking scholarly work on William Blake, which I consider only one aspect of his activity and achievement (and one that, incidentally, passed me by). From Foster I learned, instead, the principle that a truly adventurous literary critic should deal with subjects generally considered incomprehensible or "crazy," as indeed did most literature professors consider Blake in the 1910s and 1920s. Quickly assimilating this advice, I submitted to another Brown professor an honors thesis on Henry Miller, whose works in 1961–62 were not as well understood (or even as easily available) as now; this paper was returned to me with an *A* written across its title page and, curiously, nary a mark on its text, so problematic was my choice of subject. As a critic I have since specialized in avant-garde activities—those works of art that even professional critics find too outrageous, or too incomprehensible, too "crazy," to merit even a mention.

From Foster, I also learned to appreciate the idiosyncratic

qualities of American culture, at a time when America was finally realizing that its culture no longer stood behind Europe. However, this fight for treating our native art and thought so respectfully was Foster's long before I was born; and all of us who write today about Americana without apology should be partially indebted to him. Not only did he have a great appreciation of American cultural detail, but Foster also taught me that American arts would inevitably be radically different from European; and this theme has subsequently informed much of my own criticism. Similarly, I remember writing him from London in 1965, during my Fulbright year, to say that England was surprisingly dull; and he replied, both impatiently and proudly, "Come back to America, the land of the arts." This is a wisdom I've not since forgotten.

As Foster was the first man of letters ever to be my friend, he taught me what it means to be a serious writer in America— that life in literature is bound to be lonely, that disappointment is more the rule than acclaim, that the best work is privately generated, that self-sacrifice is essential, and that anything other than manuscripts after breakfast would be unthinkable. Foster's example also persuaded me of the profound and tragic truth that a thick stock of unpublished manuscripts is inevitably a sign of personal integrity; for whereas the hack creates to order, if not for the demands of a single outlet, then for the current fashions, the true writer must work, as Foster always had, principally for himself. Although Foster and I did not see as much of each other as we should, in part because we are both reluctant travelers, postal contact with him was very important to me through the 1960s. His letters were filled with so many extravagant generalizations and so much dispute with pieties and establishments that friends who have read them were convinced that this guy "Damon" must have been, like myself, a struggling writer in his twenties.

Indicatively, he alone of my undergraduate teachers continued to sympathize with my furthest-out ideas and enthusiasms; but only with my book on *The Theatre of Mixed Means* (1968), about the performance arts of "happenings" and related activities, did he start to protest, perhaps because he has not seen or personally experienced any examples of this new art. Just before his seventy-fifth birthday celebration in 1968 (where an earlier version of this memoir was read), I asked him about William Billings, the eighteenth-century American composer I planned to write about, and Foster knew things I had not encountered in the Billings literature, as well as giving me a few critical ideas. As a fellow critic and writer, he was then, to me at least, culturally younger than Edmund Wilson and Malcolm Cowley, who were respectively two and five years his junior, and culturally younger as well than most contemporary critics old enough to be his children. As William Blake's first great advocate in America, Damon was surely the hippest professor emeritus in this country.

II

[A mutual friend] tells me that Foster used to prowl up and down the study, smoking a long-stemmed German porcelain pipe, then dart to the table and write either a line of verse or a bar of music—or perhaps a sentence about Blake's prophetic books; one could never be sure which it would be.
— Malcolm Cowley, "The New England Voice" (1978)

My relationship with Foster was extremely crucial, if not necessary, during my years at Brown, which was then, let us say, not the most congenial of campuses for a student inclined toward eccentricities. When I arrived, he had begun to retire; and although he came to the main library to work at the Harris Collection a few times each week, his existence on campus was not publicized, perhaps because the powers-that-were in his field thought they passed him by. A friend of mine, majoring in creative writing but trying to avoid the profs in charge of that field, blindly registered for a class listed in the catalogue as "Verse Writing." I can still remember my friend coming to lunch after the first class, all excited, telling me about this "great old guy who seems to know E. E. Cummings and John Dos Passos. They were his buddies at Harvard before World War I." Although I was not then writing poetry, I registered too and, alas, did not do particularly well in the course.

What he had us do was imitate poetic meters from *Beowulf* to the present. These were exercises in putting words in the metrically most effective places. What the course reflected was not Foster the radical but an idiosyncratic conservative who believed in the possible music of poetry. I remember discovering his most famous poem, "The Mad Huntsman," which was published many years before; it begins:

> This is the perfect black, the borderland,
> This the Abyss, the Void—and I am here
> Watching the chaos simmer as with sand.
> But what am I?—I do not understand.

Three stanzas later it continues in the same vein:

> Across the shades; again between my knees
> I feel the surging horse; I glimpse the grey
> Night-sky above the colorless oak-trees;
> I feel my corrugating forehead freeze.

His poetry didn't get much better, alas. Nor did it change, for once he settled into Brown, among the more isolated Ivy universities, he developed bad habits that come from writing not for publication but mostly for himself. Post-World War II developments in American poetry had little noticeable effect on him, even though they were fundamentally no less disrespectful of T. S. Eliot than he was.

What Foster had to teach me was not the craft of metrical verse writing, which still escapes me (though I've done other kinds of poetry), but his experience as a man of letters. His stories and judgments were unforgettable, as well as very real and immediate; and I eagerly accepted his first invitation to drop into his sea captain's house way down on Thayer Street. I later learned that a long succession of comparably alienated Brown men had similarly found refuge there. His friendship, as well as his talk over those marvelous dinners we cooked together (and his indispensable recipes), became as important for my subsequent professional life as any course I took at Brown; for Foster represented the real world of literary writing, a domain that seemed very, very distant from both my own activities and the academic courses in literature. Indeed, it was, I suspect, through contact with Foster, rather than anything else in my early life, that I so quickly connected myself to that world. It was not for nothing that my very first book, an anthology that appeared a few years after I left Brown, *On Contemporary Literature* (1964), was partially dedicated to him or that my first book of poetry, *Visual Language* (1970), was wholly dedicated to him. (I remember going to a Rhode Island nursing home to deliver the latter book to him; and although Foster himself seemed uncomprehending, beside him, far more alert, was his wife Louise Wheelwright, John's older sister, who had returned to him only a few years before, after countless years away in a mental institution.)

While Foster was never a literary celebrity, he remained quite prominent to many of us. When the British writer Colin Wilson came to Brown in the early sixties, he met Foster and exclaimed, "I read your book on Blake years ago in Leicester. It changed my life. You can't be Foster Damon. I thought he was dead." When Foster told me this story over one of our dinners, he was more elated than depressed by this image of himself as deceased, for it demonstrated that his work and reputation had, so to speak, outlived him, as indeed it surely did. In my friend John Cage's biography of the American composer Virgil Thomson, I read that Thomson learned about his three greatest artistic influences—Gertrude Stein, William Blake, and Erik Satie—from an instructor then at Harvard named S. Foster Damon. Foster's Harvard classmate Cummings acknowledged, in *Six Nonlectures* (1953), that Damon "opened my eyes and ears not merely to Domenico Theotocopuli [commonly known as 'El Greco'] and William Blake, but to all ultra (at that moment) modern music and poetry and painting." In the late 1960s Allen Ginsberg told the world that Thomson and Damon took peyote together at Harvard in the early twenties—thus, as Ginsberg has it, placing a hip professor emeritus in the psychedelic tradition of American poetry. What I find remarkable is not just that Foster should have influenced others as much as he affected me but that Virgil Thomson is forty-four years older than I. No other teacher in America, ever, had protégés so far apart in age!

Northrop Frye (1975)

I am not suggesting that all works of literature are much the same work or fit into the same general schema. I am providing a kind of resonance for literary experience, a third dimension, so to speak, in which the work we are experiencing draws strength and power from everything else we have read or may still read.

—Northrop Frye

WITHIN THAT POPULOUS segment of the North American academic world that is professionally devoted to the study of literature, no living individual has achieved as much influence as Northrop Frye, Professor of English at Victoria College, University of Toronto, and the author of *Anatomy of Criticism* (1957), among other books. Now in his mid-sixties, he is the master mind of his field, the literature professors' literature professor. What makes Frye's influence so impressive is the fact that it was realized by himself, totally apart from any "movement," "institute," or other literary-political machine. Even more awesomely, this influence is based upon a single remarkable book, *Anatomy of Criticism*, which appeared in 1957 to no special acclaim; but as an acknowledged keystone in contemporary literary criticism, Frye's *Anatomy* has since been read by almost everyone doing graduate work, if not an undergraduate major, in any of the modern languages. It has also received an implicit honor accorded few books of literary criticism—translation into many other languages. Even in other professors' discussions of literature, his name is ubiquitous, as a fount of critical insight more popular than, say, Plato or Aristotle.

An "anatomy" is a handbook—a descriptive treatise—on the

structure of a system. Frye notes in the "Polemical Introduction" to his masterwork that wide reading in all literature led him to recognize "recurring principles" of literary structure. Viewing all literature from a great distance that enables him to see it whole, at a high level of generalization, Frye proposes an array of synoptic terms to define the structure of commonly recurring plots. His forte is offering a concise definition that applies to a large number of examples and yet excludes others. As Frye's categories cut across history and culture, they are applicable to all kinds of literary art—not only poetry, fiction, and drama but other kinds of imaginative writing, such as macrohistory and even narrative film.

Frye's *Anatomy* resists easy summary, in part because his categories are schematic, rather than systematic—to draw a crucial distinction; they cannot be neatly diagrammed or graphed. Moreover, since one set of distinctions refers to plot outline, another to the quality of extrinsic representation, and a third to the work's relation to the reader, the categories often intersect over an individual's work, in a hypothetically crossing grid. The best way to get a sense of Frye's characteristic approach, as well as his intellectual style, is to quote a few examples. "Pathos" he defines as "the exclusion of an individual on our own level from a social group to which he is trying to belong." The theme of Arthur Miller's *Death of a Salesman,* for instance, is precisely this pathos, which Frye considers "the archetypal theme of tragedy." He continues, "*Anagnoresis,* or recognition of a newborn society rising in triumph around a still somewhat mysterious hero and bride, is the archetypal theme of comedy." And with that illuminating sentence, Frye has defined the plot structure of numerous examples from literature, movies, and even comic books.

Elsewhere the art of fiction is reduced to five distinct modes—mythic, romantic, high mimetic, low mimetic, and ironic, all of which are precisely defined. In the "mythic" mode, "the hero is a divine being, and the story about him will be a *myth* in the common sense of a story about a god." In the "romantic" mode, "the chief characters live in a world of marvels (naive romance), or in which the mood is elegiac or idyllic." The hero is "superior in *degree* to other men and to his environment." The hero in the "high mimetic" mode is the leader, who is "superior in degree to other men but not to his natural environment." Then comes low mimetic: "If superior neither to other men nor to his environment, the hero is one of us; we respond to a sense of his common humanity, and demand from the poet the same canons of probability that we find in our own experience." Next: "If inferior in power of intelligence to ourselves, the hero belongs to the *ironic* mode." After drawing these distinctions, Frye offers one of those grandly sweeping conclusions so characteristic of his writing at its best: "Looking over this table, we can see that European fiction, during the last fifteen centuries, has steadily moved its center of gravity down the list." Yes.

In a different foray into spectacular generalizations, Frye divides all Western literature into four encompassing archetypes: romance, tragedy, irony, and comedy, which he then regards as "four aspects of a central unifying myth." That monomyth, which Frye finds at the root of all narrative, is the "quest for the Garden of Eden." Despite his propensity for distinctions, Frye thus regards all literature as a single unit, hypothetically with a single author (mankind). He sees literature as an essentially closed system in which new works relate largely not to life but to previous literature. As Frye persistently pursues his themes, in a charming, felicitous style full of original metaphors and sprightly wit, his *Anatomy* is strong, fearless, even megalomaniacal, mostly because its author seems to explain everything; yet the book is also so dense and full of suggestions, even in spikey asides, that someone such as myself, who has read it several times, can still find it providing new revelations.

Because of his emphasis upon the deep underlying struc-

tures of literature, Frye was initially considered a "myth critic";
but he differs from both religionists and Jungians, who are
also classified as "myth critics," in that Frye's categories are
inductive, rather than deductive. That is, his generalizations
were not deduced from prior knowledge of myth but induced
from wide reading in the world's literature. Even in dealing
with archetypal mythology, he is a rationalist, rather than a
rationalizer.

One reason for the initial neglect of Frye's hypotheses, espe-
cially in the United States, was that they had little to do with
the schools of criticism that were prominent in the forties and
fifties, such as the "New Critics" (e.g., Cleanth Brooks, R. P.
Warren), the biographical critics (Van Wyck Brooks), and the
socio-political critics (Edmund Wilson). Indicatively, it was a
younger generation, rather than established professors, who
initially acknowledged Frye's achievement.

Some commentators have connected his thinking to Parisian
"structuralism," which is similar in some respects, but really
quite different. Frye confesses to some difficulty in reading
those Frenchmen. "I wish they were more interested in litera-
ture," he says, meaning more inductive than deductive. In the
context of modern literary criticism, Frye's *Anatomy* seemed to
come out of "left field," which is to say Canada; his highbrow
homebrew is indigenously north-country moonshine.

In part because his approach is so unique, Frye's achieve-
ment resists easy classification. He is not "a scholar" in the
conventional sense, because he lacks a definable academic spe-
cialty; all literature is his mind's province. He is scarcely "a
philosopher," in spite of the level of abstraction he favors, in
part because his principal interest is literature, rather than
esthetics. He disparages both "public criticism, which assists
general readers in appreciation" and "the literary chit-chat
which makes the reputations of poets boom and crash in an
imaginary stock exchange." To this day, he has never written
reviews for, say, *The Saturday Review, The New York Times Book*

Review, or *The New York Review of Books.* "It is best to speak of me," he remarks, "as a critic of literature whose interest is putting the individual work of literature within the context of all literature. I think of 'criticism' as the systematic study of an art."

Frye's *Anatomy* is unusual, to be sure, in part because its author is likewise unconventional. At a time when most professors of English tried to become specialists in a particular period or genre, Frye became the supreme generalist; and if ambitious academic Canadians of his generation emigrated south of the border (e.g., John Kenneth Galbraith), he stayed in Canada. Descended from seventeenth-century Massachusetts Puritans who, as Loyalists two centuries ago, emigrated to Quebec, he was born Herman Northrop Frye, 14 July 1912, one year to the day before President Gerald R. Ford, in Sherbrooke, a New England-style mill city just north of Vermont. His father, a wholesale hardware supply salesman, moved his family to Moncton, New Brunswick, which then had a population of twenty thousand. North and east of Maine, the province of New Brunswick is commonly regarded as Canada's cultural backwater, roughly the equivalent of our Arkansas. Frye's mother, the daughter of a Methodist minister, introduced her son to the habit of voracious reading that he continued apart from his years in local public schools. He graduated from high school just before his sixteenth birthday; and since Moncton people rarely went to college, he entered the local business school to study typing and shorthand. The assumption was that he would become a clerk or a private secretary.

He made his first trip to Toronto in the spring of 1929, to compete in a national typing contest. With the banner of "New Brunswick" behind him, he placed second in the "novice" class, typing eighty words per minute. ("That was with a manual machine. With an electric, I can probably do 150.") While in Toronto, he visited Victoria College, which is one division of the University of Toronto, because his maternal grandfather, the Methodist minister, had gone there many years before. Matriculating the following fall, he took the honors course in philosophy and English literature, as well as participating in the debating club and the drama society; he also contributed to the undergraduate magazine.

Hardly a child of affluence, young Frye had to work his way through college, pasting book labels in the public library for fifteen dollars per week in 1930, and spending most of the depression summers writing essays to enter in scholarship contests; but in order to keep some of his scholarships, he had to maintain a top average. That requirement in turn forced him to prepare constantly for the next examination, which culminated with finals in the spring. In an off-moment he contributed to the undergraduate literary magazine a bitter denunciation of this academic regimen, blaming the mediocrity of Canadian writing upon this enforced neglect of "the awakening enthusiasm of spring which those educated here have always missed—for the average man brought up on May examinations knows as little about spring as he does about a sunrise."

Kingsley Joblin, now a professor of religious studies at Victoria, remembers that Frye, when they entered college together in 1929, seemed more self-confident than the other freshmen huddled together in an unattractive dormitory. Thus, he quickly became their spokesman in dealing with the outside world. "When we wanted a doughty champion," Joblin told me, "we chose Norrie Frye. In those days, we in Ontario wouldn't have thought of someone like Norrie coming from New Brunswick." The Canadian poet Earle Birney remembers that Frye, only a few years later, "seemed preternaturally wise, in the sense of knowing a lot, of having read more books than anyone else. Most of us were Marxist in those days; but when we argued with Norrie, he would always cite a book that none of us had read. I still remember him annoying a bright girl, a Marxist, by referring to someone named Friedell." Egon

Friedell, we remember, was a Viennese actor who wrote a multi-volume cultural history of the West. Even as an undergraduate, Frye had developed a taste for books with cosmic conceptions, such as H. G. Wells's *Outline of History* and Spengler's *Decline of the West.*

In the fall of 1933, just after graduating as the top student in the philo-lit program, Frye entered Emmanuel College, a theological school affiliated with Victoria, and studied there for three years. During that period, he was also ordained into Canada's United Church (a Protestant conglomerate). "I perhaps spent more time at Emmanuel doing English literature than theology," he remembers. "Theology for me was largely Frazer's *Golden Bough,*" from which, he acknowledges, comes much of his awareness of universal myths. He spent the summer of 1934 doing "mission field," as he calls it, in Saskatchewan, where he was issued not a car but a mare named Katie, whom he rode twenty-six miles every Sunday, preaching at three distant pastorless parishes. One summer on the ministerial road was enough. Returning to Toronto the following fall, he retired from both the institutional ministry and horseback riding.

In 1936, he went to Oxford's Merton College, like another North American, T. S. Eliot, more than twenty years before him. Frye, on a fellowship from the Royal Society (Canada's national academy of arts and sciences), took an undergraduate course in English. As a veteran student, he was scarcely pleased by yet more bouts with examinations; and as a Christian socialist, he was distressed by the growing sympathy for rightest Europe. "British morale was probably as low as it's ever been," he once told a reporter, "and everybody I ran into at Merton College seemed to be a fascist." In 1937, he returned to Victoria for a year of teaching and then went back to Merton the following year to complete his Oxford B.A. (which was automatically transmuted into an M.A. several years later).

In 1939, he returned permanently to Victoria, relieved to

be back in Canada, starting as a lecturer with an annual salary of fifteen hundred dollars. Though he never did any graduate work in English, let alone take a Ph.D., he was selected to teach the honors courses in sixteenth-century English poetry, seventeenth-century poetry, and nineteenth-century prose. Before long, he had taught, as he put it, "everything in English literature from Chaucer on." Moving swiftly up the academic ladder, he became an associate professor in 1946, a full professor in 1947, chairman of the English department in 1952, and principal (or dean) of Victoria College from 1959 to 1967. From 1948 to 1952, he also co-edited *Canadian Forum,* a distinguished monthly magazine. "It was a joe job," he says, "public service." Resigning from his principalship in 1967, he was selected Toronto's first "University Professor" and a Senior Fellow at Massey College, a nonteaching institution that is the University of Toronto's version of Oxford's All Souls. He has received numerous medals and honorary degrees.

Frye invited me to see him, one autumn weekday morning, at his office at Victoria's antiseptic New Academic Building. He had already been to his other university office, at Massey College, where he had dictated some letters to his secretary and returned accumulated telephone calls. ("Dr. Frye's office," his secretary says, even though the doctorates are all honorary.) His top-floor room at Victoria, perhaps fifteen feet square, is his more private office. The University of Toronto's other oracle to the western world, Marshall McLuhan, has an office within walking distance. Nearly exact contemporaries, they keep a wary friendship.

Greeting me with a reserved smile and a shy twinkle, Frye motioned me to a vinyl chair beside him. Medium in height and build, with gray, once-reddish wavy hair, a relatively unlined forehead and soft jowls, he switched from one set of wire-framed rimless glasses to another, lying in a case on his papered desk. His lips were thin, his mouth opening only slightly when he spoke. He wore a marine-green tweed jacket, a green tie, a green sweater, loose-fitting gray trousers, and brown suede shoes. His appearance was considerably less distinctive than his books, if not easily forgotten; the sound of his voice is equally hard to remember. A Toronto friend of mine, who met him often a decade ago, conjectures that, "If three men walked into this room just now, I'm not so sure I could tell you which was Norrie Frye." Mostly because he is so reserved, he seems a bit inscrutable; this agreeable, deferential man scarcely fit my image of the magisterial author of *Anatomy of Criticism.*

I asked how he managed to write his great book. From the study of religion, he explained, and particularly from reading Frazer, "I discovered that the Bible contained a mythological world and that eighteen centuries of European poetry continued this mythology." His *Anatomy,* he added, grew out of an earlier book on *William Blake* (1947) in which he learned that every great poet creates his own myths that nonetheless reflect traditional mythology. Frye's visibly nervous hands reached for a rubber band which he strung around his fingers until it broke; later he would take coins out of his pocket and play with them. "Some parts of the book, such as 'The Four Forms of Prose Fiction,' and the section on music and poetry, go back to intuitions I had as an undergraduate and recorded in my notebooks." His ideas were repeatedly tested in public lectures and, of course, his own classes. "You can say my writing is fertilized by my teaching." Around the walls of his office were books of English literature, a vertical set of shelves of modern poetry, another of American literature, and a third of Canadian literature. Directly behind his head was a book of mine, which he had once gracefully praised.

What is the general relevance of your ideas? Why, apart from professional purposes, should they be studied? "There are all sorts of benefits," he replied, "but they are scarcely automatic. Everybody is mythologically conditioned. Most people are conditioned by a phoney mythology of advertising

and newspaper clichés. I would like to make literary study
something that would make you aware of this conditioning. I
didn't start to get interested in my own theories until I realized
that they formed part of a teaching program that could be
taught to children." In other words, his terms inculcate more
attentive reading, of both literature and trash. "You are still
preaching gospels," I joked. "Yes," he replied, "but they are
not doctrinal gospels."

An agile mind, he moved easily from subject to subject as we
spoke, always responding promptly, but rarely elaborating—
agreeably reasonable, never provocative. Why did you spend
so many years as a university bureaucrat? "It's part of the
responsibility of an academic to do this. Otherwise, you get a
bunch of full-time administrators at the university; and when
that happens, the university goes to pieces." Who are your
favorite writers? "I don't have favorites. I find myself like a
sultan in a harem who makes his selections on somewhat ran-
dom grounds and for somewhat irrelevant reasons."

He invited me to lunch across a path, at Burwash Hall, a
high-ceiling refectory where Frye has been lunching for over
forty years. The faculty were served on a dias by white-dressed
women; the students got their own food on the floor. He told
me that he has spent nearly every academic year in Toronto,
occasionally taking off in mid-spring for a lecture tour or
to serve as a visiting professor (i.e., at Princeton, Columbia,
Oxford, Berkeley). Only two academic years have been spent
entirely away from Toronto—1950–51 and 1974–75; for the
last he was Charles Eliot Norton Professor of Poetry at Har-
vard. Some of our most distinguished universities have made
offers that no one except Northrop Frye could refuse. "This
place has always been good to me," he explained over soup.
"I have so many cultural connections here that it would be
quite an uprooting for me to leave Canada." His most recent
university sabbatical, 1972–73, was spent mostly at home.

Pleased to return to Toronto after a year at Harvard, he promptly produced several essays before classes began.

Over lunch he told me, with evident pain, about a departmental meeting the day before. Three junior professors had "come up" for tenured positions that, in the current academic depression, may not actually exist. "The demands made on young academics today, in order to grant them tenure, are so great that, if I were thirty years old today, I'd question going into academic work." He took a bite of his tuna fish sandwich. "I'd head for the Civil Service, where the requirements have a more human scale."

After lunch, we went together to his class on "Symbolism and Typology in the Bible," where he spoke totally without notes, not because he had memorized his lecture, but because the material was familiar enough for him to extemporize. This undergraduate class had over a hundred people, scattered around an ancient space, with rows of desks bolted to the floor, separated by two aisles. (His graduate class on "Principles of Literary Symbolism," later that afternoon, had over eighty students crowded into a more modern space large enough for fifty.) Everyone looked attentive; no whispers were heard. Standing erect and mostly stationary, Frye spoke leisurely, in a somewhat disjointed way, citing Biblical chapter and verse with unerring accuracy, frequently pausing to make sure his audience understood his points. He asked students for questions, his darting eyes looking for raised hands, his own hands either jangling the coins in his pocket or scratching the top of his head, his right ear leaning forward to hear the shyer voices. His answers were usually brief.

The theme of his lecture was similarities between the New Testament and the Old; and pursuing his bias that all correspondences in imaginative literature should be understood as identities, he audaciously identified such equations as Jesus with Joshua. "The only thing happening in the Old Testament is the redemption of Israel; everything else is a pseudo-happening. In the New Testament, the only thing happening is the life of Christ, which must be, metaphorically, the same event." He paused to touch the top of his head. "Nothing is in the Bible because it is historically accurate, but because it is spiritually significant." No one objected to his audacious interpretations, in part, I suppose, because the class was already several weeks old, but also because his manner was so methodical, so matter-of-fact, so conservative—so unlike what he was saying.

After class, Frye took the subway home and no doubt got lost in the post-rush-hour crowd. He and his wife Helen, a sometime lecturer on art history, no longer have a car, their last being a Studebaker; Frye himself never learned to drive. Notorious homebodies, the Fryes rarely entertain or go out socially. Their home, in a downtown residential district, is reportedly modest; they have lived there over thirty years. On most evenings Frye will play his piano, favoring eighteenth- and nineteenth-century pieces, drawn from a large collection of sheet music. ("Charles Ives?" I asked. "Too difficult for me.") He does not regularly attend church "though I do not feel like a stranger when I do." Indeed, he works on most Sundays. "I feel that church is where I am. That's a Protestant notion. The thing that attracts me about religion is the use of words like 'infinite' and 'eternal' which man has to use. Otherwise, he gets claustrophobia."

Politically, Frye has always been, as he puts it, "left of center. I suppose I'd be a left-wing Democrat in the States." He generally votes with Canada's New Democrat Party, which he defines as "roughly the equivalent of the British Labor Party." Frye thinks of Canada and, especially, Toronto as "the peaceable kingdom. If it turned aggressive, I'd consider moving elsewhere. Quebec separatism bothers me; I think it phoney." He paused. "What is called 'anti-Americanism' is really an essay in self-definition. Every Canadian has some American relatives."

His favorite recent vacation was spent in a country yet more peaceable, Iceland.

Though Frye considers himself "reclusive," he leads an active life. Early that fall, he had spent three days at a conference on Shakespearean romance at the University of Alabama, three more in New York City as an official of the Modern Language Association, two days in Kingston, Ontario, at a conference on violence in the media (that he summed up, in a quickly improvised address), a day in Boston lecturing on the Bible to the English Institute, another day in Ottawa delivering the major address at a Royal Society conference on "Preserving Our National Heritage." The day after I saw him, he would go to Ottawa again for three days to attend the public hearings of the Canadian Radio and Television Commission. He has been, since 1968, a part-time advisory member—the "tame intellectual," he says, implicitly contrasting himself with McLuhan. For the C.R.T.C., Frye has monitored programs and written critiques, among other tasks. A few days later, he told me he had nothing to contribute to the sessions, because the discussions concerned finance. "I can't tell a debenture from a debutante." He expected to spend yet more autumn weekdays with the C.R.T.C. in Ottawa and just after Christmas to attend the MLA convention in San Francisco, where he would be chosen president for a year. Almost everyone in literate North America has seen him at least once, though they, like my Toronto friend, may have trouble remembering exactly what Northrop Frye looks like. Mostly because of attention from the local media, his name is more generally familiar in Toronto than in New York, even to people who have never read his books; south of the border, he has so far been known almost exclusively to his academic trade.

Frye's essays are so exceptionally fluent that readers imagine them springing from his electric typewriter fully formed; instead, they are, in fact, composed piecemeal, often on the run—between classes, on the subway, and even in airport waiting rooms. "I'm like a squirrel burying nuts—morning, night, everywhere." He starts, he told me, with single sentences, almost aphorisms, which he collects in notebooks. "That's the way my thinking comes to me," he paused to finger his coins. "Most of my writings consist of an attempt to translate aphorisms into continuous prose." Around these kernel sentences he progressively builds paragraphs that illustrate the aphoristic generalizations, and these paragraphs are laboriously revised and expanded until Frye can no longer decipher his handwriting. Only then does he type up the paragraphs before reworking his prose some more.

On his desk were typed pages from a projected book. The single-spaced paragraphs were various in length. Some were connected to their predecessors or successors; others, not. This book, he estimated, would take several more years to complete. When he told me that he wrote without consulting the original texts, as scholars are supposed to do, I sensed that his kind of synoptic criticism was perhaps a creative art, comparable to poetry and fiction, that was particularly suitable for writers, like himself, with profound literacy and exceptional memories. His books are "teaching books," rather than "scholarly books," to quote his own distinction, which is to say that they come from teaching students, mostly undergraduates, rather than addressing colleagues.

His concentration upon pithy sentences accounts for the presence in his writing of some splendid aphorisms, which make fine epigraphs (as my own books sometimes show), even though they are scarcely anthologized as "familiar quotations":

Poetry can only be made out of other poems, novels out of other novels. Literature shapes itself, and is not shaped externally: the *forms* of literature can no more exist outside literature than the forms of sonata and fugue and rondo can exist outside music.

Politically, a Canadian is an American who rejected the Revolution.

Civilization we defined as the process of making human forms out of nature.

Criticism is to art what history is to action and philosophy is to wisdom: a verbal imitation.

In the direct experience of fiction, continuity is the center of our attention; our later memory, or what I call the possession of it, tends to become discontinuous. Our attention shifts from the sequence of incidents to another focus: a sense of what the work of fiction was all *about*, or what criticism usually calls its theme.

Literature, we said, is conscious mythology; it creates an autonomous world that gives us an imaginative perspective on the actual one.

The only way to forestall the work of criticism is through censorship, which has the same relation to criticism as lynching has to justice.

My opinion of the practice of giving a medal to any poet over the age of ten is not high.

This talent for aphorism reflects Frye's truest genius, which is a spectacular capacity for discerning the broadest structure, the encompassing pattern, the largest issues, of anything he examines.

Anyone who has read even bits of Frye gets the impression that this man has not merely read everything but deeply experienced and remembered it all as well—the classics of Greece and Rome, English literature from *A* to *Z*, Canadian literature, American literature, science fiction, romance, etc. (He has also written short critiques of film, music, ballet, and visual art.) Behind every generalization, every synoptic term, is a literacy that seems universal. He keeps selectively abreast of contemporary writing, thinking that the short stories of Alice Munro, sort of a Canadian Eudora Welty, "are about as good as anything I know in the field," and reporting to me that Thomas Pynchon's *Gravity's Rainbow* (1973) "is an extraordinary book. It is an examination of the way that the creative and the paranoid are different aspects of the same thing." He claims a "reading knowledge" of other western languages, none of which, however, can he speak with ease; and the only time an ex-student ever saw Frye panic-stricken occurred at a government function, when an officially bilingual civil servant addressed him in French!

When I asked Frye how he managed to do so much reading, he insisted, "I'm not the fantastic reader that people assume"—his characteristic modesty being less than fully persuasive. His personal library, spread over three places, is large, though not enormous. "I rarely read literary criticism," he confided, while playing with his pocket change, "and if so, then only for confirmation of my own ideas." The footnotes in the back of his *Anatomy* were, he admitted, added after the text was written. He spoke of himself as a "slow reader," which I also found hard to believe. "I read almost everything the way I read poetry. A book I don't want to read I can get to the point of in three seconds." His true forte, he insisted, was not speed reading but "an extremely tenacious memory for remembering what I've read." One reason why he reads so well is that long ago he equipped himself with Frygian structures of literary understanding; he was the first and perhaps the most successful student of his own pedagogical theories.

As an eminence in his own profession, Frye is frequently asked to give lectures—or series of lectures—particularly at universities (and sometimes over Canadian broadcasting); and these talks are often collected into books, which are customarily published by university presses. He characterizes them as "circling around the same issues as the *Anatomy,* though trying to keep them open-ended." (He published his *summa,* or summary, before most of the specific applications.) In 1963 appeared *The Educated Imagination,* which collects his CBC talks on the value of literary study, in addition to another book, *The Well-Tempered Critic.* Two years later he released both *The Return of Eden,* on Milton's epics; and *A Natural Perspective,* on Shakespeare's comedies; in 1967, both *Fools of*

Time, on Shakespearean tragedy, and *The Modern Century,* on contemporary mythology; in 1971, *The Critical Path* on the social context of literary criticism. Harvard University Press will release *The Secular Scripture* (1976), which collects his Charles Eliot Norton lectures on literary romance. Frye has also collected his scholarly essays into three volumes: *Fables of Identity* (1963), *The Stubborn Structure* (1970), and *Spiritus Mundi* (1976). His writings on Canadian art and literature were collected as *The Bush Garden* (1971); his miscellaneous book reviews as *Northrop Frye on Culture and Literature* (1978). The only book since the *Anatomy* which Frye wrote from scratch is a marvelous, often devastating monograph on *T. S. Eliot* (1963), whose politics Frye particularly deprecates. In addition, he has edited over a dozen books, including the Modern Library's selection of *William Blake* (1953) and an anthology of Blake criticism (1966). His current project—the one on his desk, his first large-scale book since the *Anatomy*—will deal with the Bible and its relation to English literature. Books, he told me in passing, are "not a synthesis of what you know but an expression of your attitude to experience"; and it is probably by his books, rather than his conversation, that this reticent man can best be known.

It is hard to measure the influence of Frye's criticism, but by no account has it been modest. The Princeton University Press sold ten thousand copies of *Anatomy* last year, mostly, one assumes, to literary professionals; sales for scholarly books nearly two decades old are rarely so high. Frye's essays are included in numerous textbooks and anthologies; his name is featured in all the recent histories of literary criticism. Back in 1966, Professor Murray Krieger, a scholarly critic of critics, could judge that Frye "has had an influence—indeed, an absolute hold—on a generation of developing literary critics greater and more exclusive than that of any one theorist in recent critical history." Four years later, Walter Jackson Bate of Harvard identified Frye as "the most controversial, and probably the most influential critic writing in English since the 1950s." Though surprisingly few of his own Toronto students have become prominent critics—"I neither want, need nor trust disciples"—several younger critics of note have acknowledged Frye's influence, including Angus Fletcher, Ihab Hassan, Geoffrey Hartman, and Harold Bloom. A few of them have since taken their own paths, and more than one has by now become, as he puts it, "anti-Frye." Ever liberal, the master does not seem to mind.

Fletcher, who is a Distinguished Professor of English and Comparative Literature at CUNY's Lehmann College, speaks of Frye's influence as "pervasive in the precise sense of the word. His is the largest single presence in North American criticism. He has unparalleled authority, and it is continually being attacked. It is hard to imagine North American criticism without him." One index of this pervasive influence became clear to me recently, when I had an occasion to read several critical books by younger American literature professors. Nearly all of them acknowledge Frye in some way; he is, literally, a touchstone. Frye's terms are also useful to teachers of literature at every level. Under his supervision, Harcourt, Brace is publishing a series of textbooks for grades seven through twelve, "The Uses of Imagination." He is also said to have influenced a flock of noted Canadian poets. The Toronto writer John Robert Colombo, who took Frye's courses two decades ago, judged, "McLuhan and Frye are Canada's Aristotle and Plato. McLuhan is the scientist, and Frye is the mystical theorist, with the eternal paradigms and the everlasting forms."

The most common criticism made of Frye's work points to limitations in its relevance. His ideas do not directly relate to issues, say, of formal innovation in literature, or social representation, or esthetic quality. "They explain structure," I've heard, "but not genius." Also, "he has only one method, classification." Other critics find that his terminology, especially in lesser hands, emphasizes the universal at the expense of the particular, whereas the quality distinguishing literature from mythology is precisely the particular. In looking at works of literary art, the derivative Frygian critic sees not individual achievements but grist for his conceptual mill. "It is not Norrie himself I dislike," one of them told me, "but the small fry."

The principal criticism made of Frye himself is that he is too distant and too cautious. For the first criticism I personally found much evidence. He does not engage issues, preferring shyly to assent, even to provocative assertions; and he is less inclined to initiate conversation than give brief answers. If only through his awesome literacy, he does tend to keep the outside world at a distance. Specifically, since he seems to know everything, one is reluctant to tell him anything. Secondly, little he does or says might upset his principal constituency of literature professors and Canadian intellectuals. Typically, he rarely disputes the canonical hierarchy of North American literary academics—Shakespeare at the top, Milton and Dickens a notch below, Blake below them. He rarely singles out for great praise any past writers whom his colleagues neglect. Solicitous of his reputation for always being smart and civilized, he won't risk appearing unsmart and uncivilized. A sociologist who studied at Toronto in the forties told me that even in his left politics at the time, "Frye was in no way out of step with the predominant mood of humanistic intellectuals at the University and in Toronto." McLuhan, who prefers a more critical, if not adversarial, stance, suggests, "Norrie is not struggling for his place in the sun; he is the sun." Frye's personal cautiousness seems entwined in both his compulsive modesty and his congenital incapacity to make serious mistakes. Whereas McLuhan recently retired from teaching, Frye received a three-year extension.

What Frye at his best has achieved is a complex structure of literary understanding that is useful not only to his fellow scholars but also to general readers and even grade-school students. Frye's schemes are almost Blakean in their dazzling, multifarious complexity, for the *Anatomy of Criticism* is, in its own way, a work of high verbal art that is, like the best poetry and fiction, a pleasurable reading experience of awesome implications and profound value. In his masterwork, Frye speaks of the mystery of art as coming "not from concealment but from revelation, not from something unknown or unknowable in the work, but from something unlimited in it." This description implicitly suits, to be sure, his own *Anatomy of Criticism*.

John Berryman (1969)

He [the poet] must be able to telescope image and symbol, if
necessary, without relying on the obvious connectives: to speak in
a kind of psychic shorthand when his protagonist is under great
stress. He must be able to shift his rhythms rapidly, the "tension."
He works intuitively, and the final form of his poem must be imagina-
tively right.

—Theodore Roethke, "Open Letter" (1950)

JOHN BERRYMAN GREETED me at the door of his
modest but comfortable, detached, three-story Minneapolis
house, situated atop a steep (and, in snow, treacherous) incline
from Arthur Avenue. A few blocks away is the University
of Minnesota where he is Professor of Humanities. It was
lunchtime; and in the course of taking my coat Berryman
invited me to join him for some Gluckenheimer, a blend mostly
of bourbon, he said, and a raid of the refrigerator. The occa-
sion for my coming was his winning the National Book Award
for *His Toy, His Dream, His Rest* (1968), his second collection
of the "Dream Songs" he had been publishing over the past
decade. Several other major honors had also recently come
his way—a Bollingen Prize in poetry (shared with Karl Sha-
piro), five thousand dollars from the Academy of American
Poets Fellowship, ten thousand dollars from the newly estab-
lished National Endowment for the Arts, and the republica-
tion of his earlier works. For this year at least he stands at the
top of his field.

We quickly settled down into two comfortable living room
chairs, before a window looking out into a street that even at
the end of March was filled with snow. Relaxing each other by

99

swapping gossip about mutual friends, I won his confidence for intimate talk by bringing regards from a girlfriend of seventeen years before. I got the impression that though the poet was a local celebrity whose name and face regularly appeared in the city newspapers, his life in Minneapolis was isolated. The telephone rang only twice in my eight hours there, once with an apology for the wrong number, while those he identified as his "closest friends here" were busy cultural officials—the chairman of his department, the director of the Walker Art Center, and the Minneapolis mayor (who once taught political science at the university). "I have a dreadful tendency when drinking to make long-distance telephone calls," he confessed at one point, "but I haven't made one in months." Berryman also admitted that he had not left his house in several days; and after describing all the socializing prior and posterior to his poetry readings around the country, he rationalized, "Doing that once a week doesn't leave you with much need for social life." On the day we met he was particularly peeved by a slick magazine's long-distance telephone request for "What ought the first astronaut to say on the moon?" "I said, 'I'm working on my lecture,' and hung up. Isn't that incredible? It's beneath contempt."

Berryman is shorter than his pictures suggest—perhaps five feet, ten inches, slight of build, though rounded in the tummy; in demeanor, both dapper and dowdy. His hair is fleecy and light brown, more thinning than balding; and the color of his full, but neatly trimmed beard runs from reddish brown under his nose to gray on his cheeks. Dressed that day in a white, button-down shirt, open at the neck, gray slacks, and black slippers, he walked gingerly, with motions that might be graceful, were they not so halting. Continually recrossing his legs, he swings his loose foot back and forth in a steady rhythm. His blue eyes look at you through fairly thick eyeglasses, and in his long-fingered, pale, visibly shaking hand is either a cigarette, a pencil, or a glass. The furniture is nondescript

American; and beside him in the living room were several piles of books which he is currently reading, an ash tray, a pack of Tareytons, some unanswered letters, and a couple of vials of pills. Rufus, a black, chubby mongrel with a brown-splotched face, walked in and out. When I first arrived, Berryman was quite lucid, through rambling; but as the afternoon wore on and all the drink got to his tongue, his conversation became more erratic, his tone more oracular, his attitude more peremptory, and his diction more slurred. There was ample evidence of his reputation for causing, if not cultivating, tension in those around him.

I opened by asking to what extent Berryman the poet resembled "Henry," the character who dominates the "Dream Songs"? "Henry, eh? He is a very good friend of mine. I feel extremely sympathetic to him. He doesn't enjoy my advantages of supervision; he has just vision. He's also simple-minded. He thinks that if something happens to him, it's forever; but I know better." This extraordinary conception of an alter ego, different from himself and yet exposing the author's attitudes, came to Berryman in the middle fifties, after two years of experiment. As we spoke, Berryman claimed to have abandoned Henry, but on the table next to him was yet another "Dream Song," scribed in pencil and dedicated "To Bernard Bowron." He explained, "Well, mostly I'm through with Henry; but the minute I say that, pains course through me. I can't bear to be rid of that admirable outlet, that marvelous way of making your mind known to many other people."

It is an unlikely but perhaps significant fact that Berryman and Ralph Ellison, whose eminence as a novelist equals Berryman's as a poet, were both born in Oklahoma in 1914, two years after statehood, Ellison on March 1 in Oklahoma City and Berryman on October 25 in McAliester, 125 miles to the southwest. Berryman's natural father, John Allyn Smith, was a banker from Vermont, who claimed descent from Ethan a banker from Vermont, who claimed descent from Ethan Allen; his mother, born Martha Little, was a schoolteacher from the South. They met in a rooming house and married, their son suspects, "as the only two literate people in that part of the state. My mother had a good instinct for things. She read Steinbeck and Faulkner before anyone else, but Dad preferred magazines." The Smiths lived in Sasakwa at the time of the poet's birth (McAliester having the nearest large hospital); and the family later moved to Anadarko, also in Oklahoma. A second son was born in 1919.

In 1925, they went to Tampa, Florida. "As a boy I liked Florida very much. Tampa had a wonderful stamp dealer; and since my father made a lot of money in the real estate boom, I had a fantastic allowance each week—something like twenty-five dollars which I got on Thursday and spent on Friday." However, his father committed suicide the following year, and his mother subsequently married John Angus McAlpin Berryman, whose surname both sons took. This Berryman family moved to New York, where young John attended public school in Jackson Heights before going to preparatory school at South Kent. Graduating from prep school earlier than expected, he entered Columbia College in 1932. By this time he had departed from the Catholic Church, into which he was born; and today he has no doubts about his youthful waywardness. "I'm not sure that God exists, and I'm very hostile to the worship of the Virgin. In New York, half the time I vaguely feel Jewish."

His first year at Columbia was spent largely in student politics, as he lost an election for class vice-presidency, and in student sports, as he ran the quarter-mile and half-mile and joined the freshman wrestling team. "I wasn't good enough for any varsity sport," he mused. Instinctively attentive to good-looking women, accomplished as a social dancer, he had a busy social life, mostly with undergraduates from Smith alumna, then a university dean, who, standing apart from her husband, spoke warmly of dating Berryman some forty years before.) As a sophomore, he switched undergraduate circles by joining the more literary crowd, contributing regularly to the *Columbia Review*. He also began to write a poem every day, even publishing a few of them in national magazines; and he wrote occasional book reviews for *The Nation*. His primary mentor at the time was Mark Van Doren, then Professor of English at Columbia and now a co-dedicatee of Berryman's most recent book. "He lent me books, advised me on various things. I like his poetry, particularly his last book, which is his best; but there was no stylistic indebtedness—Yeats being my first and last major influence. If not for Van Doren, I must not have become a poet."

It was Van Doren who urged Berryman to apply for the coveted Kellett Fellowship to study in England, and the young man won it, entering Clare College, Cambridge, the following fall. "I drew in my horns. I realized my stuff was no good." Instead, he concentrated on reading English literature, developing that fantastic literacy that impressed literate acquaintances a generation ago, and becoming the first American to win the Charles Oldham Shakespeare Scholarship (after four three-hour exams). Berryman also befriended Dylan Thomas, who had come to Cambridge to give a reading. "We drank as long as the pubs were open—no hard liquor then, just beer, for hard liquor came much later. Thomas was exactly one day older than me—October 24, 1914; and he used to make a lot of that, much to my annoyance." (In fact, however, Thomas, born on October 27, 1914, was two days younger than Berryman!) The young American abroad also took high tea with William Butler Yeats in 1936; and although not much important was said, Berryman vividly remembers offering his master a cigarette, which Yeats accepted, and then lighting it. Indeed, the incident is memorialized in number 215 of his "Dream Songs."

Returning to America in 1938, he spent his first year at his mother's Manhattan apartment, "doing nothing but writing," and the next teaching at Wayne State University in Detroit. He also became in 1939, for one year, poetry editor of *The Nation*—a position that put him in correspondence, if not personal touch, with both established figures and aspiring poets of his generation, such as Delmore Schwartz, Randall Jarrell, and Karl Shapiro. "I always wanted to be much older than I was," Berryman reminisced between cigarette puffs, "and from an early age I took to advising my seniors." The composer Milton Babbitt remembers that in the forties, "John had the most magnificent capacity to improvise elegant and very literary speech," and Robert Lowell recently wrote, "As soon as he began to publish, one heard of his huge library . . . his endless ability to quote poetry, and his work on a conclusive text of *King Lear*." Unfit for the military, because of a mental breakdown several years before, he did not go to war.

In 1940, he was offered a teaching job at Harvard, partially thanks to Schwartz's recommendation; and three years later the poet-critic Richard P. Blackmur invited Berryman to Princeton to teach for two years in the Creative Arts Program. It was there that Berryman taught his best-known former students, all of them born around 1925—the poet-translator W. S. Merwin, the novelist Frederick Buechner, and the translator-classicist William Arrowsmith. Between 1945 and 1954, when he came to Minnesota, Berryman was an academic vagabond, living largely in Princeton with his first wife, winning several major fellowships, and taking short-term teaching appointments and lecture- tours around the country. To the novelist Edward Hoagland, who studied with Berryman at Harvard during the summer of 1954, "He taught by exemplitude. He talked mostly about books he had loved with a fervor that amounted to a kind of courage. He hated stupidity and was harsher to lazy students than any teacher I've ever known, but he was also affectionate toward promising writers." During this rather rootless period, he also published several important critical essays, drawn mostly from projected books that are still unfinished, and a few short stories, one of which, "The Imaginary Jew" (1945), has been frequently reprinted. In 1950 he published a commissioned biography of Stephen Crane, which belongs among the best literary monographs ever produced on these shores—lushly written, elaborately researched, continually perceptive.

Beside Berryman's living room chair was a spread-eagled copy of Baldassare Castiglione's sixteenth-century *Book of the Courtier,* which he planned to teach the following afternoon in his only course, a twice-a-week survey for seventy-five or so undergraduates on "The European Heritage." This semester was devoted to the Renaissance and Reformation. "If poets teach, they ought not to teach poetry. That's too much like the main thing, poetry and criticism; it can be comforting and yet cheapening. A writer never does the same thing twice, but a teacher is bound to his routine. He can't change courses every year—the physical labor would be too great." He paused to sip his drink. "Writing is not routine. Each fresh experience means the possibility of absolute failure. You take your chances. Every day I open my mail to see what they are saying about me; but poetry students, unlike the public audience, can't, or don't, get up and leave. It's better to teach the classics or the history of ideas."

Berryman's closest friends in life are and were the poets of his own generation, most of whom he has not seen too often. "In America, it is very difficult to keep in touch with your friends, because of geography; they are always elsewhere. In general, I like people, and poets, my own age better." Also some of them have died in the past few years—Theodore Roethke, Randall Jarrell, Richard P. Blackmur, and Delmore Schwartz (to whose "sacred memory" the last book is also dedicated); and remarks about each of them infiltrate both Berryman's poetry and conversation. (Indeed, at times in his

poetry, the fortunes of these few people are rather preten-
tiously portrayed as a measure of the world's civility.)

"Delmore was extremely beautiful and miraculously bril-
liant, if not one of the best talkers I ever heard in my life; but
he became too well-known too soon and came to count on
fame. He began to plan his career, but a literary life is not to
be planned that way." Though productive and successful as a
young man, Schwartz in his later years became extremely
erratic, if not psychotic; and Berryman painfully remembers
bailing Schwartz, "acting like a maniac," out of a police station
in Washington, D.C. Earlier in the evening Schwartz had been
trying to make long-distance calls on a telephone he had just
pulled out of its socket.

"Roethke? A marvelous poet. We had a long session one
time in Rome. He wanted me to read his recent poems, and I
wanted him to read *Mistress Bradstreet*. However, he didn't
keep his part of the bargain. He no more cared about my work
than a hole in the head. Yes, Ted." Again a puff. "It was
impossible not to like him, but difficult to make him a real
friend, in both cases because he was so childish. He was inter-
ested in love and money; and if he had found a combination
of them in something else, he would have dedicated himself
to it instead of poetry." Berryman first met Robert Lowell in
1944, under the aegis of Allen Tate, who a few years before
had picked them both, as well as Jarrell and Schwartz, as the
promising talents of the generation then under thirty; and
Berryman proudly remembers proposing some persuasive
changes for Lowell's most famous early poem, "The Quaker
Graveyard at Nantucket" (1946).

From the beginning of his career, then, Berryman felt part
of an insurgent poetic generation that knew each had profes-
sionally to help the others constantly, or they would *all* lose.
"I still do," he added, though all four figures have very much
succeeded as poets. "In the thirties, we hated *The New York
Times Book Review,* and most of the existing magazines. All the

places where one would have wanted to publish, like *The Dial* or *Symposium* or *Hound and Horn,* were interdicted, had died. There was a need for serious magazines, and most of the new journals, like *Partisan* and *Kenyon,* came into existence around 1935. Actually you're setting your sights against the whole of American society, which is a dangerous business. Various diseases await you—women, homosexuality, silence." Was fear of risk among them, I suggested. "Yes, fear of risk. Some people hang onto their tiny reputation, sniping at everybody else; and you know where that takes you—straight to hell."

Inevitably, Berryman is haunted by the personal wreckage of this poetic generation—the high incidence of mental hospitalization, heavy drinking, broken marriages, and premature death; and after evading the equally inevitable question of why, he offered some explanations, both individual and social, none of them quite satisfactory to either him or me. "You asked why my generation seems so screwed up? But I really don't know why. They just seem to be very unhappy." His temper changed once he took another gulp; his voice grew louder.

It seems they have every right to be disturbed. The current American society would drive anybody out of his skull, anyone who is at all responsive; it is almost unbearable. It doesn't treat poets very well; that's a difficulty. President Johnson invited me to the White House by ordinary mail, but the letter reached me in Ireland, a few weeks after the ceremony. From public officials we expect lies, and we get them in profusion. American society is running the most disgusting war in history in Vietnam, and it elects disgusting public officials like Nixon, who makes you want to vomit. Don't you agree? And it puts up [Hubert H.] Humphrey, who is barely more respectable. I wanted to see [Eugene] McCarthy and [Nelson] Rockefeller; and though a lifelong Democrat, I probably would have voted for Rockefeller.

His voice became even louder and more raucous. "The protests are going to get worse and worse and worse and worse for years. Perhaps Sylvia Plath did the necessary thing by putting her head into the oven, not having to live with those lies."

Halfway through the afternoon, Berryman's daughter, six-year-old Martha (called "Twissy-Pitts," among other nicknames), let herself in the door (a son Paul by a second marriage lives with his mother in Westchester); and a short while later, Kate Berryman entered with school books under her arm. A tall, thirtyish, attractive brunette, with short curly hair, she had just returned from classes in elementary education; and not only does her constant sober cheerfulness contrast with her husband's decidedly volatile temperament, but her presence seemed, perhaps unintentionally, to dampen her husband's speech and activities.

II

You liked him to live in another city.
                —Robert Lowell, in a memorial memoir (1972)

Berryman's earliest poetry, that written back in the 1930s, came largely out of Yeats's influence, perhaps with a bit of Auden added—short, lyrical, rather formal, rhythmically intricate, and stylistically derivative. "A Point of Age," written in 1940, opens with this stanza:

> At twenty-five a man is on his way
> The desolate childhood smokes on the dead hill,
> My adolescent brothers are shut down
> For industry has moved out of that town;

Some twenty early poems were collected in Berryman's section of *Five Young American Poets*, which New Directions published in 1940 (the other poets in debut included Randall Jarrell);

and more short pieces went into *Poems* that was issued in 1942 by the same firm. Scarcely anyone outside of previous friends took notice of either book. Of his poetic aspirations during the middle forties, Berryman wrote in retrospect, "I wanted something that would be both very neat, contained and at the same time thoroughly mysterious." His next collection, *The Dispossessed* (1948), attracted slightly more attention; but not until the fifties did Berryman's work begin to infiltrate the established anthologies. Obstacles arose when he tried to publish as a single book his poems of fifty-seven eight-line stanzas, "Homage to Mistress Bradstreet," that had originally appeared in *Partisan Review* in 1953. The publisher to whom he was contracted dallied so long that Berryman took the manuscript to Farrar, Straus and Cudahy, as it was then known, where a Columbia College friend, Robert Giroux, had just become an editor; and the poem appeared in 1956, with illustrations by Ben Shahn, who was then more prominent than he is now. The years between 1953 and 1956 Berryman now regards as the low point of his life—the prolonged break-up of his first marriage, the premature death of his friend Dylan Thomas, the lack of permanent jobs; but Harvard and Iowa rescued him with short-term appointments, and then Minnesota offered his first permanent position.

The poet divides his total work into four distinct parts: (1) short poems, "to which I don't pay much attention, though some are very good;" (2) *Berryman's Sonnets* (1967), which were largely written during and about an affair with an unnamed married lady in the late forties, but not published until recently; (3) *Homage to Mistress Bradstreet*, in which, as he puts it, "The 'I' of the twentieth-century poet modulates into her voice;" and (4) "Dream Songs," which, though currently collected into two volumes, are formally divided into seven separate but untitled "books," each introduced by a Roman numeral. "All the way through my work is a tendency to regard the individual soul under stress," he explained.

The soul is not oneself, but the personal "I," me with a social security number and a bank account, never gets into the poems; they are all about a third person. I'm a follower of Pascal in the sense that I don't know what the issue is, or how it is to be resolved—the issue of our common human life, yours, mine, your lady's, everybody's; but I do think that one way in which we can approach it, by the means of art, coming out of Homer and Virgil and down through Yeats and Eliot, is by investigating the individual human soul, or human mind, which-ever you prefer—I couldn't care less. I have tried, therefore, to study two souls in my long poems.

"The point of the Bradstreet poem," he continued, in his most sustained exposition of the afternoon, "was to take a woman unbelievably conventional and give her every possible trial and possibility of error and so on, and wind her up in a crazy love affair, and then get her out of it—better, get her out of it in ways that will allow her forgetting of it after a long period of time. The affair in the whole middle part of the poem is not historical but purely imaginary. The title is a pun—homage to *Mistress* Bradstreet, namely the poet's mis-tress in the twentieth century; he works from himself into her through the two of them, back into her, out of her, to the end of the poem, which ends in the twentieth century." Berryman took a hefty gulp from his glass.

The point in Henry was to investigate a man with many opportunities, far more than those allowed to the lover in the *Bradstreet* poems—many chances to observe and to see what people of various nations are like, and what they do and are, and so on. Now Henry is a man with, God knows, many faults, but among them is not self-understanding. He believes in his enterprise. He is suffering and suffering heavily and has to. That can't be helped. And he has a friend, Mr. Bones, but the friend is some friend. He's like Job's Comforter. Remember the three people in the poem of Job who pretend to be his friends. They sit down and lament with him, and give him the traditional Jewish jazz—namely, you suffer, therefore you are guilty. You remember that. Well, Henry's friend sits down and gives him the same business.

I could have studied other things, for example, adultery, which is a big problem in the United States—people always sleeping with other people's wives. We don't use the word "adultery" very much, but occasionally it even appears in the papers. It's not in the Dream Songs, and I don't know exactly why. The whole *Sonnets* sequence is about adultery, so I felt relieved of the problem, or that it wasn't my problem anymore. Let somebody else handle it from a new point of view. Also Henry is so troubled and bothered by his many problems that he never actually comes up with solutions, and from that point of view the poem is a failure. Another problem is limitations in the narrator. I couldn't let him use fancy language. That was out. It didn't go with the blackface business. The diction is very limited. He doesn't have the language to discuss, for example, Heisenberg's theory of indeterminacy, or scholarly questions, or modern painting.

Though common themes and concerns run through Berryman's poetry, the "Dream Songs" represent a distinct break from the earlier work, almost as if the preciously literary poet suffered rebirth as a sotted sensibility, speaking in a radically different style whose abrupt shifts in both cadence and syntax suggest as well as reflect incoherent drunkenness; for Berryman's forms are now looser, the diction less formal, the general impression sloppier, the frame of reference more contemporary, and, most important, the poetic voice instantly recognizable as his:

> The bluebells, pool shallows, saluted him over needs,
> While the clouds growled, heh-heh, & snapped, & crashed,

"After having done one thing," he explained, "you want to do something as different as possible. I wanted a completely modern poem, *Bradstreet* having been an essentially seventeenth-century poem with twentieth-century interpolations. I think my later work less stupid than my earlier work." In reviewing the second volume of "Dream Songs," the critic Jascha Kessler was awed by Berryman's "increasing ability to project a writing voice as well as a voice speaking at many levels of both volume and diction, ranging from a kind of Gullah shorthand through breezy locker-room jocularity to meditative song, elegiac laments, and vision, sometimes running that entire diapason within the eighteen lines of one poem." A paradox peculiar to Berryman's own development is that as his speech became less elegant, less literary, and less coherent, his poetry became better, almost as if alcohol replaced literature as a primary oil of his poetic inspiration.

"I try to be coherent when I talk to another person, but one is sometimes incoherent regarding the sounds pushed at him by the progenitor. I feel further that we need a poetry that gives up everything—all kinds of traditional forms—and yet remains rich." He paused to draw from his cigarette. "What is wrong with poetry now is that poets won't take on observation, dealing with what is sent into individuals from the universe. It would seem to be that the job of the poet, if I may speak of such a ridiculous thing, is to handle the signs, to field them as in baseball." Why then, I asked, was he currently writing, as he put it, "a poem about heaven laid in ancient China?" "Why not?"

The "Dream Songs" are not as difficult as they might seem at first; for once the reader accepts their logic as closer to the waywardness of dreams and of inebriated stupor than to discursive prose—in Robert Lowell's phrase, "not real dreams but a walking hallucination"—the relation among the parts often becomes more credible, if not coherent. "Both the writer and the reader of long poems need gall, the outrageous, the intolerable," he declared upon receiving the National Book Award, "and they need it again and again. The prospect of ignominious failure must haunt them continually." The central figure, Henry, who speaks, in Jonathan Cott's phrase, in "the singing brawl of a declamatory sot," concerns himself with a multitude of matters; and in the entire work, now stretched to 385 published songs (which their author regards *not* as individual poems but as parts of a whole), is a cumulative impact. Berryman has declared that the first collection of these songs "concerns the turbulence of the modern world, and memory, and wants," but to Cott the theme of the entire work is "nothing less than the decline and fall of the contemporary West."

Though quite unlike anything else in poetry, the "Dream Songs" nonetheless reveal Berryman's continuing debt to the modern masters. "From Pound," judges Lowell,

He learned the all-inclusive style, the high spirits, the flitting from subject to subject, irreverence and humor. I feel the presence of Stevens, in sonorous, suggestive, nuance-like, often not quite clear lines; in cloudy anecdote about fanciful figures, such as *Quo,* or in the sections on Clitus and Alexander the Great. . . . The resemblance to Cummings is in the human, verbal contortion, and pathos. There is also Joyce.

Those critics who write regularly on poetry have by and large preferred this later work to the earlier Berryman; but perhaps because the "Dream Songs" are so idiosyncratic, representing a style valid and relevant only to their author, their visible impact on contemporary poetry has so far been negligible.

Kate Berryman invited me to stay for dinner, which she made from a Chinese recipe; and at first the poet paid more attention to a beautiful, but politely unresponsive, young woman who had come to join us. Over a desert of cheesecake he chanted a Bessie Smith blues, authentically reproducing the original subtle rhythms and intonations, and then brilliantly declaimed selected passages from his favorite younger poets— James Wright, W. D. Snodgrass, Adrienne Rich—as well as from his own "Dream Songs," including the great one, number 18, subtitled "A Strut for Roethke."

Indicatively, though he speaks of abandoning traditional forms, he prefers the more conservative fortyish poets to the radicals, and confesses to not reading/knowing/appreciating any American poets under the age of thirty-five. "I don't keep up with contemporary writing, except my friends. I don't read much. I sit and think. Reading is for young people." After getting up from the dinner table, he settled down with another glass of Gluckenheimer with water, which he consumed quickly. "It's rather useful for poets, relaxing after their labors." What about psychotropic drugs? "Know nothing about them." Kate chimed, "I don't know anyone who uses alcohol to such good advantage as you do, John." He smiled, evidently proud of his wife, and extended his glass, "Make me another drink."

> Turning it over, considering, like a madman
> Henry put forth a book
>
> ....
>
> Bare dogs drew closer for a second look
> —John Berryman, Dream Song number 75

P.S. (1990) A year later he joined Alcoholics Anonymous; three years later he jumped off a Minneapolis bridge to his death.

As I reread this portrait two decades later, I realize how deeply Berryman came to represent in my own mind the kind of poet/person I didn't want to be.

Notes on the Poetry Biz,
1985–89 (1990)

THE ONLY GENUINE measure of a poet's importance is the authorship of works that survive; anything less does not count. Once we move outside the classroom (with its gradations of *A-B-C-D-F*), there is no sure means for calculating distance from the top; there is only everything else. The surest medium for testing the possible permanence of poetry is the memory, both individual and collective, of serious, experienced readers of poetry. Simply, if you, as a regular reader of poetry, have read a poet's work, and yet cannot remember anything that he or she has written, dollars to donuts there is nothing worth remembering. Moreover, if this poet's work cannot be remembered, it does not matter what others say about him or her, or how many prizes he or she has won, or what position he or she might have in the academy or any other cultural bureaucracy; that work has no hope of survival.

May I propose a simple experiment any of us can do alone: Look at a list of putatively important American poets, and then try to connect particular poems or even lines of poetry to each of their names. Then do a converse experiment with a colleague: Each of you show the other a typical or best poem by a prominent native poet, with his or her name deleted, and then see which authors can be identified by work alone. You may be surprised by how many well-known individuals flunk these simple tests of memorable example and signature.

What is puzzling is not that so few do distinguished work but that more poets don't try to realize a unique signature, thinking instead that their education, professional position, or charming good looks will compensate for esthetic deficiencies. It is amazing how many otherwise intelligent writers made the mistake, or are conned into making the mistake, of thinking that their work must be "important" if it resembles widely accepted models. Everyone complains that the number of poetry writers in America exceeds the number of poetry readers, which is to say buyers of poetry books, as though the modesty of the latter figure reflected cultural failure. However, consider the opposite that is likewise familiar to everyone—few American poets do work that is worth reading, even by other poets. My own sense is that this mad quest for counterproductive uniformity accounts for why the American poetry scene as a whole seems uninteresting except to the poets themselves and their lovers.

In *The End of Intelligent Writing* (1974), I argued that the principal post-World War II machines of literary reputation-making were breaking down; they were no longer effective at pitching writers born after 1933 to top pedestals. Right though I was on that score, I did not see that nothing would replace them and then what the effects of that vacuum would be. One effect apparent now is that no poet of younger generations than my own (b. 1940) could gain great prominence with the lay public. None among us has the celebrity of Robert Lowell or Allen Ginsberg, let alone Sylvia Plath or Joseph Brodsky (whose peculiar celebrity is discussed elsewhere in this book). Nothing seems capable of propelling any one of us youngsters to the skies (thus visibly frustrating those with regal ambitions). Indicatively, commercial publishers are presently no more effective than noncommercial at making major reputations (to the disappointment of those who thought that famous imprints would automatically grant them lasting fame). Even at courting our elders, our successes must have been limited, for at last count the youngest native-born poet currently in the National Institute of Arts and Letters, traditionally a repository of literary-political pressure, is Mark Strand (b. 1934).

As a result, even though some hundred of us have modest prominence, we are all swimming in a crowded cauldron out of which, no matter what we write, none of us can climb or, for the while, expect to climb. It seems that the present impact of what we do will never include any extravagant professional surprises. No, no, I hear you saying (and I tell myself), that cannot be so; but it is. Since there is nothing to do but write the best poetry we can, it is wrong to insist, as my colleague Greg Kuzma does, that "it is about impossible *not* to become a careerist in poetry." No, the truth is quite opposite. It is eminently possible, especially now, though, apparently, psychologically difficult not to do.

The paradox is that now is a good time for poetry, because many American poets receive more remuneration for poetry and immediately related activities than their predecessors had; but now is a bad time, because little poetry succeeds, as poetry. The two sides of this paradox are perhaps one. The system of rewards supports work that is more acceptable than distinguished, more conventional than innovative, even though most of us know that important poetry transcends conventionality and acceptability. More pointedly, let me suggest that the academic effort to uphold certain critical "standards" is primarily responsible for the general decline in standards for individual creative functioning. Unable to realize much literary influence (i.e., poetic success), too many poets hunger for tokens of career success while cautiously obeying whatever conventions are dominant around them. Perhaps a decade ago we heard claims for "a new golden age of American poetry." Nobody makes such claims anymore; such talk died with the disintegration of the vision it was summoned to bring.

Just as most poets known to me are more inclined to discuss matters of career than art, so esthetic issues rarely engage us any more. Even the radical challenges posed by "the beats" have by now been fully assimilated, not just by emerging poets but by veteran academics. There is nothing, even for contentious personalities, to discuss. One cause of this current stagnation is, of course, the difficulty of our common publishing situation, where every manuscript that becomes a book seems the beneficiary of a fortuitous accident; a second cause of the paralysis is that the deepest, most divisive theoretical issues have been cut out of the discussion.

It pains me to repeat that the principal symptom of the insularity of the poetry community in America is its neglect of decidedly innovative work. It remains revealing, if not scandalous, that minimal poetry, visual poetry, sound poetry, media poetry, language-centered poetry, and the like are not taught in the poetry classes. It is not for nothing that its practitioners do not have teaching positions in the writing programs. The simple truth is that such poetries pose such strong, radical challenges that, merely for the preservation of current privileges, they cannot be acknowledged. Everyone knows that, the victimizers as much as the victims; but few acknowledge it. When conventional work is all but totally forgettable, while radical work exerts no pressure, an art scene is decadent, if not dead.

One truth more familiar to the other arts holds that resistance to an immediate sale can be a sign of a work's integrity (whether that sale be publication, prizes, or teaching positions). We poets differ from visual artists in our reluctance to suggest our work might initially be for only a few. To account for this difference, remember that visual artists supply their work to retailers, who know their customers personally, while writers have traditionally serviced wholesalers, who sell their produce not to ultimate customers but to intermediary retailers. If only to entice wholesaling publishers, we writers must pretend that our work is destined for the masses. Furthermore, since most poets have leftish sympathies, we claim to be potentially popular, while a professional fear of being taken for "elitist" induces some oddly self-deceptive postures.

It is not for nothing that of the dozen-plus personal grants I have received in the past decade only one has been for the creation of literature, and that grant came from the Deutscher Akademische Austauschdienst Berliner Kunstlerprogramm. Simply, with such disparities I must be doing something right. More precisely, the sort of poetry (and fiction) I do has a more central place in European literature today (while American poets who celebrate Europe scarcely enter its literary scenes). In continental Europe especially, genuinely experimental writing is published and reviewed, and read on radio and even television. One clear difference between Germany and America now is that, in regard to this sort of work, the former is evidently less exclusionary, or should we be more precise and say *less fascist*.

In truth, there is no surer measure of the radicalness of certain literary activity than professional neglect. Innovative poets would not be so ruthlessly excluded from the rewards here unless their work were strong enough to represent a threat, perhaps even stronger than that posed by the "beats." Donald Hall included a book of my essays on poetry, *The Old Poetries and the New* (1981), in his University of Michigan Press series to expand its scope. Instead, the book fell outside it, with, he tells me, the lowest sales in the entire set. I felt more disappointment for Hall than myself. Since rewards for experimental poetry are paltry, if not nonexistent, in America, its practitioners find it not hard but easy, believe me, very easy "not to become careerist." We take comfort from knowing that no social condition is more suitable for the creation of major art than some enthusiasm and personal comfort amidst general neglect.

Nonetheless, when neglect comes from those who appear to be your friends, you (at least I) think twice. It could be said that the principal direction of my own creative writing in the past decade has been into publishing my texts in media other than printed pages, beginning with audio/radio and video in 1975, film in 1976, and holography in 1978. In all these arts, I function not as an adapter (on a production team) but as the principal producer (and generally work with only one assistant). I also try not to duplicate in the new medium what I have done on the page, but, instead, to engage, if not exploit, the medium's particular capabilities for realizing the esthetic essence of my work. It is scarcely surprising that such language works are never reviewed in the literary press (even though they have been occasionally acknowledged by critics of those new media). What was more surprising to me was that a recent sampling of previously published criticism of my work, in the twenty-eighth volume of *Contemporary Literary Criticism* (Gale, 1984), includes reviews of my poetry, fiction, numerical art, experimental prose, criticism, and anthologies, but *nothing* about this literary media art, which is not mentioned either in the editor's otherwise comprehensive biographical note. What makes this omission of my nonprint publishing even odder is the fact that this *CLC* series prides itself upon acknowledging "screen writing" among literary activities worth crediting. Doesn't this neglect of my audio, video, and film mean that I must have made a genuine conceptual leap in my poetic activities—a leap so far beyond current literary practice that not even a sympathetic bibliographer can accept it? Can we expect the machinery of the poetry biz to acknowledge such work, whether by me or others, a decade, or two, from now?

What is the social vision behind certifying ever-increasing numbers of young people with M.F.A.'s in poetry? Is there a commendable purpose, or is the popularity of this degree merely a reflection of the academic opportunism of teaching anything anyone will pay for? Isn't one likely result of mass M.F.A.-ing going to be the morass comparable to the Gresham's Law of economics, where bad money (poetry) completely drives out good? What is going to happen to all those aspiring writers who think that since they got good grades in creative writing courses, they ought to become successful writers (much as good law students become successful lawyers)? Isn't another result going to be the creation of a disappointed, angry class of intelligent young people? What will they do when they wise up? Bomb the universities? The commercial publishers? Initiate class action suits to get their tuition money back? (Could it be that the proliferation of M.F.A. poetry programs reflects an insidious Communist plot to destabilize, if not America, then at least our literary culture?)

At this point in history I can no more predict the future of the literary profession than the future of literature.

The Republic of Letters
(1984)

GRANT WEBSTER'S *THE Republic of Letters* (1979) is subtitled "A History of Postwar American Literary Opinion," which is misleading, because the book is really about the professional careers and literary politics of "critics" and, as such, is the most profound specialized treatment of its subject that I have ever read. (Its competition, my own *The End of Intelligent Writing* [1974, 1977], is more general.) The subject is the life cycles of a critical career and a critical school—how both function, develop, survive, and decline in America. Its author is a professor of English at State University of New York at Binghamton, and his name was previously unfamiliar to me. *The Directory of American Scholars* says that he was born in 1933 and that his other specialty is eighteenth century English literature.

There is no need to characterize Webster's extraordinary literary-political intelligence when passages from the introduction to his book can nicely illustrate it:

Perhaps the most potent "ideology" motivating critics who also happen to be writers of fiction or poetry is the set of literary values implicit in the literature they themselves write.

In science, as in literature, specialized journals serve as the institution that authenticates originality, creates influence and hence establishes the importance of critics.

The careers of modern American critics develop in fairly uniform pattern through four stages: apprenticeship, Journeyman, Man of Letters and superannuation.

Post-World War II America has witnessed the development of two dominant types of critic: the writer-critic and the scholar-critic. The writer-critic's apprenticeship is an extension of the traditional Grub Street or newspaper cityroom route to criticism. Beginning by writing and publishing poems, novels, stories and essays in little magazines or the underground press, he progresses to criticism to defend a new literary charter of a rising generation, or to make his reputation. Hence the writer-critic tends to begin by writing reviews. In contrast, the scholar-critic serves his apprenticeship by going to graduate school and getting a Ph.D. in English, and his progress to criticism represents an escape from the factual world of the historical scholar to a discipline where he can assert his literary values directly and explicitly in critical essays.

In addition to being a stage in all critics' development, the Journey-man period can also be perpetual. Some critics never progress beyond this stage because they fail either to choose a critical charter or to develop their own critical voice.

The mark of the Man of Letters is that because his opinion is accepted as being worth something in itself, he is asked to do things he once appealed to do as an apprentice.

Despite the sobriquet "little magazine," the aim of every editor is to expand his magazine in size and eminence as much as possible. This explains the practice of luring famous names to the magazine to add authority to the editor and other contributors, as well as the publishing of lists of famous past contributors.

The remainder of *The Republic of Letters* consists of provoca-tive, detailed analyses of the careers of the major "New Critics" and "New York Intellectuals": T. S. Eliot, Cleanth Brooks, Allen Tate, Philip Rahv, Irving Howe, Edmund Wilson, et al. These commentaries are full of detailed perceptions. Webster seems to have read everything (except the book of mine mentioned before) and to have discovered the sort of unfamiliar, yet appropriate, quotation that reveals he has done his own research and his own thinking. In sum, this is the liveliest book about literary criticism since Stanley Edgar Hyman's *The Armed Vision* (1949); it leaves both Elmer Borklund's *Contemporary Literary Critics* (1977) and John Gross's earlier *The Rise and Fall of the Man of Letters* (1969) back in the stacks.

By now, however, *The Republic of Letters* relates very ancient history. Webster scarcely acknowledges recent developments that fit clearly into his scheme. He says nothing about the radical new literature of the past two decades—a literature that incorporates the visual and the aural, that often initially appears in media other than books, that conservatives dismiss as "not literature" (which is a subspecies of "not art"). Since traditional criticism has been unable to deal with these literary intermedia, let alone provide conceptual equipment for understanding such innovations, younger critics and theorizing practitioners have evolved, along Websterian lines, approaches and terms more appropriate to this new art and its peculiar mixes. In other words, for the same reasons that a new literature has emerged, literary criticism continues to evolve. Nonetheless, Webster, as a judicious academic in spite of himself, discusses only those writers and movements that his elders and predecessors have certified. But that's show business—I mean *academia*.

False and True:
Criticism of Avant-Garde
Writing (1986)

Language is made up of words and their configurations (the
clause, the sentence, the poetic line—as well as the subtler, style);
to these might be added the spaces between the words (for
measurement's sake) were these not properly to be considered them-
selves words—of a sort.
—William Carlos Williams, *The Embodiment of Knowledge* (1974)

I N THE PREFACE to *Poets, Prophets, and Revolutionaries*
(1985), his new book purportedly about, to quote its sub-
title, "The Literary Avant-garde from Rimbaud through Post-
modernism," Charles Russell announces,

My intention has not been to present radically new interpretations of
the writers' individual works or careers, but rather to see what is
often familiar about an individual's or movement's career within a
framework of an ill-perceived and misunderstood tradition of aes-
thetic activism that makes up the record of the avant-garde.

In addition to disavowing any interest in new discoveries,
that passage also broadcasts Russell's critical style, which is as
belabored and tentative as his entire presentation.

Elsewhere in this preface, Russell identifies the avant-garde
with "the writers' self-conscious extremism," an epithet cer-
tainly applicable to the subjects of his initial chapters: Rim-
baud, Apollinaire, the Italian futurists, and the literature of
Dada and Surrealism. Those are good places to start; however,
when Russell gets to Russian futurists, he jumps track, focus-

ing not upon the most extreme poet, Alexei Kruchonykh, who pioneered nonsyntactic writing, the distribution of phonemes in poetic space, book-art books, etc. No, instead, Russell represents avant-garde Russian futurism with a poetically far less adventuresome figure: Vladimir Mayakovsky. One likely explanation for Russell's mistaken choice is his unfortunate reluctance to broach new critical territory; you see, critical interpretations in English on Mayakovsky have been far more plentiful than guidance about Kruchonykh.

Given Russell's initial departure from his ostensible track, it is scarcely surprising that his next chapter is devoted wholly to Bertolt Brecht, whom Russell correctly acknowledges "was not an extreme innovator." By his concluding chapter on "Postmodernism," Russell has propelled himself into a retrograde ditch, focusing upon writers who are *not* extreme, whose works represent not extensions of the avant-garde tradition but, as he puts it, "rejections of modernism, even while the premises of modernist innovation still serve as a foil to the new creations." What is neglected here are those writers assembled in Russell's own anthology, *The Avant-Garde Today* (1981), which, oddly and inexplicably, is not even mentioned in this new book's "Selected Bibliography," so far backwards has this critic "progressed."

Remember, friends, if it isn't extreme, if it doesn't cut an edge, if it isn't (or wasn't) "unacceptable" to most everyone, it isn't avant-garde, regardless of what its authors or their salesmen say.

In its concern with the "politics" of avant-garde writers, *Poets, Prophets, and Revolutionaries* addreses the myth more common a dozen years ago—"the idea of the organic struggle of society in which artists had an integral role." Since then, in the past decade, everyone familiar with vanguard art knows the truth of what Russell peddles as a fresh discovery: that the politics of avant-garde artists has, alas, more effect upon the evolution of art than upon the general populace, or as Russell puts it, with characteristic zestlessness: "Most of the conflicts were fought within and about the separate space of art, even if they represented an effort to change the nature of that space, to merge art and life."

What makes Russell's wrong turns doubly unfortunate is that he handles genuinely innovative writing considerably better than less extreme literature. To his credit, he rarely makes the sort of gross mistakes often found elsewhere in "critical" writing about the avant-garde. Perhaps the most prevalent goof nowadays, after the still-chronic misspelling of *Finnegans Wake* (which, don't forget, has no apostrophe), is the misinterpretation of John Cage's so-called silent piece, *4'33"*, which is not about silence, but about the continual presence and joyous, esthetic acceptance (as *music*) of miscellaneous, unintentional mundane sounds within its time-frame. Nonetheless, Professor Frederick Karl in his recent *Modern and Modernisms* (1985), writes,

The suicide of lovers Villers' *Axel* foreshadows that rejection of the world, that embrace of a higher reality, that would become such a strong attraction in Modernism. . . . If we jump eras, we can see something like John Cage's book *Silence* in a direct line from Villers, however tortured the route. Silence was to be an essential ingredient of Modernism, the furthest extreme.

If that Cage book was actually read past its title, it was obviously not digested well. As suicidal silence is far from what Cage had in mind, there is no question that his work was neither experienced nor understood. Give this professor an *F*. Too often in reading "criticism" of the avant-garde, I'm reminded of white academics writing about black American culture—whites who believe that as long as they have proper credentials they can say anything, regardless of its truth to reality. Had the academic "profession" genuine standards, for egregious fakery it would revoke Ph.D.'s, not to mention tenure. If only because Russell does not fall to such Karlian sins, this new book should have been slicker, becoming the introductory text on the literary avant-garde that everyone could use that is necessary still.

The scholarly purposes missed by Russell are exemplified by Gerald Janecek's *The Look of Russian Literature* (1984), which documents the development of visual devices mostly in futurist writing of 1900–1930. Professor of Slavic and Oriental languages at the University of Kentucky, Janecek begins modestly with a close analysis of Andrei Bely's expressive punctuation, less in *St. Petersburg,* his most famous novel, than in his *Kotik Lateav* (1922), which is available here in Janecek's own translation (1971). From this opening analysis he progresses into examining the more extreme innovations of Alexei Kruchonykh, making fresh connections between the new futurists and earlier symbolists such as Bely. With the fullest discussion known to me of Kruchonykh in English (for which Russell would have done well to have waited), as well as elaborate visual documentation, *The Look of Russian Literature* provides not only a revelation about previously uncharted territory but a model of avant-garde scholarship reflecting original research and thinking.

The book that Janecek supplements, as it surpasses, is Vladimir Markov's *Russian Futurism* (1968), which I first devoured in 1970. By reading between Markov's lines at the time, I could tell that the most radical and thus most interesting futurist poet was not Mayakovsky, the most famous, or Khlebnikov, whom Markov favored then (and Marjorie Perloff for one has favored since), but Kruchonykh, whom I have come to appreciate as the most radical single poet in all modernism. Don't consider this choice of masters trivial, because the three are as essentially different as, respectively, Langston Hughes, T. S. Eliot, and such extreme eccentrics as Gertrude Stein or Abraham Lincoln Gillespie.

Whereas Russell seems more interested now in conservative

departures from the avant-garde, Janecek announces future work on the visual documentation (scoring) of sound poetry and on the most radical poetic concept, *Zaum*, which Markov long ago called "the most extreme of all Futurist achievements." Janecek translates Zaum as "transrational language," which is to say words that make sense exclusively within the spirit of poetry. If only because *Zaum* remains unacceptable to 99 percent of the professors of poetry in America, Janecek deserves credit and support for the genuine courage we associate with avant-garde. Friends, accept no substitutes.

Ezra Pound: A Person
of Arts (1981)

All through his life he was equally praised and blamed for his
many-sidedness, which was as natural to him as breathing. He shuf-
fled his different jobs like a deck of cards, getting innumerable
combinations but finding them all part of the same game.
       —Sibyl Moholy-Nagy, *Experiment in Totality* (1950)

O NCE EZRA POUND died, in 1972, and the legal entan-
glements of his later life unraveled, it became possible
for others to collect the miscellaneous writings that he could
not, or would not, bring together on his own initiative. Three
fat annotated volumes of these works have so far appeared:
R. Murray Schafer's edition of *Ezra Pound and Music: The
Complete Criticism* (1977); Leonard Doob's edition of *"Ezra
Pound Speaking"* (1978), which reprints the notorious wartime
speeches for which Pound would have been imprisoned or
executed for treason had he not been committed to a hospital
for the insane (speeches which would have remained justly
forgotten, were not their author a major modern poet); and
Harriet Zinnes's new *Ezra Pound and the Visual Arts* (1980).

This last volume is disappointing, being neither as rich as
the first collection nor as revelatory as the second. Also shorter
than its two predecessors, this book is filled with Pound's short
businesslike letters to the New York lawyer John Quinn and,
sometimes, other art entrepreneurs and then Pound's reviews
of London exhibitions just before World War I. Most of the
last appeared in the London periodical *The New Age*, some-
times under the pseudonym of "B. H. Dias." More than sixty
years later, nearly all of Pound's reviewing remarks are no less

dispensible than the artists he mentions. Written for peanut fees that were nonetheless necessary to the Pound family economy, these pieces have that "jerky confectionary quality" that Schafer found in Pound's miscellaneous music reviews.

It is better today to regard these reviews of visual art as contributions to a certain historic episode in British cultural history. Just as Pound's early poetry criticism aimed to emancipate modernism from the soft Georgian remnants that were still fashionable in Britain in the 1910s, so his strongest art reviewing focused upon those astringent artists, called the vorticists, who most successfully transcended the flaccid post-impressionism that was dominant at the time. In longer, more considered essays, where Pound functions not as a journeyman reviewer but a true critic, he deals with Henri Gaudier-Brzeska (1891–1915), a French-born London sculptor whom Pound knew personally, whose premature death he mourned in a book-length essay (1916); and Wyndham Lewis (1882–1957), whose painting preceded his writing and who remains the only Englishman after William Blake to produce first-level work in both painting and writing.

Ezra Pound and the Visual Arts also contains many of these penetrating, illuminating sentences that we associate with Pound's finest critical prose. Simply to quote a few of them conveys a sense of his esthetic intelligence at its best:

Parody is, I suppose, the best criticism—it sifts the durable from the apparent.

By genius I mean an inevitable swiftness and rightness in a given field.

Serious art is unpopular at birth. But it ultimately forms the mass culture.

The one thing that would purge (purge, not kill) the Academy would be the awakening of a critical habit in the public.

The vorticist principle is that a painting is an expression by means of an arrangement of form and colour in the same way that a piece of music is an expression by means of an arrangement of sound.

A volcanic and disordered mind like Wyndham Lewis's is of great value, especially in a dead, and for the most part rotted, milieu. The curse of England is fugg.

Our respect is not for the subject-matter, but for the creative power of the artist; for that which he is capable of adding to this subject from himself; or, in fact, his capability to dispense with external subjects altogether, to create from himself or from elements.

The only thing one can give an artist is leisure in which to work. To give an artist leisure is actually to take part in his creation. It is a question of making freemen, in the only sense that that word is worth while. It is NOT a charity.

Otherwise, Harriet Zinnes's notes to *And the Visual Arts* scarcely compare with R. Murray Schafer's for *And Music*. Whereas the latter is so elaborately introduced, footnoted, and annotated with a running commentary that it becomes Schafer's brilliant book around Pound, Zinnes does much less, in part because she seems to know less about Pound and his milieu but also because she cares much less. For instance, she fails to confront such obvious issues as relating Pound's critical method and esthetic ideas to those of other critics at the time or even to relate Pound's arts criticism to his literary criticism.

One remaining stone in the Pound mausoleum will be Schafer's long-promised collection of Pound's musical compositions, including *Le Testament* which Schafer regards as "an unduplicated little masterpiece of musical composition." A second necessary addition would be a complete collection of Pound's fugitive *literary* essays and reviews; so far, only selections of these have appeared. A final stone would be a full editon of Pound's remarkable letters, as the D. D. Paige edition, published in 1950, covered only the correspondence from 1907 to 1940 (and thus the beginnings of Pound's treason).

These three recent Pound books confirm our sense of his

expansive esthetic career; for in addition to writing poems and poetic translations that will never be forgotten, he wrote considered criticism of literature, music, and the visual arts and then extended essays on economics and politics; he edited magazines and anthologies and even produced a series of musical concerts for several years, and much, much else. He was not just "a man of letters," as some would say, but, like his contemporaries Wyndham Lewis and Herbert Read, a genuine Person of Arts.

Claims by Poets? (1985)

Poetry feeds the imagination and prose the emotions, poetry liberates the words from their emotional implications, prose confirms them in it. Both move centrifugally or centripetally toward the intelligence.

—William Carlos Williams, *Spring and All* (1923)

OVER THE PAST six years Donald Hall has been editing an ambitious series of uniform books, collectively titled *Poets on Poetry*, that publishes individually the prose of over twenty living poets. One simple measure of its value is the conjecture that if a similar collection were done sixty years ago of the prose of a comparable generation of earlier poets, our sense of what they thought they were doing would have been considerably accelerated, if not enhanced. (It follows that there ought to be a comparable series devoted to the theoretical writings of current fiction writers, edited by someone whose generous temperament is married to a similarly strong and yet catholic devotion to fiction—say, Jerome Klinkowitz, David Madden, or George Garrett.)

As Hall's multiple enterprise on behalf of contemporary poetry is coming to rival that of Eric Bentley's on behalf of theater (and is equally commendable), he takes the next step of editing *Claims for Poetry* (1982), a one-volume anthology of poets' theoretical and critical prose. Here Hall must first of all be credited with a mix broader than his series, alphabetically interspersing the innovative poets (who are usually excluded from compendia pretending to definitiveness, and are never invited to teach in the universities) with the professor-poets. This landmark volume represents the first time that Jackson

Mac Low, Dick Higgins, Bliem Kern, and Ron Silliman have appeared between the same covers as, say, Louis Simpson, John Hollander, and Richard Wilbur. For officiating over such shotgun marriages Hall should be rewarded in heaven for sure, elsewhere perhaps.

This volume, like the series behind it, depends upon our fascination with intelligent artists talking about their purposes and, behind that, upon the current custom in the creative literary world of trying to talk intelligently, rather than playing dumb. However, Hall has a thesis, reiterated by others here, that the best theorists of poetry are practicing poets. As much as I would like to agree with my fellow unionist on this last point, some of the awful thinking in these pages is embarrassing. The principal problem appears to be the apparent belief that the practice of poetry provides privileges, if not pomposities, that would normally be unacceptable. Take Robert Creeley's "I had gone through a usual education in the East." Since no details were given, I checked into *Contemporary Poets* to discover that Creeley attended Harvard for three years which must have provided an *unusual* education that was quite different from, say, the University of Maine or Fitchburg State. (Isn't it pretentious to treat false modesty as anything more than false?)

Take Louis Simpson's "the style is the man," which echoes Hayden Carruth's "style is the property of the poem that expresses the poet's personality." No, poetry is not made that way and never was, while wishing does not make it so. Properties of language and then structural techniques are what essentially distinguishes one poet's work from another's, for style can be imitated (and even parodied), while personality cannot be. Perhaps one difference between poets and nonpoets, in writing about poetry, is that the former feel obliged, or permitted, to emphasize the poet's *personality*. It is a problematic custom that apparently afflicts both the professor-poets and nonprofessors alike.

And now listen to Robert Duncan:

Though I am unread in contemporary verse of the conventional persuasion outside of the work of Marianne Moore, T. S. Eliot, and Robert Lowell, I realize that beyond these there is marshaled an imposing company of arbiters and camp followers, lady commandos of quatrians right! and myrmidons of the metaphysical stanza, holding the line against any occurrence of, much less the doctrines of, poetic genius or romantic imagination, handing out prizes (booby and otherwise) to balance the accounts and bolster standards.

Notwithstanding the flourishes of Duncan's style (which incidentally comes from language, not personality), one is put off by the apparent assumption that the poet, unlike the normal person, is permitted to deprecate what he does not know and allowed as well to admit his ignorance prior to drawing dismissive conclusions. That is another way of drawing the unacceptable, dangerous premise that, in areas outside poetry, the poet need not obey the rules.

Take Denise Levertov, who declares, "The poet—when he is writing—is a priest." No, when he or she is writing, and especially when he or she is actually writing, the poet is working primarily with the problems and possibilities of poetry. To say otherwise is to deceive the innocent much as advertising does, and for the same reason—aggrandizement. Levertov later devotes an entire paragraph to this anecdote:

"Form is never more than the extension of content." At the Vancouver poetry conference this summer (1963) I proposed to Robert Creeley, the originator of this now famous formula, that it should be changed to read: "Form is never more than the *revelation of content*" (to which he agreed).

Since I had not heard elsewhere of Creeley's concurrence, or the canonization of her revision, in the two decades since, the question is whether this Levertov self-testimonial should be regarded as history, pseudo-history, or merely evidence of Creeley's *politesse?*

There is more of this, which I would rather not reprint, because it pains me to record the inanities of colleagues—idiocies that in the context of such claims for the powers of poetry really discredit them. Can I be alone in believing that something is wrong here—profoundly wrong with the perception of the figure of the poet and his or her relation to poetry and to the world?

"Herd of Independent
Minds" (1987)

Any bright young man can be taught to be artful. It is impossible to teach taste, but you can teach most anybody caution. It is always the lesser artists who are artful, they must learn their trade by rote. They must be careful never to make a false step, never to speak out of a carefully synthesized character. The greater poetry is notably disheveled.

—Kenneth Rexorth, "Poetry, Regeneration and
D. H. Lawrence" (1947)

BEHIND STEPHEN BERG'S *Singular Voices* (1985), a new anthology of contemporary native poets writing about their own work, is the voice-theory of poetry, which holds that a poet is valuable not for his perception, his language, his formal skill, or inventive intelligence but the uniqueness of whatever "voice" is heard on the page. From this assumption follows Berg's claim that since his book includes "living American poets whose work exemplifies strong new styles," their voices must therefore be indubitably singular.

To test this claim, I compiled the following sequence of opening sentences from the prose essays, using just less than two-thirds of the book's thirty "singular voices":

Up in my eyrie-room atop the Chapel of the Madonna of Monserrato, perched on a cliff higher than the hawks above Lake Como, listening to the sweet bells of Bellagio's San Giacomo, I begin to cast into air and mind for an explanation of "Awakening," a poem written years ago in homage to the great Japanese Rinzai Zen master Hakuin. Sometimes I think communication is all we have—a voice like a silver wire extending through the dark or one chunk of flesh pressing against another chunk of flesh. I write prose poems when I long for intimacy. I want it from my friends, and I want it in poetry. The life in detail, the small moment, the texture of a thing—that, it has seemed to me, is where the poetry is. Poems begin when something in the present—event or object, word overheard—calls power to itself by association with somethng alive in the mind's recesses, some connection potent but unavailable to consciousness. The ideas that make a poem present themselves as images. My insights on what I perceive to be the themes of this poem are already expressed: the poem embodies them. Something you are writing, after it is done, or begins to feel close to done, you can lean over and breathe on it and try to bring its main moves, its trajectory, into the center of your attention. Usually my poems are very difficult for me to write. Poets often admit, with something like a parental sense of surprise, pride, pleasure, that once a poem is finished it becomes someone else's, becomes something else. Like many other writers of this century, my obsession has been with the lost and neglected forces of the world, what is dark and hidden, and unseen, although I'm not sure if my own passion is the result of political or psychological or religious impulses, or a particular combination of the three. There are aspects of the writer-reader relationship which sometimes drive a poet into apology and denial. Only a few months ago a graduate student at a Midwestern university sent me an elaborate commentary on an early poem of mine, requesting my seal of approval for his interpretation. This poem, "Recollection Long Ago: Sad Music," is literally a recollection. I find that many poems have a germ in a recollection, but this is as literal, even in detail, as recollection permits after some three score years have done their work. It is true that there was a brief period, three or four years perhaps, when I thought of myself as a Southern writer. Then, as young men in our twenties, we were quite besotted with poetry, writing it constantly, continually theorizing about it, and translating each other's work. "Elegy for N. N." was written in 1962 but for a long time it remained in manuscript, as I hesitated whether to publish it at all. Most of my life-as-a-poet I have avoided writing poems about paintings, pieces of sculpture, sonatas, or other people's choreography out of a Calvinistic sort of purism, thinking always that to give in to the impulse to embellish another's art diminishes rather than enhances it. "Klimt" began on a day in Arcata, after a long rain, the sun suddenly blazing every wet thing.

As these nineteen opening sentences go, so proceed whole essays, collectively realizing a certain uniformity of solemn, if not pompous, tone and diction (and even of subject, as Europe in some form appears in half of them). What we hear are cultivated Anglo-American voices in postures quite familiar to us—indeed, the voices of teachers addressing students. It follows that most of these poets have been or are (or expect to be) professors of poetry at America's colleges. The spectacle reminds me of Harold Rosenberg's classic image of a "herd of independent minds."

Such uniformity is realized primarily by Berg's nearly total exclusion of poets who deviate from current classroom manners, not only in their poetry but in their prose. In his thirty-person regiment the only exceptions to this pervasive voice are Etheridge Knight (who remains the sole non-white contributor), Hayden Carruth (who contributes an arch dialogue), and then Carolyn Forché and Robert Haas (who both write as though they are addressing colleagues, rather than students). Indeed, to my senses, the principal unintended theme of *Singular Voices* is precisely the general inability of so many prominent American poets to realize a unique voice, let alone to think about transcending current fashion, not just in the writing about poetry but in writing of poetry itself; and it is precisely this artistic failure that, to me, dramatizes the continuing stasis, if not decadence, of the American poetry scene.

The truths lost on these professor-poets are that success in academia requires acceptability, whereas success in art requires individuality that risks unacceptability, and then that success in the former does not guarantee success in the latter. This second truth accounts for why so many professor-poets nowadays are embittered about the lack of commensurate success for their poetry. Isn't this bitterness itself another sign of decadence?

Given Stephen Berg's evident ease in marshalling uniformity, it is not surprising that he neglects other parts of his editorial task. In the bio notes, he writes that Galway Kinnell "now runs the Columbia University Graduate Writing Program," whereas Kinnell actually teaches at N.Y.U. On page 275 is a Robert Penn Warren sentences that suffers from a missing word: "The scene is an evening picnic of college in a distant woodland." On page 291 is a wrong pronoun, as Theodore Weiss writes of visiting his father: "I recall one day when I and my wife were visiting my [*sic*] home." In the preface, Berg claims, "These poems and essays are also a substantial introduction to what is happening in American poetry today." Now a careful editor, especially of such a narrow-minded book, would have removed that sort of disingenuous claim that was initially made, one suspects, to impress commerical publishers (and their sales managers). Reprinted here, a puff so false becomes outrageous and, need I say, infuriating.

Unloaded Canons
(1980, 1989)

Unlike most modernists Kenneth Burke has always understood the political and historical costs of "tradition" and "canon-formation."
> —Frank Lentricchia, *Criticism and Social Change* (1983)

THE HARVARD GUIDE to Contemporary American Writing (1979) is an incredible mess; it must be read to discover the number of ways in which a collaborative survey can go wrong. It is misconceived, soporific, incoherently divided, underedited, dangerously exclusive, factually unreliable and egregiously dumb. Considering that America's most prestigious university press invested not only its good name but thousands of dollars producing this 618-page, three hundred thousand-word volume, this *Harvard Guide* is a cultural disaster comparable to the pilfering of the National Gallery or the secession of New York City.

HGCAW, as it shall be known, has twelve chapters divided among ten authors. Some of the chapter titles reflect the success of minority-monikered literary politicking: "Jewish Writers" and "Southern Fictions." Others reflect the patronizing isolation that indicates historic literary-political failure: "Women's Literature" and "Black Literature." Some chapter titles encompass a single genre: "Drama" and "Literary Criticism." Fiction that is not black, Jewish, female, or southern falls into two more chapters: "Realists, Naturalists and Novelists of Manners" and "Experimental Fiction." Poetry, blessed poetry, is exiled into three concluding chapters, 159 pages in sum, all authored by the book's editor, Daniel Hoffman (b. 1923), poet-in-residence and Professor of English at the University of Pennsylvania. Prefacing these eleven chapters is Alan Trachtenberg's "Intellectual Background" (50 pages), which is perhaps the only appropriately placed and accurately titled chapter in the entire book. Otherwise, in mixing ethnic and geographic categories with procedural ("experimental"), *HGCAW* resembles a carcass mangled by cross-purpose butchering. Norman Mailer, for instance, is sliced several ways.

One senses that these chapter titles were assigned in advance and then doggedly retained, even when the actual contribution scarcely fit them. Josephine Hendin's forty-seven-page section on "Experimental Fiction" discusses William Burroughs, Robert Stone, Richard Farina, Truman Capote, Joyce Carol Oates, John Gardner, William Gass, Flannery O'Connor, Kurt Vonnegut, Richard Brautigan, Donald Barthelme, John Barth, Vladimir Nabokov, J. D. Salinger, John Updike, John Hawkes, Thomas Pynchon, et al.—a whole gallery of commercially successful and academically acceptable writers. A checking of Hendin's earlier critical book on recent fiction, *Vulnerable People* (1978), reveals that her *HGCAW* chapter discusses the same writers she featured before, in roughly the same order, with many of the same critical comments; but whereas the epithet "experimental" hardly appears in her own book, it is here inserted, almost randomly, into nearly every paragraph, generally to describe literary phenomena that are scarcely experimental, let alone unusual. Indeed, "Unexperimental Fiction" would be a more appropriate title for this bunch.

In my judgment, anyone classifying *these* fictioneers as "experimental," especially at a time when *other* American writers are courageously redefining the formal extremes of fiction, is patently exploiting, if not vulgarizing, an honorific term. If there were Justice in the literary world, her professional license would be revoked for misusing critical language and her doctorate taken away. Also, any book editor accepting this essay should have his contract canceled. Any book publisher issuing it between hard covers should have his or her advice system overhauled. Chapters like this can make "Harvard" synonymous with misguided mediocrity.

"Jewish Writers" is likewise a misnomer here, as its author, Professor Mark Schechner of SUNY-Buffalo, uncritically accepts the Jewish-American literary movement's exclusive promotion of itself and thus devotes his entire forty-nine-page essay to Bellow, Podhoretz, Mailer, Malamud, I. B. Singer, Trilling, Howe, Philip Roth, et al. In Schechner's essay there is, by contrast, hardly any mention of literary Jewesses (not even Gertrude Stein) or of Jewish-American poets (none of the Shapiros—Karl, Harvey, or David—with Delmore Schwartz noticed only in passing) and no mention at all of such religious novelists as Chaim Potok and Arthur A. Cohen or of contemporary American writing in Jewish languages— Yiddish, Hebrew, and Ladino (Singer, of course, excepted). Since Jerome Rothenberg is not acknowledged, it is scarcely surprising that most of the alive-and-kicking American-Jewish writers included in his remarkable anthology *A Big Jewish Book* (1978) aren't mentioned either. Indeed, by ignoring American-Jewish writers younger and more experimental than Philip Roth (b. 1933), Schechner is either excluding them from Jewish-American literary history (for shame) or converting them, mostly unwillingly, into literary goys.

However, Schechner is not alone in his generational neglects. His coconspirators, Professor Nathan A. Scott, Jr., of the University of Virginia and Professor Lewis Simpson of Louisiana State University, hardly mention younger writers in their putatively exhaustive surveys, respectively, of "Black Literature" (44 pages) and "Southern Fiction" (38 pages). The latter, incidentally, is the only contributor to this book who does not presently reside in an east-coast state.

Factual errors are inevitable in any compendious book, but

this has more than its excusable share. Many of these boners appear in Daniel Hoffman's own chapters (and thus did not pass through a senior editor). He has Ezra Pound living "with his daughter in Venice until, at eighty-seven, he died in 1972," but the woman was, instead, his (illegitimate) daughter's mother Olga Rudge. On page 553, he writes, "Ashbery was curator at the Museum of Modern Art and O'Hara an editor at *Art News*," reversing their positions. Eight pages later, Hoffman casts Ashbery as "spending all his years attacking academicism," which is scarcely true, either in print or conversation. Josephine Hendin portrays Richard Farina as "a talented jazz musician who was killed at the age of twenty," but he was a folksinger who lived to be twenty-nine. In the other nonsectarian fiction chapter, Leo Braudy identifies "John Phillips" as a pseudonym for John P. Marquand; however, the former is, in fact, the latter's fiction-writing son. One wishes that any scholarly book that resembles a telephone book—chock full of names and titles—would be as accurate as my local telephone directory.

Even though *HGCAW* contains a large number of individual names, it can be faulted for its omissions. Anyone looking through the index, name by name, will notice that remarkably few people born after 1938 are mentioned at all. Somewhat familiar with the literature of my own generation, I counted only thirty-five, perhaps missing ten others, out of approximately 850 names in *HGCAW*'s index. Checking again I notice that nearly all of these youngsters are mentioned only once, and that most of them are poets whose names appear at the end of Daniel Hoffman's survey paragraphs: ". . . by such poets as Daniel Halpern, Larry Levis, William Matthews, Gregory Orr, Linda Pastan and Stanley Plumly."

By contrast, the index acknowledges an abundance of references to Robert Bly, Louis Simpson, Kenneth Koch, A. R. Ammons, James Baldwin, Robert Creeley, John Hollander, Richard Howard, Galway Kinnell, Adrienne Rich, James

Wright, et al.; for this book, particularly in the poetry chapters, is finally not about "Contemporary American Writing" in general but about writers who were, like Hoffman, born in the 1920s. Indeed, in both its interest and its attitudes (and especially in the treatment of minority literatures), *HGCAW* reminds me of the emerging fashions of 1964, which I hesitate to note was a decade and one-half ago!

Indeed, there is good reason to question to usefulness of any contemporary survey that does not mention at all such consequential, established, and mostly prolific writers as Rita Mae Brown (Adrienne Rich being this book's token "radical feminist"), James Tate, Nicholas Delbanco, David Ignatow, Sharon Spencer, John Leonard, Harvey Shapiro (the editorship of the *NYTBR* evidently being good for business but bad for one's liteary reputation), Stanley Berne (too experimental), Emmett Williams (ditto), Paul Zelevansky (ditto), Bern Porter (ditto), Bliem Kern (ditto), Robert Wilson (ditto), Michael Kirby (ditto), N. H. Pritchard (ditto), Aram Saroyan (ditto), Alain Arias-Misson (ditto), Arlene Zekowsky (ditto), Philip Lamantia (ditto), Kenneth Gangemi (ditto), Robert Lax (ditto), Raymond Federman (ditto), Charles Doria (ditto), Samuel R. Delany (and, by extension, all speculative fiction), Rochelle Owens, Jonathan Culler, Edward Said, David Antin, Michael Mewshaw, Donald Hall (surprise), Charles Newman, Len Fulton (and, by extension, alternative publishing), William Everson (another surprise), Lawrence Lieberman, Matthew Bruccoli, Ed Sanders, Gilbert Sorrentino, Frederic Tuten, Marvin Cohen, Tom Veitch, and *all* Hispanic-American writers. Though this list of absentees is scarcely complete, it is obvious that critical commentary about these other writers could make an equally fat but far more up-to-date book about "Contemporary American Writing."

HGCAW is misnamed, its contents misrepresented. Were there a Fair Trade Commission in Literature that insisted upon truth in titling, the book would be renamed: "An Oddly

Organized and Curiously Incomplete Collection of Older Contemporary Names and Titles Inexplicably Published by Harvard (yes Harvard)." However, no hardback volume with that title would be worth $18.50.

II

Not unlike other writers, I suppose, I began reading the 1,263-page *Columbia Literary History of the United States* with the index. It runs 50 full pages, double-columned, with roughly fifty items to a page, most of them proper names. Finding my own name spelled correctly—what a relief—I looked around for other contemporaries and began to notice omissions that fell into several categories:

1. Poetry professors at Ivy League universities: Theodore Weiss, Edwin Honig, Daniel Hoffman, John Hollander, Michael S. Harper, Keith Waldrop, Daniel Halpern, Helen Vendler, Robert Fitzgerald, Richard Eberhart, Stanley Kunitz;

2. Sometime writer-editors of prominent literary reviews: John Leonard, George Core, Andrew Lytle, Frederick Morgan, Harvey Shapiro, Gordon Lish, William Phillips, Daryl Hine, Stephen Berg, George Plimpton, Steven Marcus, Robie Macauley, Robley Wilson, W. J. T. Mitchell, Robert Boyers, Herbert Liebowitz;

3. Highly visible litterateurs of various cultural persuasions: Donald Hall, Andrei Codrescu, Howard Moss, Eric Bentley, Harry Levin, Louis D. Rubin, Howard Nemerov, James Atlas, R. V. Cassill, D. Keith Mano, Theodore Solotaroff, Reynolds Price, George Steiner, Robert Coles, Walter J. Ong, James Dickey, M. L. Rosenthal, Brad Leithauser, George Garrett, Peter Davison, John Simon, Philip Lopate, William Jay Smith, Winfield Townley Scott, Rosellen Brown, Frank Conroy, Wilfrid Sheed, Richard Gilman, Anthony Hecht, Geoffrey Wolff, Dana Goia, Anne Waldman, Thomas Merton, John Ciardi;

4. Younger pop novelists prematurely inducted into the putatively prestigious National Institute of Arts and Letters: Anne Tyler, Paul Theroux;

5. Avant-garde heavies: James Laughlin, Dick Higgins, Richard Foreman, Ed Sanders, Rosmarie Waldrop, Charles Amirkhanian, Norman Henry Pritchard II, Emmett Williams, Pedro Pietri (even though there is a full, if peculiar, chapter purportedly about "The Avant-Garde and Experimental Writing"), who, since their kind has always been excluded from such histories, can now, so to speak, welcome the others to the humbling Club.

Welcome.

Thomas Merton (1978)

THAT THOMAS MERTON was an extraordinary man no one doubts. Born in France, 31 January 1915, the son of a New Zealand artist and American mother, he grew up in Flushing and Douglaston, in outer Queens, New York, before attending a French lycée and then a British public school. After two years at Cambridge University, he returned to New York and entered Columbia College, where he became editor of the 1937 *Yearbook* and art editor of the undergraduate humor magazine. Converting to Catholicism in 1938 and taking his M.A. the following year, Merton taught English at St. Bonaventure University and began contributing to literary magazines.

On 10 December 1941, three days after Pearl Harbor, he entered the Abbey of Our Lady of Gethsemani, near Bardstown, Kentucky, where he lived for twenty-seven years as a Cistercian of the Strict Observance ("a Trappist"), taking his simple vows in 1944 and his solemn vows in 1947. He was ordained a priest ("Father Louis") in 1949. Free to write only a few hours a week for most of his highly scheduled monastic life, Merton nonetheless produced nearly fifty books, including an enticing, best-selling autobiography, *The Seven Storey Mountain* (1948), and numerous essays on theology, religion, the contemplative life, and even worldly politics. Although he could have petitioned to rejoin the secular world as a popular writer, collecting royalties that went instead to his monastery, he remained a faithful monk, subservient to his abbott and to the physical hardships intrinsic in his vows. He even let his writings pass though a hierarchy of Catholic censorship (that reportedly deleted, among other passages, much of the original manuscript of *The Seven Storey Mountain*). In the years just before his 1968 death, by accidental electrocution, Merton had also become a prominent advocate of ecumenism, not only within the divisions of Christianity but with Eastern religions as well. Throughout his life, Merton also published poetry, all of which is gathered in *The Collected Poems of Thomas Merton* (1977).

A labor of publishing love, over a thousand pages in length, this is a disappointing volume. Bad lines abound from the book's opening poem, "The Philosophers," which begins:

> As I lay sleeping in the park,
> Buried in the earth,
> Waiting for the Easter's rains
> To drench me in their mirth
> And crown my seedtime with some sap and growth

A more conscientious craftsman, with more time to rewrite, would have cleaned such doggerel up, or out.

It was commonly joked that Merton, having taken the vow of silence, then produced heaps of garrulous prose. His poems are similarly verbose, generally more prosy than poetic, and undistinguished in both language and idea. Indicatively, Merton's poems are scarcely anthologized, and his name rarely appears in histories of American literature, his general eminence notwithstanding.

One trouble with the poems is that they are incorrigibly derivative, in a variety of styles. Little here has sufficient per-

sonal signature to be instantly attributable to Merton; even less
is memorable. His religious poems, which one might expect to
be extraordinary, pale beside T. S. Eliot's or those of either
St. John of the Cross or, more recently, Brother Antoninus;
and Merton's later poems are not much better than his earlier
ones. There is nothing here as distinguished as the post-
Joycean "macaronic" language, say, that enhances his novel,
My Argument with the Gestapo (1969, though written in 1941):

Rouse. Wreck. Sturz. Bekom. Gross lettercatchers i the orders of the
day. Guess you no comprenny, you jigsfrench. Youse of the lapin
races, aside, hide in your lascivious newspapers. Faz dolor di honta
rossu figaro. Ecartez vous, cheaps. Hoc es fe Trowel-spiel, or the
Roarspiegel. Begins in the first with Latin declensions, fur monstrar
la natura clásica de la fiesta. Continua mit whole speeches from
imitation marble paradigms, eventually concatenating intself up-
wards into a Durchbruch of the meistens emotive hocking and chok-
ing: it y a des scènes dans la rue, et d'autres encore dans la maison.

The Collected Poems suggest to me that Merton's true medium
was not poetry at all but *prose*. The best passages here are such
prose aphorisms as: "The way of man has no wisdom, but the
way of God has." Or, "An age in which politicians talk about
peace is an age in which everybody expects war." The best
individual "poems" are composed of curt prose paragraphs—
not only the "Original Child Bomb" (1962), which has been
widely reprinted for its political sympathies, but my own favor-
ites: "Chants to be used in Processions Around a Site with
Furnaces" and "Cables to the Ace." (The latter is dedicated
to his college classmate Robert Lax, whom I regard among
America's greatest experimental poets, a true minimalist who
can weave awesome poems from remarkably few words.
Though a survivor, Lax remains the last unacknowledged
[and, alas, uncollected] major poet born in the 1910s.)
The Collected Poems also includes a section of "Humorous
Verse" (which is rarely funny), "A French Poem" and transla-

tions, along with several "concrete poems" that Merton wrote in the final year of his life. (Only one of the last, "Awful Music," is passable.) The vain attempts at "songs" particularly indicate that poetic music was not Merton's forte. His poems in general suffer from both a general remoteness that perhaps reflects the monastic life and the facile indulgences that are more typical of a literary recluse immune to professional criticism.

The strongest theme of *The Collected Poems* is neither religious nor political but autobiographical, suggesting that what remains most interesting about Merton is not his art or his thought but his unique experience. Quite simply, his life was his most extraordinary creation, his example making credible an extreme behavorial option, with its rigorous efforts toward spiritual perfectionism, that would strike most of us as unthinkable. His example also earned the devotion of several loyal publishers and thousands of readers who eagerly consumed whatever he wrote. For them too, however, the man (or the myth of him) loomed larger than his work.

Merton's college friend Edward Rice revealed glimpses in his charming, largely photographic memoir, *The Man in the Sycamore Tree* (1970), and Merton's clerical colleagues contributed to Brother Patrick Hart's informative anthology, *Thomas Merton, Monk* (1974). However, the book to be written now, clearly, is a definitive biography, describing not only his religious development and Trappist spiritual athleticism, but explaining how Merton managed such an active literary life despite such adverse environmental conditions and recurring rotten health.

The Collected Poems itself is peculiarly underedited. Although previously published poems are chronologically arranged, "Uncollected Poems" are not, and their present order is inscrutable to me. Though it is common knowledge that the appearance of Merton's writings was often delayed, if not by the hierarchy then by Merton himself, there is no effort to identify dates of composition, especially if they radically differ from the publication dates and there is no indication whether dates of the "Uncollected Poems" refer to publication or to composition. "Ceremony for Edward Dahlberg," undated on page 694, should be dated either 1967 (authorship) or 1970 (publication), and the footnotes on page 547 should have been repaginated for this new book.

Merton's poems initially in French are translated by "William Davis," who is acknowledged on the copyright page, though not otherwise identified. One wonders whether the translations of poems originally in French, Spanish, Portuguese, Latin, Classic Greek, Persian, *and* Chinese were done totally by Merton himself, or whether he had helpers? If the latter, as one supposes, shouldn't these helpers be acknowleged? Since this book has neither a preface or an afterword, Lord knows who did what here. Finally, though this *Collected Poems* has an academic value, Merton's memory and literary reputation might be better served with a new *Selected Poems* that would be more selective than the garrulous self-selected volume that appeared a decade ago.

Joseph Brodsky: "I Keek It, I Vin It" (1987)

> Style, in other words, is an expression of the writer's literary personality. If it be too consciously chosen, it becomes a fake, a mask, a persona, a fabricated self-image. And of course that is what often happens to "style." It becomes simply a bad habit by which an author reverts mechanically to the parody of his own *opus*, like the dog to his vomit.
>
> —Thomas Merton, "Writing as Temperature" (1969)

TWO DECADES AGO, the general managers of professional football teams discovered that the highly specialized job of place-kicking could be done by sometime soccer players, most of them born and raised abroad; and the bench-warming place-kicker, we remember, is often called upon to deliver a field goal whose three points, especially in the game's concluding moments, can tilt the final score from one side to another. This place-kicker would then be mobbed by his teammates; newspaper headlines could then proclaim that he had "won the game," discounting the performance of the other players who did a lot more consequential work. It was Alex Karras, then a star tackle, now a television star, who charged that, with such place-kickers, a great American pastime has disintegrated to the level that guys who never played any other position in the game, young men who can hardly speak English, now scream, "I vin it, I keek it."

This bit of ancient history comes to mind with Joseph Brodsky's new book of essays, *Less Than One* (1986). In slightly over a dozen years in this country, he has become the most worldly successful poet of his generation. He took an early MacArthur

Prize, he was in 1979 the youngest poet in our National Institute of Arts and Letters, his new books get reviewed on the front page of the New York *Times Book Review,* he received an honorary degree from Yale, etc., etc. Brodsky is a good poet, accomplished in undistinguished ways, somewhat obvious and bombastic. To judge from the translations published here, he is by no measure better than a hundred others his age, a generation that, at least in America, has an abundance of good poets, though none commonly recognized as great; but since a lot more remuneration has come his way, some examination is in order.

The truth is that he is admired by people who understand personal history better than poetry, as the former is easier to merchandise, especially in America. The immigrant, especially from an Iron Curtain country, has a "bankable" biography unavailable to the native-born; and it would seem that the major purpose of this book of essays is contributing to that self-myth of the young Russian who learned literary English in Leningrad, translated some of it into his native language, was imprisoned for independent literary activities until he was kicked out of Russia and, at the Vienna airport, rescued by a generous American professor-publisher who got him a midwestern university teaching job for the fall. Soon afterwards, Brodsky befriended native literary powerhouses able to grant not just encouragement but substantial rewards.

If Brodsky has actually written any masterpiece poems, I cannot find them in the English translations I have read. (Much reportedly remains untranslated, as well as untranslatable.) I notice that his admirers are no more sure. While reviewers quote passages from individual poems as illustrative of something or other, they are reluctant to identify any poem as great. That accounts for why Brodsky's poems do not appear in anthologies of American poetry, not even Helen Vendler's *Harvard* (1985), which strives like hell to be a compendium of received opinion. I know of only one American poet colleague who reads his work with pleasure, and have thus concluded that it ultimately is no more written for us than for the common reader. Emigre literati I know insist that Brodsky's reputation here is based upon tokenism, our publicity machinery rewarding one and only one member of every identifiable minority (e.g., black, midwestern, etc.); and if Solzhenitzyn is to be America's favorite emigre novelist, so Brodsky has become our token Russian poet, even though other emigres are equally consequential artists.

The occasional essays collected in this new book are no more substantial. They range from perfunctory back-slapping appreciations of older poets (Derek Walcott, Eugenio Montale) to extended analyses of two poems (one in Russian by Tsvetaeva, the other by W. H. Auden). There is a memoir of his native city, Leningrad, and another of an awful trip to Constantinople. There are brushes at political commentary, but nothing as classic as the political prose of another emigre poet—Czeslaw Milosz's *The Captive Mind* (1953). If Brodsky has read any American poets younger than Robert Lowell, he does not say; it is probably safer for his self-myth (and specialized position) not to. In the end, *Less Than One* has no cohesive subject, other than his own celebrity.

Most of these essays were originally written in English. Those initially in Russian were put into English by Barry Rubin, an otherwise unidentified figure whom Brodsky credits with "editorial counsel" in his last poetry collection, *A Part of Speech* (1980). The principal distinguishing mark of Brodsky's prose is a grandiosity that comes largely from exaggeration and from taking poetry, and language, far too seriously. It is a kind of so-called "grand manner" I associate first with poets generations older than himself, especially in Europe (and perhaps accounts for the publicist's image of Brodsky as "cosmopolitan") and then with the illusion that from a grand style necessarily follow great ideas. Consider the book's opening paragraph: "As failures go, attempting to recall the past is like trying to grasp the meaning of existence. Both make one feel like a baby clutching at a basketball: one's palms keep sliding off." This last metaphor is a confection inconceivable to me, who has never seen (and cannot imagine) infants ever having the opportunity to clutch a grandiose *basket*ball. (A *base*ball would be more appropriate.) Now, of course, to impressionable minds, what seems an unnecessary affectation can become more acceptable if you can say "I keek it; I vin it." However, in English, such inflated phrasing reflects the mentality of the limited specialist; and within the world of American poetry, Brodsky has never been more than a place-kicker, a sideshow import whose praise-winning boots appeal particularly to those more inclined, alas, to appreciate overly publicized flashiness to substance.

P.S. (1990) When the above review initially appeared, it was attacked by contentious people who refused the challenge issued in the essay itself, to quote (or even identify) a poetic masterpiece. Instead there were *ad hominem* attacks that reveal to everyone smarter than dunces the lack of strong contradictory evidence. At the time I replied: "The one colleague serious (or courageous) enough to quote examples, albeit in conversation, was Brodsky's Leningrad compatriot, K. K. Kuzminsky, who identified remarkable sonic qualities that, he knew as well as I, did not show (sound) up in English translations—a demonstration that did not refute as much as confirm my thesis about Brodsky's marginal place in American letters." That is another way of acknowledging that Brodsky's name belongs in the history not of American literature but our literary publicity.

With a singular lack of self-awareness, Brodsky wrote the following in a recent memoir of Isaiah Berlin in *The New York Review* (August 17, 1989):

This is not how I first saw him, though, seventeen years ago, when he was sixty three and I thirty-two. I had just left the country where

I'd spent those thirty-two years and it was my third day in London, where I knew nobody.

I was staying in St. John's Wood, in the house of Stephen Spender, whose wife had come to the airport three days before to fetch W. H. Auden, who has flown in from Vienna to participate in the annual Poetry International Festival in Queen Elizabeth Hall. I was on the same flight, for the same reason. As I had no place to stay in London, the Spenders offered to put me up.

Wow, Brodsky has either reduced famous people to nonentities ("nobody") or indulged a helluva lot of *chutzpah*, or fake innocence, to portray them as such, also incidentally demonstrating that you need not write English well to be a literary celebrity here, so stuporous, or decadent, have our cultural gatekeepers become. "What a country" another emigré/comedian continually reminds us.

As for the Nobel Prize, consider that perhaps the Swedish judges read the poetry of their Baltic neighbor in the original Russian, or that Brodsky's work might translate better into Swedish than English?

Autobiographical
Addenda

Literature is not merely language, it is principled language, whatever the principle in a given case.
—Denis Donoghue, *Ferocious Alphabets* (1981)

Poetry is potentially the most powerful technology to realize the multidimensionality of reading values—to sound the sonic, measure the lexicon, and refuse a standardization and regimentation that deafens us to the living past in language and diverts us from enacting living presents—decentered and plural—*for* language.
—Charles Bernstein, "Blood on the Cutting Room Floor" (1984)

The work of each poet, each poem, is a response to a determinate coordinate of language and history. Each writer possesses in his or her imagination a subjective conceptualization of this *matrix* (inevitably partial, inevitably a distortion), usually termed the tradition. The locus of the work to be written is felt as a blind spot, a primal lack toward which the writer is driven. This is the essential truth in the cliché that poets write only those poems which they *need*. Each successful poem abolishes (but only for a time) the lack and subtly reorganizes the structure of the subjective matrix.
—Ron Silliman, "Disappearance of the Word, Appearance of the World" (1987)

I have shaped my endeavor with ever widening fields for research and since I enjoy the exhilaration of work I have not been oppressed by the apparent endlessness of my task.
—William Carlos Williams, *The Embodiment of Knowledge* (1974)

Interview (1983)

RICHARD KOSTELANETZ HAS been present on the edge so long that he is coming to seem the Lou Gehrig of American Avant-Garde Literature. For the past two decades, he has been hyper-active, publishing poems so unusual that creative writing professors unanimously grit their teeth at the sound of his name, fictions so innovative they have been widely published but never reviewed or anthologized, experimental prose that every teacher of expository writing would find unacceptable, and pointed cultural criticism that makes everyone's enemies wince. A complete literary radical, he has also edited over two dozen anthologies of the stuff he likes in literature, art, criticism, and social thought. Given that his work is challenging and noncommerical, that people of power often do not like what he stands for, that ass-kissers resent his independent success, perhaps the most incredible thing about Kostelanetz is that he has survived intact, if scarred, apart from academia, apart from hackwork, apart from jobs, apart from patrons—apart from all those pseudo-benefactors that deplete the literary spirit in exchange for lucre. *Woodrose* found him exhausted from a European trip, just barely breathing, in his SoHo loft, surrounded by thousands of books, piles of mail, and a spate of unfinished projects.

We wanted to interview him as he moved around the space, forever "cleaning up" as he put it; but since we were in Madison and didn't know anyone in New York, he reluctantly agreed to do it himself.

Let me open with the question that must occur to everybody, though I suppose few ask it. How do you survive?
In truth . . . simply by having resolved a long time ago to function on my own terms. I had no choice, once I made certain perceptions. When I was nineteen I had a bad job experience that led me to believe that I could never be employed; and although that assessment may or may not have been true, the fear of the need to take a job became a boiling cauldron under my desk, so to speak—a cauldron into which I am, even now, always on the verge of falling. I worked not for fame or money but, literally, for my life, living cheaply, initially in a Harlem housing project, making sure I found things that paid me, while, then as now, I spent most of my time on work that is not immediately remunerative.

What paid?
Two decades ago, I got book contracts that had advances of a thousand dollars or so; I did articles for slick magazines, usually about the contemporary art I liked. Towards the end of the 1960s, I began to give lectures and illuminated demonstrations of visual poetry; and even though I don't have any bait that enables me to play swapsy games with the academics, I've done an awful lot of touring over the past fifteen years. Financially, I hit bottom around 1976, when the commercial book business dried up, though small press business was booming, while my expenses had increased from moving to SoHo. It was then that I actually accepted my first and only full-time job, as Visiting Professor of American Literature and English at the University of Texas for the spring of 1977. I enjoyed Austin, especially as a vacation from this factory here in New

York; but I also felt that if I didn't get my butt out of there, I would disintegrate from inactivity. Fortunately, I began to receive grants around this time, not only from the NEA, which has rewarded me a few times now, but from several private foundations. One of these grants took me to Europe for the first time as an adult post-graduate—to West Berlin, as a guest of its DAAD Kunstlerprogramm; and this last episode has had a great effect on my creative activity and how I think about it.

How so?
I was able to do sorts of work I've always wanted to do, but could never do here and, better yet, get paid for it.

How could that be?
One thing I'd been doing since 1975 is experimental audio. During a residency then at a new Rochester FM station, I made in a few evenings several short pieces that were remarkable enough to be broadcast over National Public Radio network, and then over Australian radio and later over German radio too; but I was unable to do any new radio work for several years. Private studios were too expensive, while grants were unavailable. My audio work was already too original for Earplay, which had a monopoly over American radio drama at the time and was trying, opportunistically, very hard to be antiexperimental and thus acceptable to the conservative funders, who not only favor more conventional activity but, in addition, have always been predisposed to klutzy documentaries.

However, when I met Klaus Schöning, the leading producer of *Neue Hörspiel* or New Audio Art, for German radio, he invited me to work for Westdeutscher Rundfunk. Before long, I was able to realize experiments that I had thought about for years. Formerly unable to do pieces more than a few minutes long, I could now produce works that were a full hour in length, and even longer. Better yet, these pieces were broadcast, and sometimes rebroadcast, often in prime time, without the sort of condescending explanations or apologetic introduction that might be required in America, and for the first broadcast there I was paid, incredibly and indicatively, more money than I had previously earned for *all* my radio work.

Since this is a literary magazine, rather than a record or audio cassette, can you describe some of these audio pieces?
Invocations, done in 1981, is about the sound of the language of prayer. Commissioned by the public radio station in West Berlin, which assigned me an assistant for field work, I recorded prayers spoken by sixty ministers in twenty-five languages, and then mixed these on a twenty-four track machine into duets, quintets, choruses that were then strung together roughly on the principles of J. S. Bach's *St. Matthew Passion.* What sounds so simple in retrospective summary actually took weeks of full-time, painstaking work. Sixty minutes long, *Invocations* has since been broadcast on German radio, Dutch radio, Australian radio, Canadian radio; and I have commitments from stations in Yugoslavia and Sweden, as well as queries from Italy and Denmark. I offered the work here to NPR, which, even though it had broadcast me before, predictably found *Invocations* too experimental. Remember that its taste has always been so relentlessly middlebrow. (When NPR recently stumbled over its own greed, even filching money from its employees by keeping their withholding taxes, you could not count me among the mourners. Especially in its cultural programming, NPR has not failed from thinking too high.) The only time *Invocations* has ever been aired in America was over New York's Pacifica station, WBAI, when I brought the tape in myself, gave it to the announcer to play while I watched, and then took it home. The pay for this was, you guessed it, nothing. Fortunately, an American record company, Folkways, has recently issued the piece; so as with much other avant-garde American sound art nowadays, you are able to buy on record what you can rarely, if ever, hear on the air.

Is European radio really that different from American?
Yes, yes, yes. Let me tell an illustrative story. When Glenn
Gould died last year, the senior producer of the NPR sunday
arts show called and asked me to talk about Gould's achieve-
ment as a musician. Well, I have this personal rule against
doing anything that anyone else can do better, and so I recom-
mended other people to do this job for NPR. However, I
added, there is one aspect of Gould's achievement that I would
like to talk about (and that nobody else known to me can cover
better), and that is his radio art. Since it was radio art month,
or something like that, at NPR, I figured they would leap for
a short introduction to extraordinary programs that are hardly
known here. Two days later, they replied that only Gould's
music would be covered, because they felt obliged to discuss
"what everybody knows." A few months later, I proposed to
Westdeutscher Rundfunk a much longer feature on Gould's
audio art, and my proposal was immediately accepted, not
only because I said the work was so excellent, but mostly
because, as Klaus Schöning told me, "We don't know anything
about it and should." I swear that is what he said. If the same
bone is fed to two purportedly similar dogs, and one of them
bites, while the other refuses, don't you think that certain
almost-scientific conclusions can be drawn?

What else have you done for German radio?
In 1982, I did a fugue of the Gospels, the first four books of
the New Testament. Since they tell the same story, I always
wanted to experiment with the experience of hearing them
simultaneously. However, in order to do the piece in English,
I had to agree also to do it in German. Since I don't know
much German, this took a lot of work with a diglot Bible. The
60-minute German version that is called *Die Evangelien* was
broadcast later that year over Westdeutscher Rundfunk. The
English version, which runs 120 minutes, was broadcast only
once, again over New York's Pacifica station, WBAI, where as

before the pay was an infinitesimal fraction of what WDR had paid me for something it had not even broadcast, which is to say nothing. I hope that *The Gospels,* as the English version is called, eventually becomes at least a two-record set.

This past summer I did for WDR another piece that, given its subject, should have been done here, but couldn't have been, for all those reasons I mentioned before. I've wanted for fifteen years to do a photograph book about images particular to New York City—a visual exposition of those sights and juxtapositions that make my home town so visually different from everywhere else in the world. However, that project never had any takers, while I've never had sufficient resources to do it on my own. As I became more involved with audio art, it occurred to me to try to realize the same principle on audiotape—to compose an extended piece of sounds particular to New York. Klaus Schöning commissioned it and assigned me John David Fullemann, the engineer who had worked with John Cage on his *Roaratorio,* a masterpiece that, need I say, has scarcely been heard in the United States, even though its author is widely counted among our greatest living artists. Fullemann and I spent months recording sounds here in New York, and then nearly three more weeks working around the clock at the Electronic Music Studio of Stockholm. We put sounds together along certain themes, such as the New York style of selling, or the frequent experience of languages other than English, or the density of crowds, or answering machines, among others; and these thick mixes were tied together with interludes composed of an immense variety of solo subway sounds. The initial result was a tape 87 minutes long. Schöning wants 60 minutes; I want 120 minutes, if not for radio stations, then at least for a concert performance in which the visual element will be perhaps a thousand slides of those particularly New York images mentioned before. I'd like to think that *New York City,* as it is called, is the best audio piece I've ever done;

but since it really isn't finished yet, perhaps I should wait before making any further claims.

How does this new work relate to your writing?
It follows some of the same principles, the first and most important being *to do what has not been done.* My work is so different it challenges everyone's ideas about appropriateness in art. Just as my poetry is continually undermining all encapsulating definitions of that art, these audio pieces implicitly pose the question of whether or not they are music. One aspect of my style as an artist is continually challenging conventional categories, less to destroy the categories than to expand them; and my persistence in pursuing this vision, not just in my art but in my anthologies as well, is, of course, what makes my work so difficult and unacceptable to narrow-minded professionals. Indeed, if perchance it were more widely accepted, there would be good reason to question my entire esthetic enterprise. A second quality that the audio work shares with my writing is its conscious attempt at being about the essences of the thing, in this case acoustic experience. Perhaps one result of this European activity is that I am no longer just a writer but an artist who has done, and continues to do, writing along with other arts—an artist who has evolved for himself a plural situation that enables, or encourages, him to work in any one of several areas at any time. This last achievement, which is personal, or professional-personal, is probably what makes me different, profoundly different, from 99 percent of the other writers in this country, let alone Europe.

What else did you do in Europe?
More things that I could not do at home, such as two films. The first extends from a project I have been doing these past five years—a large number of single-sentence stories that I call *Epiphanies,* because they are meant to be the Epiphanies, in

the James Joycean sense, of otherwise nonexistent stories. As
I have nowadays been thinking of working in more media
than print, I envisioned from the beginning that these stories
should be "published," so to speak, on radio, in video, in an
exhibition, and in a film. Back in 1980, I began a video version
which drew upon a technology unique to that new medium—
the character-generator, which electronically makes the letters
you see on the television screen. I say "began," because these
first forays were done on a character-generator so elementary
that it quickly became clear to me that, to realize the potential
of this technology with my *Epiphanies* text, I really had to use
a more sophisticated machine, with more technical possibili-
ties. As usual, I applied to video workshops, but they were all
really more inclined to sponsor those earnest documentaries.
(How the hell these masquerade as "art" mystifies me.) Some
no doubt regard my decision to put words and only words
on the small screen as "not-video," confirming my guerrilla
reputation. I even wrote the companies manufacturing such
character-generators, offering to become their artist-in-resi-
dence at no expense to them; but none of them replied.

When I got to Germany, I realized how to do a film version
of *Epiphanies:* I would find in other filmmakers' outtakes mo-
ments that had the same epiphanic quality I was trying to get
in my stories. So I gathered mountains of sixteen-millimeter
footage from all sorts of sources, and from them selected
nearly a hundred moments that went into a 26-minute film.
This was shown the following spring in Berlin. The following
summer, I gathered more footage and mixed new selections
with the old film to produce a 70-minute version. By this time,
the producer in charge of the experimental *Projektionen* series
at the local television station, Sender Freies Berlin, asked for
a 20-minute version. He even sponsored the production of a
German sound track with sixteen readers. It was broadcast
this past summer, late one Friday night, and lots of Berlin
friends told me they saw it. This was incredible. Such success

would never happen here in America, where, as I said, "independent film" means not experimental art, not anything attempting to discover possibilities intrinsic to the medium, but politically sympathetic documentaries.

I also began in Berlin another film, a sort of documentary, I'm ashamed to say, this funded indirectly by the Berlin *Senat,* which is the government of Berlin. (Try to imagine any *city* here funding noncommercial film, especially by a foreigner, and you will quickly get another sense of how Europe differs from here.) This film deals with the great Jewish cemetery of modern Berlin, the *Judische Friedhof im Weissensee,* which, with over 110,000 graves, is the largest Jewish graveyard between Poland and America. Begun in 1880, it is also, to the eye, the principal surviving representation of Berlin's most golden age. The visual track of this film shows mostly gravestones (and thus relates to the visual poetry I've been doing these past fifteen years)—but I've also wanted to convey through images of gravestones alone what Berlin life in that period must have been like, the stones, as well as this film about them, constituting visual history. What makes this film unusual is that it depends upon words that must not be only read; they must be interpreted, often for subtle inferences. On the sound track, which was composed apart from the visual track, are heard ex-Berliners, now between fifty and ninety, remembering the cemetery and the Berlin represented there. The film eschews those talking heads which are, needless to say, the current convention in funded documentaries (because, to my mind, the current faces of my informants aren't the visual dimension of the historic subject). We've completed a 20-minute version with a German sound track for the *Senat* grant and have now applied to the National Endowment for the Humanities here for support for an English version, probably twenty-eight minutes long. I cannot afford to be sanguine, as aware as I've become of the differences between Europe and the United States toward independent art, but also because of our own different attitude toward so-called minorities. Here we use that last word to refer to people who represent a *large* segment of the population—women, blacks, hispanics—in the belief that their claims must be appeased. There the term minority refers to genuinely marginal groups, such as blacks (there), Armenians, Jews. Europeans are simply more sensitive to the survival of small minorities and the need to acknowledge their existence. Another difference is that German sponsors in particular seem more eager to have the best, or the best first of all, whereas here the Endowments feel obliged principally to support the most acceptable, esthetically and politically, often with the most vulgar considerations informing their decisions. There is here a lot more waste of taxpayers' money and a lot more sabotage of national cultural interests than, if you think about it, should be tolerable, especially to a Republican administration.

You have no idea how all this complaining about America profoundly disappoints me, because I have over the past two decades always defended American society, promoted American art, etc., often when fashions were quite contrary. I'd made a professional point of avoiding Europe, etc.; but now that I've gone myself, I see that I spoke out of ignorance, I made a mistake. Now that I have worked there, it has become clear to me why the greatest American avant-garde artists always went to Europe, back in the nineteenth century, in the twenties, in the fifties, and even into the seventies with, say, the music of Steve Reich and Philip Glass or new jazz. It became clear why, unless there are more changes than our National Endowments have so far brought us, avant-garde artists, especially major ones, will continue to go abroad— not to embarrass America, though their success abroad does undermine our cultural pretensions, but simply to discover, as I did, opportunites and acceptances, alas, unavailable here.

Arenas, etc.:
An Introduction (1982)

The student of classical Chinese poetry—particularly that of the
Tang dynasty, or "golden age"—will be aware that much of it is
intended to be read (in the original) vertically, horizontally,
diagonally, backwards or forwards and yet make sense in each
context. The Chinese generated a continuum of resonances as
opposed to more visually oriented Occidentals. With the
typewriter (and instant-graphic technologies), contemporary
poetics may approach this Oriental mode of composition:
abstracting language back into acoustic, iconographic space.
    —Keith Rahmmings, "Five Hundred Words or So" (1980)

THE NUMBER OF words in the initial series of these
rectangular poems was limited to four, each of them
placed at right angles to one another in the four corners of an
invisible rectangle, floating in the space of a larger page that
is bare of other imagery. Two questions a reader might legiti-
mately ask of such constellations exclusively of words are: (1)
Which way is *up*? (2) In what order should the words be
read? In writing them, I tended to put the initial word of the
collection in the upper right-hand corner of the vertical page,
but that was solely for my own reference. I could imagine a
publisher or reader inverting one of these poems, or turning
it by 90 degrees or 270 (or 45, 135, 225, or 315), to discover
a different version of the same poem and perhaps resonances
that escaped him or her before (or the surprise of an utterly
different poem with the same words!). Secondly, the words
may be read in any order—clockwise or counter-clockwise, or

by one diagonal and then another, at any speed. Ideally, let me suggest, *all the words could be seen and read simultaneously.*

In doing a large number of these poems, I wanted to explore the various ways in which four spatially separate words might become more than the sum of their parts. Sometimes, it seems to me, they reinforce one another through complementary relationships and sympathetic overtones; other times, one word stands out from its companions precisely because it is not a complement—perhaps, instead, a word that comments critically upon the other three. Occasionally, the words cohere in terms of sound; sometimes, in terms of image or other visual qualities (such as length); once, by common neology. This summary scarcely exhausts the variety of intended relations; unintended ones no doubt exist as well. (Trust the tale, not the teller.) If one crucial difference between poetry and prose is that the former need not be linear, and if one purpose of poetry is exposing readers to essences of language revealed apart from linear syntax (which is the domain of prose), here, ideally, the *poetry* occurs both among and between the words.

I personally think of the rectangular arrangement of four words in the title poem as both defining and epitomizing the entire set; what is there, in that title poem, is what the others, in general ways, are all about. That should not forbid the use, in identifying this body of work (apart from others), of such convenient shorthand as "*Fields,* etc." or "*Turfs,* etc." However, a verbally more complete title in sequential form—*Fields/Arenas/Turfs/Pitches*—would be contrary to my purposes, for it establishes a definitive sequence for reading these four words. The only accurate way to represent the title in an expository essay would be with a photographic replication of the original rectangle. Indeed, precisely because nothing represents the title poem (or any other poem) in this set better than that poem itself, this work cannot be anything but poetry. Another reason for their status as poetry (as distinct from essays) is that they are *fields,* not "windows" or "codes," that do not necessarily reveal anything outside themselves.

Sometime later I made two more groups of poems—one with eight words to a rectangle (the four extra words forming a compass in the middle) and then another with sixteen words to a frame (with the initial form multiplied into quarters); and in these as well, the words within each poem relate to one another in various ways. While I feel, on one hand, that four words to a page may be too sparse, I am not at all sure that the more populous poems are necessarily more successful (or more poetic).

These poems represent a departure from the kinds of visual poetry I had written before—among them, a single word or, occasionally, a related collection that is visually enhanced, shapes filled with words, and handwritten visual-verbal portraits. In point of fact, these poems came to me after a period in which prose and other art were plentiful, but poetry rare. The dedication of these poems to Anton von Webern acknowledges my love and experience of his style of an aural pointillism informed by linguistic rigor. Another influence I will gladly acknowledge is Islamic art.

If this poetry is as radical as I think it is, it would render the current standard vocabulary and strategies of poetry criticism irrelevant, and yet raise provocative questions about general issues: Have there ever been poems more restricted in form than these? Are these forms of just four, eight, or sixteen discrete words more rigorous than even those of Japanese haiku? Is it important to compose poems in ways drastically unlike those used in poetry before? Is it consequential to enlarge, in Viktor Shklovsky's phrase, the "geometric devices" of poetry? Isn't the purpose of poetry the offering of experiences of language that are not common but uncommon? Do these poems exploit the possibilities of nonsyntactical vectors? Exhaust them? Is the abandonment of traditional syntax a necessary prerequisite to current research into the poetic essences of language? Hasn't real poetry, great poetry, always been not about self-expression but revelations of the machinery of poetry?

These single-page texts could appear in any or all of several media. In periodicals publishing poetry, they could be gathered in one continuous sequence or distributed through the magazine, between other items (feasibly *without* author identification on the pages where they appear, as no one else's work resembles them). Selections from this work could be published in spine-bound books, with individual poems in a fixed order, or as a pack of cards, with the poems in an unfixed order. The words could also appear as black letters on a white page or, in a radical reversal, as white letters against a black background. During a 1980 residency at Davis and Elkins College, I produced a four-track audiotape in which four words and then eight were distributed to each of four tracks to resound simultaneously, much like a chord of music. Although distinguishing all the individual words in an aural cluster is admittedly hard at first, it is possible, after repeated hearing, to identify particular parts, much as people experienced with music can identify individual notes in a chord.

Other forms of "publication," as well as other poems in this form, are no doubt possible. The poems could be enlarged for mounting as either rectangles or diamonds on a wall of a gallery where the audiotape could be played in a continuous installation. (In 1988, I made a character-generated videotape in which four and then eight words appear on screen at roughly the same time that they are heard on the soundtrack recorded several years before; the tape concludes with the sixteen-word poems appearing in silence.) Now that I have become involved in public art, it occurred to me to print a new one each month on billboards that would rotate ninety degrees every week, each time pushing a new word to the top. Another suggestive "page" for these words would be the sky itself, with the letters in white, ideally produced at the four points of a compass by four skywriters simultaneously, thereby ensuring that none of the four words would have more presence than any of the others in their brief life, which is to say that the initial compositional constraint of equally weighted words would not be violated.

Notes on "Duets, Trios & Choruses" (1988)

Possibly what basically distinguishes poetry from prose is its greater range of geometric devices: A whole series of arbitrary semantic resolutions can be replaced by a purely formal, geometric resolution.
—Viktor Shklovsky, "Poetry and Prose in Cinematography" (1927)

O NE RECURRING THEME of my poetry has been the search for unusual forms that would prompt, if not generate, discoveries in the poetic presentation of language—discoveries that must be classified as poetic, because they are not prosaic, which is to say practical. The first move, in explorations that began over two decades ago, consisted of visualizations of a single word—the "imaged word," as I called it at the time. Among the most reprinted poems of this kind were "Disintegration," "Nymphomania," and "Echo." The next development I called "worded images," because an image was made exclusively of words, or letters functioning as words, as in my most reprinted poem, "Tributes to Henry Ford," the triptych in which the capital letters A and T, in this case representing successive models of automobiles, are arrayed in three patterns typical of successively more complex automotive traffic. Some of these earliest poems were cast into silk-screened prints, forty inches by twenty-six inches, which have been exhibited, representing a form of alternative publication different from the smaller formats of traditional poetry. Another kind of early visual poetry is the handwritten portrait, in which something is visually-verbally represented in the space of a page. My first poem in this vein was "The East Village (1970–

71)," which was reprinted in *I Articulations* (1974); a second was "Portraits from Memory" (1974), which appeared as an entire book under that title (1975). A fourth early development involved synonyms visually arrayed, as in the pyramid and inverted pyramid of "Live-Die" that is likewise reprinted in *I Articulations*. A recent variation on this strategy is a two-sided hologram, *Antitheses* (1985), in which words suggesting warmth protrude into space from one side of the picture plane (that is suspended in space), while words connoting chilliness protrude from the other side. In a fifth departure, numbers were substituted for words, making a poetry that consisted entirely of numerals. A sixth alternative involved extended strings of letters, "long poems" so to speak, composed of continuously overlapping words, each new word containing at least three concluding letters of its predecessor. Six of these "strings" exist so far—not only three in English but one in French, another in German, and a third in Swedish. Typed out, they are over a hundred uninterrupted inches in length. Published in public spaces, such as, say, in four-inch letters along the edge of a train platform, they could be at least two hundred feet long. Related to this is a video poem, *Partitions* (1986), whose kinetic action is revealing short words buried within longer words, all within the sequential structure available in that time-based medium. There were no doubt other unusual moves in my poetry, some of them less conscious than others, a few whose premises were forgotten, and some that were inadvertent by-products of intentional departures; and should a subsequent critic define the innovations of my poetry in different ways, or recognize discoveries unfamiliar to me, there is no reason to dispute his or her authority—trust the tale, not the teller.

In the late seventies, I began working with visual forms that are not representational but geometric and thus rigorously abstract. In the cycle whose title poem is "Turfs/Arenas/Fields/Pitches," I put individual words in the four corners of the page and expected poetry to arise from the relationships among them. As is typical with me, once I established a radical premise, I tried a variety of solutions, in part to discover the possibilities of the form. One departure within the structure involved eight words, with four in the corners as before, and four others in the middle arrayed like points on a compass; and a step beyond that involved sixteen words, with the initial rectangle divided into identical quarters. One quality all these poems have for me is that I still do not know for sure which ones are better, or why. One provocative question that remains unanswered in my mind is whether the more populous poems are better/richer/more complex than the sparer ones?

Though scarcely finished with this last experiment with the geometric structuring of language, I recently tried several other tactics. The first involved putting two words adjacent to each other, so that they interact not only in terms of meaning but as simultaneous weights on the page, which is to say that they make a *duet* in which, as in music, adjacent notes fairly equal in appearance may assume varying volumes when heard together. A second tactic involved the use of three words, likewise laid out horizontally (though vertical arrays are also feasible), functioning in the same way; to me these are *trios*. The last recent alternative involved the form of the circle (which I had previously used for "Manifestos," a personal favorite in my earliest work, and for *On Holography* [1978], my initial hologram, which contains syntactically circular statements about holography). In these new poems I set words only around the circle's circumference, all of their bottoms facing the center; and in some of them I also cast progressively smaller second and third circles of words parallel to the outer circle. In all these circular poems, there is an abundance of individual words, all related to one another in various poetic ways, more harmonious than dissonant—all, as in the earlier geometric poems, ideally making more than the sum of their parts. One quality that these last poems share with their rectangular predecessors is that no word is more important to the whole than any other. To my mind, all this is *visual poetry,* to cite a category I still find useful (while "concrete" has passed), in that the art very much depends upon how the words are displayed on the page and the poems must thus be read as paintings are read, which is to say not as lines or other units with beginnings or ends but as circumscribed spatial *fields.*

When either *Turfs* or these newer poems appear in print, I prefer that my name not accompany them on their pages; nothing should distract attention from the poetry. However, since no one else is working in these ways, it is possible that my name simply may not be necessary beyond the table of contents. One publisher of a fine poetry magazine told me that she recently gave a fresh copy to an older poet, an Ivy League professor proud of his conservative prejudices, who upon flipping it open to four-word poems without a name spontaneously exclaimed, "Oh, you publish Richard Kostelanetz." With enemies so sharp, who needs fans to tell you that a poetic territory you have staked out for yourself does indeed belong to you! One ambition I have as a poet is, in truth, not to repeat my poetic discoveries for profit and prominence but to discover more distinct and distinctly alternative terrains, perhaps more than anyone before me. I am not done yet.

Why Audio Theater Now
(1986)

Radio begins its existence with experiments to find out what it is
made of.

—Klaus Schöning

THE THREE PRINCIPAL charms of audiotape for me
as a theater artist are, first, that you work with fewer
people at any time; second, that you can create and reconsider
elements apart from the others; and, third, that you can pro-
duce definitive performances of your conceptions.

Every time I have gotten involved in making live theater or
film, the working situation suffered from too many people—
too many egos which had either to be persuaded or bossed if
the show were to go at all. Bossing I find politically disagree-
able; persuading, often at the last moment, consumes too
much valuable attention. If I need to work with anyone else,
there should be no more than one, either a colleague or an
assistant.

In producing radio theater, I can record a person at one
time, edit that recording at a second time, and then integrate
it with other tapes at a third time, further reconsidering each
of these latter two moves on my own time, working with at
most an audio technician. In producing a radio play from
separately gathered fragments, of sounds as well as texts, I
can compose an audio play much as tape composers produce
music.

It was Glenn Gould who pointed out that recordings enable
the musical performer to make such a definitive interpretation

of a work that further live performance of it becomes unnecessary. Audiotape can have the same effect upon the performance of written, time-based texts.

Back before World War II, Guillaume Apollinaire made "conversation poems" composed of snatches of speech heard around him. Into continuous printed language he pieced together fragments initially gathered separately. Regarding this effort now, we can judge, "Poor Apollinaire. Too bad he didn't have audiotape." We could now make the same remark about Edgard Varèse's *Ionisation* (1931).

One issue confronting the radio dramatist in our time is whether he or she wishes to imitate in audio alone the conventions of live drama or realize, instead, illusions possible on audiotape. My own feeling is that in the age of wire recording (prior to 1952) it was credible, say, to portray characters in dramatic conversation—talking to one another in live time; by now, however, that essentially theatrical convention, and others like it, seems indubitably archaic. To my mind, an audio play is more true to itself if its presence in the listener's head is purely acoustic. We don't want to hear what we cannot see; we want to hear what can hardly be imagined, whose visual image is indefinite, like that of music, which is to say that we experience what can only be heard. In this age of television, listeners should close their eyes and relax blind, letting audio alone animate their imaginations.

Audio artists want to be able to create acoustic worlds that do *not* suggest theatrical images (or film or video), but portray in time relationships of voices and other sounds that can be heard, but scarcely visualized, such as a person talking to himself, or a dialogue between two people who are perhaps in different physical spaces, or an individual progressing through a fantastic environment. We can even create scenes, if not whole narratives, primarily, if not exclusively, of sounds other than speech. Audiotape thus becomes a medium for realizing not just acoustic literature, or literary language to be heard aloud, but also articulated sound, which is to say semblances of music, all at the service of dramatic conceptions that are both literary and musical, but need not be theatrical.

Among the recent North American works defining this new terrain are Glenn Gould's *Schoenberg: The First Hundred Years* (1974), Francis Schwartz's *Caligula* (1975), Peter Schickele's *P.D.Q. Bach on the Air* (1967), The Firesign Theater's *Don't Crush that Dwarf, Hand Me the Pliers* (1970), John Cage's *Roaratorio* (1978), Doris (Sorrel) Hays's *Southern Voices* (1980), Charles Dodge's *Any Resemblance Is Purely Coincidental* (1980), Alison Knowles *Natural Assemblage and the True Crow* (1984), Dennis Williams's *The Search for the Colossal Man* (1984), and my own *New York City* (1984).

One remaining question is whether radio might be a less appropriate medium for disseminating audio theater than disc or audiocassete, especially for works that do not immediately reveal themselves and thus must be heard more than once.

Video Writing (1987)

> Of course, in this electric age of computers, radio and television, the writer can no longer be someone who sits up in his garret pounding a typewriter.
>
> —Marshall McLuhan (1966)

THE PRINCIPAL ADVENTURE, or strategy, for my creative writing over the past dozen years has been exploring the use of language in media other than the traditional one of 8½-by-11-inch rectangular manuscript pages. For those dozen years, and then another dozen before that, I have spent most of my working days manipulating words—words for articles and books; words for journalism and criticism; words for poetry and fiction, experimental prose and much, much else. It should be understood, at the beginning, that I love language, and I love to work with language.

From my earliest essays as a critic of literature and the arts, I have been committed to appreciating the innovative, to work that did not fulfill conventions but transcended them, often radically; and so it became inevitable that when I came to do my own creative works, the first around 1967, I began at a point far beyond the conventions of the time. My opening moves were visual poems, which is to say language enhanced primarily in terms of design. Among the more familiar examples were "Disintegration" (1967) and "Tributes to Henry Ford" (1967), both of which have been widely reprinted.

My next steps involved visual fiction, which is to say worded images in sequence, as in "Genesis" (1971), which summarizes the opening books of the Bible in seven images, or the "Football Forms" (1968), whose letters portray the evolution of an offensive play in four images; and "Development" (1972), whose abstract shapes fall into a sequence that suggests a narrative about various kinds of constructive processes. At the same time I was working with radical kinds of exclusively verbal fictions that were severely truncated, or minimal, with only two words or less to a paragraph.

Also, by 1974, some of the better visual poems, including "Disintegration," appeared, enlarged, as silk-screened prints that are forty inches by twenty-six inches in size; and one subsidiary benefit of that last move into visual art, as it is commonly perceived, was propelling me out of the literary tradition of doing "writing" only on small rectangular pages. Indeed, what I had also discovered with these prints was alternative forms of making public my work with language; that is to say that I found another way to publish my writing. A final foundation behind my initial video writing was a 1975 residency at a public radio station. Here I took some of my earlier literary texts—the minimal fictions, especially—and exploited the unique resources of multitrack audiotape to publish them acoustically, in ways that I hoped would be appropriate not just to the verbal text but also conducive to the unique possibilities of audiotape.

Having established my willingness to explore writing in the new media, I was invited, later in 1975, to be a guest artist at the Synapse video studio at Syracuse University, where I worked not with a single engineer-producer, as I had at the radio station, but with an institutional staff of young instructors, graduate assistants, and undergraduates. With their help, I realized video versions of earlier literary texts. "Excelsior" (1970), for instance, was initially a skeletal, minimal story in which two people seduce each other in one-word paragraphs: Let's /No /Yes /Stop /Now /Please /Later /Relax /Insist /Don't / Dislike/No/Like/Pooh. . . . And so on. To visualize the text on videotape, I created two abstract designs and then swiftly alternated between them, letting the sound track eroticize the rhythmic abstract imagery. Another skeletal story, "Plateaux," tells of the development of a love affair in single-word paragraphs. Since the original text ends with the same words with which it begins—the phrases "Introductions," "Pleasantries"— I decided such a circular form needed the technology of video feedback to create a kaliedoscopic moiré pattern that changes slowly in no particular direction, complementing visually the directionless development, so to speak, of the fiction's plot.

For my third early piece, I drew upon a more difficult literary text—a piece of experimental prose called *Recyclings* whose first volume had been published the year before. Its pages were made by subjecting earlier essays of mine to selective processes that destoyed their original syntax, while retaining their characteristic language. What I did in writing this text was extract words out of their original sequence, and by this method make of the words for each past essay a single page of new nonsyntactic prose—literally, a recycling. As words on these pages have no grammatical connection to one another, the texts of *Recyclings* can thus be read not only horizontally, like normal prose, but also vertically or even diagonally, as one's eyes, moving down and around the page, can perceive not only consistencies in diction but repeated words that usually indicate an identifiable ulterior source or subject. The subtitle of *Recyclings* is "A Literary Autobiography, 1959– 1981" since the 320 pages of its definitive text (1984) recapitulate, or recycle, everything I had written to that point.

During the earlier residency at the radio station, I decided to use multitrack audiotape for its particular capabilities. Essentially, I read a page of *Recyclings* text horizontally, one word after the other, in the conventional way. When that reading was complete, I could go on to a second page of text, which I read *twice*, likewise in conventional ways, this time, however, amplifying my voice differently from before. For this duplicate declamation we rewound the multitrack tape so that I could begin the second declamation approximately one line (or a few seconds) behind its predecessor, making a duet with myself. For the third page, I triplicated the same delay procedure on the third text, thus making, again thanks to multitrack, a trio canon with three different amplifications of my own voice. By the time I got to a seventh page of *Recyclings*, adding six delays of me reading a seventh text, I had transformed myself into a choral septet. With this fugal technique, I was aiming not for any specific juxtapositions of one word with another, but just for continuous vertical relationships among different parts of the same text.

For the video *Recyclings* I created the image of pairs of lips speaking; and as the voices in the audio realization were all mine, so were these lips. However, videotape differs from audiotape in that it doesn't have separate tracks; there is no audio equivalent of multitrack audiotape. Rather than laying the versions apart from one another and then mixing them together, as I did on audiotape, I had with videotape to lay them literally on top of one another. However, with each new generation of imagery, the video signal of the previous generations becomes less stable. As a result, the prior images become progressively weaker, which means not just that they become fuzzier but that they lose their original colors. That degeneration of the signal strength explains why, by the time four voices are speaking, and four lips are on the screen, they all have different colors, incidentally epitomizing a self-surrealism as only contemporary technology can make it. As this work is far more difficult than its predecessors, it also demands a lot more explanation. However, it is not impenetrable; it is not impossible to understand. Like so much else in contemporary art, *Recyclings* must be seen, or heard, or read, more than once to reveal itself. Indeed, the more often you hear it, the more of itself will be revealed.

The last videotape that I made at Synapse in 1975 is based upon my book *Openings & Closings* which also appeared in that year. It is a collection of single-sentence stories that are alternately either the openings of hypothetically longer fictions or the closings, again of equally nonexistent fictions. While each of these stories radiates either forwards or backwards, they have no intended relation to one another; and there are no intentional connections within the entire work, other than the principle of scrupulous discontinuity. Here I decided to read the stories on camera, one after the other, the openings in alternation with the closings. To enhance my reading in ways that would be impossible live, and also impossible on audiotape, I instructed a crew of Synapse technicians to alternate between color cameras for the openings and black-white cameras for the closings, and connected each coloring system to its own camera crew. Thus, one class of stories could not be visually confused with the other. My second instruction was that each crew make its current visual image of me as different as possible from the one(s) before. My aim here was to realize visually the enormous leaps of time and space that characterize the book's text. *Openings & Closings* is, incidentally, the only creative videotape I have made so far in which an image clearly recognizable as me appears on the screen.

Beginning in 1976 I began to tour with my videotapes, or rather to play them instead of reading aloud from my texts whenever I was invited to do a literary recital. Since my first show of these tapes, at the Anthology Film Archives at the end of 1975, involved an Advent video screen, I began to insist that my hosts find similar two-piece projection systems in their own communities or institutions. I remember on the eve of Jimmy Carter's election, at the University of California at Santa Cruz, my tapes were shown on a university-owned screen that no one in the audience had seen before; and once my show was done, we watched the political news on this new medium (whose light is projected onto the screen, rather than from behind it, as in normal television). At Arizona State, eighteen months later, my hosts discovered that the only video screen available on campus was in the nursing school; so my audience traipsed by plastic cadavers on the way to my show.

After my experience at Synapse, I wrote a theoretical text in which I tried to define what I was doing and incidentally distinguish my tapes from other video art. Entitled "Literary Video," this essay appeared in several magazines at that time, as well as in program notes to my own screenings and later in anthologies about video art. In 1977, in a private New York video studio run by Joanne Caring, I also put the manifesto on videotape, in a visual form (with only my mouth visible) that incidentally illustrates one of its points (about video differing from film in favoring close-ups over long shots and parts of bodies over full figures). Another piece from this period, "Milestones in a Life," is, in essence, a reading of a truncated verbal text, in which the words for numerals alternate with paragraphs mostly a single word in length; but again, rather than subscribing to the literary convention of showing the author at a lectern or in some other formal, pseudo-literary situation, I decided that for my video realization of me reading this text it would be best to show only my eyes.

During a literary residency at Eastern New Mexico State University in 1979, two professors of English interviewed me about my writing for their television program. To illustrate my work, they invited me to do a conventional reading of my poetry or fiction, my eyes no doubt glancing earnestly from my text to the camera. However, that presentational form is no more acceptable to me on camera than it is in live performance, so often confusing as it does the writer with his or her work, and therefore vulgarizing the reception of that writing. I insisted instead upon doing something else, which would involve declaiming a text as difficult as *Recyclings*, again superimposing image over image, which here would be four pairs of bearded lips, all visibly different in size; but now I used a video technology that was new to me—the character-generator that electronically produces letters that appear on the screen. Since this text, titled "Declaration of Independence," was so difficult, I decided to add continuous lines of explanatory gloss that would crawl from time to time along the bottom of the screen.

Since 1979 I have been writing a text called *Epiphanies*, which are single-sentence stories that, unlike those mentioned before, are not the openings or the closings but the epiphanies, in the James Joycean sense. That is to say that these are the resonant moments that illuminate the entire, but here nonexistent, story. In my video writing of these texts, I used the character-generator, or electronic letter-making machine, to put the words of these epiphanies directly on the video screen, one story at a time, in various typographical arrangements; and I let them dominate the screen for durations roughly equal to the length of the stories, while J. S. Bach's keyboard music is heard in the background. Someone remembering silent movies has joked that my video *Epiphanies* is "all titles, no action," and that is true, in that the visible words contain the entire action of each story. Nonetheless, this videotape is very much about an alternative experience of reading, not only in concert with others (usually) but at a speed of presentation that (unlike the conventional reading experience) cannot be controlled by the reader. Literally printing these stories on videotape also represents a viable alternative to traditional publishing. This *Epiphanies* was produced wholly within the realm of video technology and like most of my other later tapes could be characterized as *cameraless* video.

The character-generator I used in these video *Epiphanies* is rather primitive, compared to what is available—it could use only one style of lettering, in one size, only with white letters on a black field, in a fixed grid of twenty-four characters across and ten lines high. More sophisticated character-generators, by contrast, contain various typefaces, expandable to any size that can fit within the screen, in a variety of colors. These letters can be programmed to enter the screen from any place along the edge and then change size in the course of moving across the screen's face, in, say, a visual crescendo or decrescendo; the letters can even be made to perform such acrobatic tricks as flipping over or turning inside out. Or so I am told, as I have not yet been able to use one.

I also want to compose by myself a new contemporary sound track, replacing the classical piano which sounds too much like old-time movie music for my taste. Instead, I want to use computer-assisted speech resynthesis to take the single word "epiphanies" and extend, combine, and vary it in a multitude of ways, with each variation equal in length to one of the stories. Such a sound track would necessarily be composed apart from the visual track and would thus draw upon the techniques I have been developing in my audio art and upon, as well, a bias toward separately composed sound and image that is also evident in my films.

My sense of my video art now is that the character-generator is my principal tool, and that my principal creative interest will be exploring it for a video writing that will not supercede the printed page—that's not possible, because the book will always be with us—but become yet another possibility for presenting heightened, poetic language. What I like about video in general is its capacity to complement my literary interest with visual elements in addition to the temporal and kinetic.

During recent residencies at the Experimental TV Center in Owego, New York, I have been producing visual realizations of both poems and stories, using not only elementary character-generators but, more important, rather sophisticated processing equipment to put my words on screen in unusual shapes. Perhaps the most successful of these experiments so far has been "Stringfour" whose text is composed from overlapping English words. To be precise, each new word in this continuous string of letters contains at least three letters from its predecessor:

stringfourselvestrymandolingerbillowbrowboatmealtimetablemish
apelessence . . .

As the character-generator enabled me to write its several
hundred letters as a continuous feed that runs from the
right edge of the screen to the left, we decided to make a
second version of the text, enlarged to a greater height; and
it too flows across the screen, with fewer letters visible
from vertical edge to vertical edge, as a kind of harmonic
compliment. As the words of "Stringfour" move across the
screen quite quickly, some of the verbal sequences are more
visible, or more accessible, than others; some are also more
witty. As a video realization of a text that was originally
composed for paper (and has been published in literary
magazines), "Stringfour," with language in such an extended
structure, works far better on videotape, which here becomes
an effective alternative vehicle for publishing certain works
of literature. May I also recommend viewing it, as well as
other works of mine, on a two-piece video projection screen,
where the imagery indigenous to television becomes yet
more fantastic and powerful, precisely because, as in the
silk-screened prints of my visual poems, language assumes
special qualities when it is seen so large at such close range.
A graduate student currently researching a thesis on
American poets using video has recently told me that no
other "published poet" in America today has been producing
his or her own videotapes, as distinct from performing
before video cameras, which is to say that no other native
writer has become a video artist in his or her own right.
Because this technology has been available for over a decade,
I find this hard to believe, but then professional self-
limitations are a literary fashion in America today, which is
to say that the opportunistic poet would avoid the opportuni-
ties of new media as scrupulously as any other stylistic
deviance. The only published poet known to be working in

holography is a young Brazilian, Eduardo Kac, and the only writers to be making their own videotapes are European. It would seem that less out of genius than default, in the world of contemporary American literature, video writing has become my own terrain.

Literary Holography
(1990)

As a sensitive person, the artist first observes the world around
him. In his mind he makes conjectures, conceptualizes images or
forms, and then translates his vision into a cognitive, positive
thought. This image is then transferred to some medium. . . . To
effectively translate ideas, one must develop an understanding of
the capabilities and limitations of the medium in which one works,
and develop skill with the use of one's tools.
                    —Fred Unterseher, et al., *Holography Handbook* (1982)

FOR MORE THAN fifteen years now, a principal theme
of my artistic activity has been working with language and
literary forms in media other than small printed pages. I
have, instead, produced drawings, large graphics, audiotapes,
videotapes, films, photographic sequences, and even proposals
for public art, all containing words and/or literary structures
such as narrative (as in photographic sequences). Among my
purposes has been the discovery of alternative possibilities for
organizing words and then for "publishing" my writing, which
is to say to do in these media what could not be done in print.
Behind the last thought is my assumption that in transcending
the printed page is one future for literature. Even though I
consider myself less interested in expressing a particular vision
or in exploiting an idiosyncratic "look" than in exploring these
media for literary experiment, the results invariably reflected
earlier poetic ideas of mine, if not particular poems.

Since I had no official training in any of these media, most
of this work was produced during residencies at professional
installations—at radio stations, electronic music studios, video

production facilities, and film schools; it was produced in collaboration with technicians professional in these media. My customary way of working involves defining first the character of the new medium, then the particular potentialities available at the host studio, and finally the tastes and competences of my technicians. Once these factors are in mind, I generally favor technically optimal possibilities. For instance, in my very first residency, at WXXI-FM in Rochester, New York, in 1975, I was introduced to an eight-track tape recorder, which had just been installed there and had never been used. The machine itself inspired me to produce an eight-voice realization of a text of mine. When we discovered that one track of this new machine appeared to be dead, I coined my motto for such situations: "I'm the visiting artist; I'm here to test your machinery" (or "your technicians").

Though I remember clearly the first laser I ever saw, in 1967 at Bell Laboratories in New Jersey, my recollections of holography are hazier, probably because little impressed me until a decade later, when I saw a rotating cylindrical (360-degree) white-light transmission hologram. As the three-dimensional image suspended within the cylinder was continually revealing the other side of itself, the impression here was not just photographic, like too many other holograms I had seen; this was a three-dimensional representation in time that could not be grasped in a single viewing. The cylindrical hologram differed as well from a panoramic photograph, where the camera spins around an axis, rather than, as in the hologram, focusing upon the axis. The second advance in my holographic awe came a few years later, when I saw three-dimensional imagery extend not back from the visible plate, as in most holograms (and three-dimensional photography before them), but forward to points between the plate and the viewer's eye. The third epiphany came from noticing that parts of an image could be hidden from view, forcing the viewer to move, usually from side to side, to complete his perception of the whole. Finally, I continue to remain impressed by the medium's basic mystery to implant in lucite "a strange pattern that has the capacity to play back an image under certain conditions."

With the first discovery in mind, I produced in 1978, during a residency at the Cabin Creek Center in New York, my first hologram, *On Holography*, a rotating cylinder with five syntactically circular statements that, as the cylinder continually turns to the left, pass endlessly before the viewer's eyes. In each of the statements, the words were about holography, and the ends were tied to each other to make a continuous circle:

. . . holos = complete; gram = message; . . .

. . . representation in depth = hologram . . .

. . . the hologram creates a world of incorporeal activity that exists only within . . .

. . . the illusion not only of depth but of equal focus to all distances are characteristics particular to holography which creates . . .

. . . by capturing on photosensitive material the amplitude, the wavelength and, most important, the phases of light reflected off an object a hologram reconstructs a three-dimensional image . . .

Both in form and in their self-referential subject, these syntactically circular statements about holography echoed the four circles of the visual poem-manifesto introducing my first collection of poetry, *Visual Language* (1970), in which:

. . . the poetry of life copies . . .

. . . artistry belies argument dupes . . .

. . . art creates worlds made entirely from . . .

. . . the truth of fiction is the power of artifice is . . .

One difference between the circles of this poem and the holo-
gram is that whereas the language of "Manifestos" must be
read at angles that some of us find uncomfortable—upside
down or sideways—the circular statements of the continuously
revolving hologram could be entirely horizontal. Similarly,
whereas the printed poem is best read from a location perpen-
dicular to the face of it, the circular hologram lacks fixed
perspective, which is to say that it is equally legible from every
side of its stationary base. It became clear to me that, for
the presentation of language, holography offers advantages
unavailable on a flat printed page.

Once *On Holography* was completed, I discovered two prob-
lems. The first and most obvious was that I had hardly utilized
the medium's capabilities for creating the illusion of depth.
Instead, the words appeared to emerge from behind an invisi-
ble door on the right and then pass across the face of the
cylinder to disappear behind another invisible door, now on
the left. While shorter statements, higher within the hologram,
do appear to lie further back in space, few would notice a
second, more complicated perceptual problem that must be
described in fuller detail.

I thought initially of stacking the statements into a single
pyramid, with the shortest one on top and the longest one at
the bottom; but to fill the cylinder with only a single rotating
image struck me as clumsy (and unholographic). Were the
words at the bottom level of a single pyramid to move across
the viewer's eyes at a legible speed, the upper levels would
have been boringly slow; conversely, to key the motion of
words to an upper level would have necessitated making the
bottom levels illegibly fast. I decided instead that each line
should revolve independently, in the ratios of 1:2:3:4, count-
ing from the bottom up, so that statement number four
(twenty words) would be seen twice for every rotation made
by number five (twenty-nine words), and then have number
three (twelve words) be seen thrice, and number two and

Photo: Robert Haller

number one (each four words) be seen four times during each rotation of the cylinder. (This was realized by having each circle of words filmed individually on a drum to exactly equal lengths. However, the film of number four was step-printed, as they say, to omit alternate frames, and then duplicated to equal the length of number five. The film of number three was step-printed to omit two of every three frames, and then triplicated; the single film of number two and number one was step-printed to omit three of every four frames, and then quadruplicated. These four films were then superimposed to make a single continuous film whose images were then anamorphically compressed into vertical slivers that comprise the holographic film that lines the inside surface of the exhibition cylinder. The imagery on this film becomes apparent only when illuminated from below by a single-filament light bulb.)

While this restructuring of the holographic representation of five statements was conceptually very clever, the inadvertent result was a remarkably unclever illusion (no, delusion). Instead of moving before the viewer's eyes at different speeds, the letters in five rows appear to move roughly in unison. (Twenty-nine at the lowest level is roughly equal to two times twenty and three times twelve.) That means that viewers initially perceive all five lines as belonging to a single rotating pyramid, all contrary to fact! Now, of course, if the viewer examined the relationships among the lines closely, he or she would realize that a four-word statement could not possibly rotate at the same frontal speed as a twenty-nine-word statement. Likewise, if the viewer made vertical comparisons among the lines, he or she would notice that whenever the word "holos" appeared in the top (first) line, a sequence, or cycle, of four different words would appear directly below it in the bottom (fifth) line. However, few viewers would "read" *On Holography* that closely, in part because the tradition of perceptually photographic holograms accustoms them to a more painterly, instantaneous kind of looking. Instead, this hologram offers visual-verbal experience that can only be appreciated in time and is, in that respect, perceptually closer to film or, of course, literature.

When *On Holography* was initially exhibited in a crowded group show at New York's Museum of Holography, I noticed that it could scarcely compete with the pseudo-photographs whose images were quickly recognized, whose ideas were readily grasped. *On Holography* not only required more patience literally to be "seen," it posed perceptual problems that were not immediately apparent. To make its presence more competitive in the gallery, I decided to add a multitrack audiotape accompaniment of five voices reciting the same five lines of words repeatedly and simultaneously at a rate roughly matching the rotational speed of the hologram, so that viewers could hear in five-voice unison the same words they see simultaneously in five-line unison. If nothing else, they could hear that "hologram = representation in depth" occurred far more often than the longest statement; and I figured perhaps that the addition of an aural-verbal element might generate questions about visual-verbal perception. When *On Holography* has been shown along with works of mine in other media, as in a traveling exhibition *Wordsand* (1978–), the audiotape remained an option. (My collaborators in producing *On Holography* were Hart Perry and Neal Lubetzky; the audiotape was made in collaboration with Charlie Morrow.)

II

On the most basic level, you don't look at a hologram—you look into it. A holographic image can project in front of the plate (a real image), in back of the plate (a virtual image), or it can straddle the plate (an image plane).
—Rosemary H. Jackson, "Through the Looking Glass" (1976)

To make a second hologram in 1985, I first had to win another residency competition, this sponsored by the Dennis Gabor Laboratory at the Museum of Holography for "artists who have had limited or no experience in making holograms, yet have a strong body of work in a different medium." An invitation in hand, I decided to work more with the medium's awesome capability for generating literal three-dimensional experience. Since holography transcends three-dimensional photography in allowing the viewer to look literally around and behind a foreground image, my first notion was to put words behind other words, thus requiring the viewer to move his or her body up and down, if not from side to side, to find back words that would complement the front words; for one of my aims was realizing an unfamiliar kind of *reading* indigenous to holography. (The trade epithet is "laser limbo," which differs only in degree from the physical activity normally associated with reading—turning the page.) I also thought of working with letters whose parts (lines) evolved out of one another, so that, say, as you moved to the left, the left-hand vertical line of an *E* would become the right-hand vertical line of an *H* while the middle horizontal lines would flow into each other. One difference between the Gabor Laboratory and Cabin Creek was that the former had only pure holography, where original images were shot directly with laser light; there was no intermediate transfer onto movie film.

However, the same holographer who gave me that vision of words behind words, Dan Schweitzer, also showed me how images could be projected forward to rootless points between the viewer's eye and the hologram's plate and then how the side parts of this forward-image could be made to fall outside the viewing field. In a subsequent conversation, the holographer Scott Lloyd gave me the structure of a two-sided plate, with different images on each side. Necessarily illuminated from behind, this would become a transmission hologram, in contrast to a reflection hologram that is illuminated from the front. Moreover, in requiring illumination from both sides, my two-sided image would create the illusion, utterly false, that the lamps illuminate the otherwise clear glass *facing* them, rather than the plates *behind* them. When I came to work with Fred Unterseher, the coauthor of the standard *Holography Handbook* (1982), we decided to put each set of words on four planes. Here, as in other media work, I was dependent upon professionals to tell me what the machinery could do (or they could do with the technology).

Once I had in my mind this last form of two sets of words on four planes apiece, the question became how best to fill it with language. In recent visual poems, I had been using the form of constellations of individual words that relate to one another in various ways; and that seemed appropriate here. Which collections of words would be most efficacious? I thought in terms of antitheses such as "love/hate" or "good/ evil" or "white/black," but my biases toward symmetries found such plus-minus combinations wanting. If one side were more sympathetic than the other, in prejudicial ways, I could have made of this unbalance a hologram in which the imagery on the plus side came forward, while the other (minus side) retreated.

Though I might later use that out-in form, I chose instead to project both sides forward with an antithesis of equal value: Warm and Cold. Upon those pegs I wrote thirty-five additional pairs of words of roughly equal length: Summer/Winter, Chaud/Froid, Char/Numb, Love/Hate, Devil/Ghoul; Flamma-ble/Frigorific, Eat/Diet, Febrile/Niveous, Mead/Beer, Home/ Jail, Incandesce/Glaciate, Pussy/Putty, Calid/Gelid, Head/Feet, Bonfire/Icecube, Punctual/Dilatory, Ecstasy/Stasis, Palm/Pine, Reverberate/Evaporate, Conflagration/Congelation, Erect/ Supine, Sultry/Boreal, Knife/Spoon, Sanguinary/Sanguinity, Leap/Dive, Ginger/Yogurt, Bubbly/Sleepy, Right/Left, Patri-mony/Parsimony, Demagogue/Politician, Independence/Sub-ordination, Seethe/Shiver, Scramble/Leisure, Affection/Obedience, Antinomies/Congruences. While I wanted through words alone to make one side feel warmer/colder than the other, I also wanted to use striking words in unfamiliar relationships. The next idea was to typeset each pair in a typeface unique to it, so that each word, in addition to contributing to its field, could be connected to a word in the opposite field, not only in terms of antithetical meaning but similar typeface.

I figured that since the last twenty pairs were verbally the most interesting (and less obvious), they should go to the back planes; the next ten pairs should go on the planes one up from the back; on the third planes forward should go the first five pairs; and on the front planes, as far forward as possible, should go "warm" and "cold." Another idea was that each of the two front words would be so large, and so far forward, they would never be entirely visible—parts would fall outside the viewing field. Thus, if the viewer deciphered the letter A, he or she would be prompted to move to the left to find the W and to the right to find the R and M. Another preliminary calculation was to make black letters on an illuminated field, which would make a shadowgram (that visually echoed the photograms of my artistic hero Moholy-Nagy).

To realize the sort of forward projection I wanted, it was necessary to make a hologram of a hologram. This technique required locating an "image plane," which would be the level with the greatest illumination. Confronting the question of where to place the image plane, Unterseher favored the second levels, each with five words; I insisted that it go to the back group, as those words required the most illumination for legibility (in part because they had to be visible behind other words), but also because within my structure of verbal values I could let the forward planes be increasingly less illuminated (and thus less legible). One risk of putting images behind one another is losing the back row, but one advantage that words have over abstract imagery, say, is that recognition of a few letters prompts the viewer to find the rest of the word (and thus move beyond an immediate perception). A second problem involved the thickness of the front letters, which were initially set boldface four inches high with scarcely any space between them. Since we feared that even with less illumination they would block out the back planes, we decided to rescreen those letters at 40 percent benday dots. However, when that turned out to lack presence, Samuel R. Delany, the literary colleague to whom *Antitheses* is dedicated, proposed increasing their visibility with strips of black tape along the letters' edges (and then actually sat down and started taping!).

One inadvertent result is that the words on the three front planes have a peculiar visual-verbal status. As holographic imagery differs from photographic and few viewers are accustomed to perceiving objects floating unattached in space (illustrating the holographic truth that visualized objects exist only in the eye), these words are not immediately seen. (Indeed, some people discover much faster than others that words are sharing their space, so to speak; and a few people won't discover them until a guide physically positions their head in an appropriate place.) For each plane forward, the letters lose density, their thick bold lines becoming progressively more vaporous (an effect that must be seen to be believed). My sense is that words partially dematerialized have a status I have yet to understand. Clearly they require more time to be "read," while they individually lose semantic presence (and thus become more dependent upon others in the field for their communicative value). I also wonder how many will recognize that every word in one field has a typographic mate on this other side, for this cross-referencing over physical space also transcends photographic perception.

The two very front words, which are poetically the least interesting, are perceived initially as vertical lines that flash into the visual field and the eyes move from side to side. Simply to decipher the individual letters of "warm" and "cold," the viewer must move his or her eyes and head, refocusing away from the image plane and then following those flashing lines until they reveal whole letters. (And in the course of such movement discovering yet other letters, no more than two of which are visible at any time.)

The fear, of course, is that viewers expecting pseudo-photographs will never examine these mysterious floating lines; perhaps *Antitheses* has turned out to be as perceptually problematic as its predecessor. Another result of such extreme dimensionality is a holographic image that cannot be still-photographed adequately, because cameras are designed to focus upon a particular level, especially in such darkness. It would be more effective, but less feasible, to film it through a succession of focus-changes. Perhaps such nonphotograph-ability, to indulge a Teutonic coinage, should be considered a sign of holographic integrity.

For me as a writer, the principal peril of holography involves set-up time. If a writer is accustomed, as I am, to having an idea and then realizing it immediately in words, the painstaking procedures of holography can seem tedious. The laser, once turned on, takes time to warm up; the plates must be appropriately positioned. In making a shot, the laser beam must be split into precise ratios and then routed over a table in the most precise ways. Exposure meters must check that the entire plane is equally illuminated, etc., etc. Simply preparing a shot can take an entire evening; and then as soon as all the parts are appropriately calibrated, the system is subjected to an episode unique to holography—at least fifteen minutes by itself with all doors closed to make sure that all ambient vibrations die down, simply because anything that moves only slightly will show up on the recording plate as a black hole. The shutter is switched from a control unit located in another room. And then we tested shots with horizontal fractions of plates before risking a full-sized impression.

If I had come to dislike shooting film (as distinct from

editing it) for requisite set-up times that are too long for my literary temperament, holography tested my patience yet more. Taking several times longer, holographic preparation is tolerable, to be frank, if and only if the worktable conversation is good or the technician allows the writer to go off and read. Otherwise, no art known to me has posed so many mind-boggling challenges, precisely because it demands so much of my verbal, esthetic, and technical expertise; no art known to me is so recalcitrant in posing so many obstacles, some of them paralyzing, between conception and realization. Nothing illustrates the obtacles of this medium more than a simple comparison. Video and holography appeared at the same time, in the late 1960s; but while the world is filled with video artists, most of them amateur, there are far fewer holographers, few of whom are amateur. Any child can make a video-tape by himself; to make a hologram, any hologram, requires more elaborate training and considerable trial-and-error practice.

Finally, as I chose to make a state-of-the-art image that is best illuminated by a laser installed in a precise way, I lessened the work's possible "distribution," to use that publishing term. Even to install *Antitheses* in my home became a project requiring a professional consultant. Nonetheless, it would be possible to make a reflection version that, while reducing the forward depth projection, could go onto walls or even, more appropriate for me, on the front and back covers of a book's worth of similarly structured constellation poems.

Within the context of my poetry, I think *Antitheses* the best of the constellations, in part because in three dimensions, with the spatial experience of language, I can better realize my earlier poetic idea of complementary words within a single visual frame, as well as my general purposes of reading in unfamiliar ways and doing with new media what could not be done in print. One way that this complements and yet surpasses not only my visual poems but *On Holography* lies in revealing the medium's capacities for unusual verbal-visual experience.

Addendum

In 1987, Fred Unterseher and Rebecca Deem invited me to a Hamburg installation where they were working. Here we shot a series of masters with the pulse technology that reduces considerably the set-up time, enabling us to shoot several masters in a few days. However, once I got these masters, I had to deal with the problem of making "transfers," or copies that can be viewed under normal light. A holographic master, it should be noted, can be viewed only under laser light; otherwise, it looks like a large sheet of thick cloudy film. Everyone new to holography imagines that copies are made by a kind of photographic process, where light passing through a negative produces a positive. For all its conceptual correctness, that assumption is too simple. What is required is that a hologram be made of a hologram, which is to say that the master becomes an object situated between a laser beam and a photographic plate. Once this arrangement is made and tested, in a procedure taking several days, the door to the lab must be shut until the situation "settles," as they say. Once the shot is made, with a half-minute exposure, the glass plate is then developed, washed, bleached, and washed again before being deposited in a "fotoflo" fixative. Once removed from the last liquid, the plate is dried, initially with a squeegee and blotting paper; then with a hair-dryer. I know, because for a second residency at the Museum of Holography, once my colleague Doris Vila set me up I did all this myself.

These new holograms deal with withholding parts of words, forcing the viewer to move to complete linguistic understanding. For instance, you see a horizontal string of only the letter

A, move a bit and you see *BR*'s, move further and you see *C*'s and then *D*'s. It becomes apparent that the word represented here is *ABRACADABRA*. Another device has letters appearing in continuously overlapping sequence, from *HO* to *HOG* to *LOG* to *LAP* to *RAG* to *RAP* to *HAP* to *HEP* to *HER*, in sum revealing a multitude of words embedded within *HOLOGRA-PHER*. In another case, the white letters on the black background of *MADAM* slide into the black letters on a white background of *ADAM* over a shifting horizontal divider, creating at one point the letters *MAD* in white on one side of a line that has *AM* on the other. I call this sequence *Hidden Meanings* (1989) for its various poetic explorations of a certain holographic capability.

There are more poetic possibilities to be discovered in holography, with more words to fill them; by no count am I done yet.

On Anthologies (1987)

Of the making of books, there is no end.

—*Ecclesiastes*, 12

IN MY DICTIONARY "an anthology" is defined as a collection of literary pieces; the word comes from the ancient Greek and means, literally, a gathering of flowers. By now, I have edited over two dozen anthologies, with various subjects, sizes, and purposes, in addition to co-organizing a dozen book-length compilations called *Assemblings* which, while not anthologies in the strict sense, somewhat resemble them. This memoir entwines my thoughts about the issues of anthologizing in general along with my sense of each of these books:

On Contemporary Literature. New York: Avon, 1964. Freeport, NY: Books for Libraries, 1971. Revised edition. New York: Avon, 1969.

The New American Arts. New York: Horizon, 1965. New York: Collier, 1967.

Twelve from the Sixties. New York: Dell, 1967.

The Young American Writers. New York: Funk and Wagnalls, 1967.

Beyond Left & Right. New York: Wm. Morrow, 1968. In Japanese, abridged. Tokyo: Diamond, 1973.

Social Speculations. New York: Morrow, 1971.

Human Alternatives. New York: Morrow, 1971.

The Edge of Adaptation. Englewood Cliffs, N.J. Prentice-Hall, 1973.

Piccola antologia della nuova poesia americana. Varese, Italy: Nuova Presenza—Editrice Magenta, 1968.

Possibilities of Poetry. New York: Delta, 1970.

Imaged Words & Worded Images. New York: Outerbridge and Dienstfrey, 1970.

Moholy-Nagy. New York: Praeger, 1970. London: Allen Lane-Penguin, 1971.

John Cage. New York: Praeger, 1970. London: Allen Lane-Penguin, 1971. In German. Koln: DuMont Schauberg, 1973. In Spanish, abridged. Barcelona: Editorial Anagrama, 1974.

Future's Fictions. Princeton, N.J. Panache, 1971.

Seeing through Shuck. New York: Ballantine, 1972.

In Youth. New York: Ballantine, 1972.

Breakthrough Fictioneers. West Glover, Vt. Something Else, 1973.

Essaying Essays. New York-Milano: Out of London, 1975.

Language & Structure in North America. Toronto: Kensington Arts, 1975.

Younger Critics in North America. Fairwater, Wis. Margins, 1976.

Esthetics Contemporary. Buffalo, N.Y. Prometheus, 1978. Revised edition. Buffalo: Prometheus, 1989.

Assembling Assembling. New York: Assembling, 1978.

Visual Literature Criticism. Carbondale: Southern Illinois University Press, 1979.

The Yale Gertrude Stein. New Haven, Conn. Yale University Press, 1980.

Text-Sound Texts. New York: Morrow, 1980.

Scenarios. New York: Assembling, 1980.

Aural Literature Criticism. New York: Precisely—RK Editions, 1981.

American Writing Today. Washington, D.C. Voice of America Forum Series, 1981.

The Avant-Garde Tradition in Literature. Buffalo, N.Y. Prometheus, 1982.

The Literature of Soho. Brooklyn, N.Y. Shantih, 1982.

The Poetics of the New Poetries. Tel-Aviv: Poetics Today. New York: Precisely, 1983.

Assemblings (annually from 1970 to 1978, except for 1974, but with two volumes for 1978; and then another in 1980).

A Critical Assembling. New York: Assembling, 1980.

Eleventh Assembling: Pilot Proposals. New York: Assembling, 1982.

II

No one starts out adult life with the intention of making anthologies. One imagines oneself a poet, or a novelist, or perhaps a critic, but certainly not an anthologist. The initial idea for making anthologies inevitably comes from someone else. In my case, the muse was a young editor at a commercial publishing house to whom I claimed, over twenty-five years ago, that I could put together from extant sources a good critical book on the major figures and developments of post-war world literature—indeed, a book that would treat its subject better than any that then existed. He asked for a possible table of contents, a list of essays that I prepared mostly from memory and then sent to him. Having already acquired a taste for reading anthologies, along with an aptitude for structuring large amounts of fugitive material (thanks to graduate education in intellectual history), I quickly envisioned how the parts should go together. However, no further would this proposal go with my muse's firm. Apologetic, he suggested that I submit the outline to another young editor who in turn showed it to a third editor, a young man named Peter Mayer, who in 1963 had just assumed an editorial position at Avon Books. Even though I was only 23 and had not done any books before, Mayer commissioned my proposal. Once I had a contract and an advance of a thousand dollars, I went to work requesting permissions, rechecking my initial selections, considering alternative essays, and then commissioning a few pieces that repaired holes in the critical picture (e.g., surveys of postwar Spanish writing, Canadian literature, etc.). I also spent considerable time reading contemporary literature previously unknown to me, if only to check the veracity of the essays I was publishing, but also to discover worthy subjects I might have initially missed. Although I was also in graduate school that year, swamped with reading to do for its classes, I stayed up every night until dawn, reading, reading, reading. For this anthology alone, I must have read several hundred books. As criticism was my initial literary ambition—the poetry and other creative work did not begin until later—I wrote a few short essays myself.

The manuscript was delivered in the spring of 1964. *On*

Contemporary Literature, as the book was called, appeared that fall with an archery target on its cover in a distinctive package with rounded outside corners that Avon thought would be an innovative marketing success—they were wrong. Nonetheless, by 1968, as the book's original edition had sold out, Avon commissioned me to do a revision which had several new essays and short appendices to selected earlier essays (and corners with right angles, thankfully.) Rights to do a hardbound reprint of this earlier edition were sold to Books for Libraries, which years later was sold to Arno Books, which kept *On Contemporary Literature* in print through the 1970s. My last royalty check from Avon came in early 1974. The amount on its face read one dollar; and rather than collect the pittance, I affixed that check to my study door, where it still is, to remind one and all about the scale of remuneration for doing serious literary anthologies.

Looking back at *On Contemporary Literature,* I think I was perhaps too impressed with the then-current promotions of the commercial publishers' publicity departments and of the fad-making flacks (who are in turn responsive to clues from the publicity departments); for in that book are individual essays on John Updike and Philip Roth, both of whom were then scarcely over thirty. A little wiser now, I would be more skeptical about the futures of fresh high fliers; for even though Roth and Updike have survived, thankfully, it would have been perilously easy for an ambitious young man (me) to get conned into selecting an inflated hotshot who might quickly disappear. Nearly two decades later, I remain impressed with some of my selections—essays on Thomas Pynchon and Doris Lessing's *The Golden Notebook,* Leslie Fiedler on John Barth, Stanley Edgar Hyman on Anthony Burgess's *A Clockwork Orange,* Maurice Blanchot on Samuel Beckett, Roland Barthes on Alain Robbe-Grillet, etc. Perhaps the only individual featured whose reputation has not since survived was Muriel Spark; and it is my recollection that it was she, and only she, whom the publisher insisted be treated with an individual essay (that, indicatively, its author has *not* reprinted in any of her own books of collected criticism). In *On Contemporary Literature,* unlike later anthologies, I was by and large not establishing new taste or making courageous selections but, instead, reifying sophisticated literary taste of the middle 1960s. It was therefore a book that both publishers and professors immediately liked, some of the latter even recommending it as the "best single book on the subject." Perhaps that acceptability explains as well why more copies of it were sold than any other anthology I have published since; yet other books of mine have had more impact, while, more crucially, other anthologies are more commonly connected to my name. (As I write, yet another publisher is considering it for reissue with its contents as is, but with a new title: "On Early Contemporary Literature.")

The next collection, *The New American Arts,* would likewise cover with several hands a territory that would not be grasped with one. Fundamentally, however, it was a different sort of book, for my purpose here was making taste, rather than cleaning up behind the taste-making of others; and most of its contents were fresh, rather than reprinted. What happened was this. In 1963, *Contact,* a new California magazine, commissioned me to do a comprehensive critical survey of recent American theater—of the playwrights and theater groups who had just emerged. My essay turned out to be several thousand words long; and once it was done, I remembered that, while in college a few years before, I had received from Ben Raeburn, the chief of Horizon Press, a letter flattering my undergraduate review of a Harold Rosenberg book he had published and incidentally asking whether I had any book-length manuscripts for him to see. Well, there were none at that time, but that was the sort of invitation that an aspiring writer does not forget. (That perhaps was precisely its purpose.) So, I sent him the theater essay, proposing a collection of similarly comprehensive critical surveys on new developments in the other arts. To my surprise, Ben Raeburn contracted my proposal. I agreed to do a comparable essay on new fiction, in addition to the lengthy introduction, and got Jonathan Cott to cover new poetry; Jill Johnston, modern dance; Eric Salzman, music; Max Kozloff, painting; and Harris Dienstfrey, film. (Since I took an additional single share for editing, four-ninths of the royalties were mine.) I remember editing their contributions closely, though perhaps not as thoroughly as I would come to edit previously unpublished contributions to anthologies of mine. The essays on poetry, modern dance, and music taught me much about those arts, as my own later critical writings on those subjects no doubt show. That on painting is the toughest to read—I remember working very hard to repair it and then hearing its style ridiculed after publication—while Dienstfrey's is essentially slight. My own essay on fiction takes too long to get to its positive points. Nonetheless, the book was up-to-date at the time of publication, introducing readers to advanced American arts in the early 1960s; and several years later anyone can judge that we were generally accurate in its portrayal of the emerging scenes. *The New American Arts* must have been provocative, too, to witness Jonathan Miller's vehemently negative review in the New York *Times Book Review*. The paperback edition, which Collier published in 1967, remained in print through the 1970s.

Twelve from the Sixties was commissioned in 1964 by Avon, which published *On Contemporary Literature;* but it was returned to me in 1965, for reasons I can no longer remember. It took my first agent, Perry Knowlton, a year or so to find a new publisher for it, and that remains my only anthology to find its publisher through an agent. By and large, for the kind of serious gatherings I want to do, agents are ineffective, not only because there is not enough profit to stimulate their enthusiasm, but because for books of this kind the editor's sympathy for the proposal (or me) is more persuasive than any agent. When I began work on this project, *Twelve from the Sixties* was meant to be the most advanced fiction anthology around—a selection of emerging talents, a definition of a new kind of story. However, by the time the book appeared in 1967, some of this edge was blunted. The selection of Tillie Olsen, Kenneth Koch, Bernard Malamud, John Barth, Thomas Pynchon, et al., seemed considerably less adventurous only a few years later. What does impress me about this book, even now, is less the contents, most of which would become or remain available elsewhere, than my introduction in which I trace the evolution of short fiction from the traditional arc story to the modern epiphany story, epitomized by James Joyce, to the totally flat contemporary story in which every part of the uninflected narrative contributes to the whole. This must have been pioneering criticism at the time; my ideas were plagiarized in more places, and in more ways, than I care to remember. By 1978, over a decade later, this introduction was reprinted as the concluding essay in someone else's academic anthology of critical essays on the American short story, which is to say that my essay survived long after the paperback book containing it disappeared from common print.

From the beginning of my critical career, I thought that I should keep track of the literature of my generation, much as Edmund Wilson or Malcolm Cowley did forty years before me; and for several years I tried to get magazines to commission an extended critical essay on those serious writers who were, like myself, born around 1940. No one ever commissioned it, in part because the literary moguls in the 1960s were not interested in the literary young—that was one key difference between the 1960s and the postwar 1920s—but also because the kind of serious young literary magazine that might be predisposed to commissioning it did not exist in the 1960s. That is to say that there were no descendants of *The Dial* or even *The New Republic*. Instead, those years witnessed the birth, on one hand, of the *New York Review of Books* which succeeded

by exploiting well-established reputations, rather than fo-
menting new ones; and, on another hand, the "underground
press," which was sub-literary, if not sub-literate. (Not *minds,*
but "heads," as we said at the time.) Instead, the essay I wanted
to do (and stand) by itself became the introduction to an
anthology, *The Young American Writers* (1967), whose purpose
became an extension of the essay: presenting the best work of
poets, novelists, and literary essayists then under thirty. This
book's publisher was an old dictionary house that had a brief
fling with tradebook publishing before it was swallowed by
another conglomerate. And my anthology sank in its wake.
Sometime in the future, those who keep track of such trivia
might credit me with the early recognition of Jerome Charyn,
Frank Chin, Jonathan Cott, Louise Gluck, Dick Higgins, Robin
Morgan, Joyce Carol Oates, David Shapiro, and Ed Sanders,
among others. One principle that became apparent to me
then was that anyone anthologizing his or her contemporaries
should not feel threatened by anyone else's excellence or
success.

Not unlike others, I sympathized with (and learned from)
the radicalism of the late 1960s, but it seemed to me that most
"Movement" people had naive notions of social change in
modern society. For one thing, they did not know much about
technology and thus had little sense of how it was changing
the world, largely for the better, I thought; and partly to
expand their intellectual horizons, but also to discover my
own synthesis, I edited an anthology of technology-conscious,
future-centered writings about social change. Whereas *The
New American Arts* was about advanced art, this was about
comparably avant-garde social philosophy. I titled it provoca-
tively, *Beyond Left & Right* (1968), even though I considered
myself more left than right, because I thought that certain
left prejudices were intellectually (and thus radically) limiting.
Also, this book had less public influence than I hoped, al-
though individuals here and there have told me that it meant

a lot to them. I also think it the best—the most original and most substantial—of my four anthologies on this theme. Its successors were *Social Speculations* (1971), *Human Alternatives* (1971), and *The Edge of Adaptation* (1973).

One way in which these four anthologies differ from *On Contemporary Literature,* say, is that they are, to repeat my theme, even more decisively about the making of taste, rather than the sweeping up of tastes already made by others. My synthesis was original and independent, and it was not subservient to any established political interests, either of the right or of the left. That last observation may explain why these books (and most of my later anthologies) were scarcely reviewed—reviewers are, after all, very inclined to accept what they already understand, what neatly fits their intellectual preconceptions, whether positively or negatively, especially if the book is also prominently promoted. By the 1980s, I find these four books naive and dated (especially in their 1960s optimism); and since my feelings towards my anthologies of literature and criticism are not so distant, perhaps it would be wiser for me to stick to what I know best. I think I have.

In 1966, an Italian literary magazine that had published critical essays of mine, *Nuova Presenza,* asked me to edit a "Piccola anthologia della nuova poesia americana," which is to say a little anthology of American poetry. Somehow, somewhere, I got permission to have the Italians translate poems and excerpts by John Ashbery, Allen Ginsberg, Galway Kinnell, Robert Mezey, W. D. Snodgrass, Gary Snyder, and James Wright—poets who were mostly around forty years old at the time. These selections were then prefaced by an eight-hundred-word essay that I now find embarrassingly perfunctory in style and conventional in thought. The selection could have survived as well without the introduction. On second thought, if a selection has more weight and purpose than the introduction, then perhaps the anthology was unnecessary.

Having read all the full-length anthologies of post-World War II United States poetry published here, I knew that a better one could be done. On one side were several books representing the academic traditions, beginning with the first selection of Hall-Pack-Simpson (1955); on the other were the anthologies of nonacademic poets, beginning with Donald Allen's *The New American Poetry* (1960). My initial hypothesis was that since both sides had good poets (as well as bad), a better book could be done that included the best of both schools and then several newer poets whom both sides neglected. Once the contract was in hand, I went to Puerto Rico with a large suitcase full of books, reading them all day at the beach and then making notes toward an introduction in the evening; and before I let myself go home, I hit upon a theme that would organize not only my opening essay but also the entire book (and incidentally give it a title). Like all good critical ideas, this theme gave the project an intelligence that literally exceeds my own. Put simply, my theme was to regard American poetry in the post-World War II period as a series of reactions to the rather formal and restrictive post-T. S. Eliot establishment of 1945, and the cumulative result of all these alternatives was a new pluralism in which a variety of poetic styles was feasible. My title was *Possibilities of Poetry* (1970). In the long introduction I sketched each of these alternative styles and then identified their major practitioners. The book itself has ten discrete sections, each introduced only by a Roman numeral, and within each section a particular sort of poetry is gathered. My recollection is that the publisher wanted me to give each section a verbal subtitle, but that struck me as making too explicit what ought best remain implicit. This anthology, like some others of mine, closes with an elaborate bibliography, listing not only titles of the chosen poets' books but selected articles about them, plus a general bibliography of books about modern poetry and American poetry. My thought is that since my anthologies are mostly designed not to close but to open their subjects, I would also mention where else their readers might go.

By 1967, I had begun to do my own creative work—initially visual poems; and once I sent them around to magazines, I had immediate reason to notice that such poems were not being published at the time—they were simply too, too "avant-garde" for the current notions of acceptable poetry. (From time to time, even nowadays, some editor reminds me that they [we] are still generically unacceptable.) I also found the earlier anthologies of "concrete" to be embarrassingly weak in either concept or selection; and whenever I identify weaknesses in the presentation of something dear to me, there arises within me the feeling that perhaps I can do better. After all, the contrasting example of the success of visual poetry in Europe persuaded me to think that the neglect of it in America was scarcely inevitable, and one of the best ways to remedy neglect of a certain kind of work is a book-length persuasive selection. Rosalie Frank, then the publisher of the little magazine *Panache,* asked me to edit a special issue. I proposed to devote it to visual poetry. Meanwhile, a new book publisher, Outerbridge and Dienstfrey, asked to publish the collection of visual poetry that I had gathered for Rosalie Frank (who then gave me permission to do something else for *Panache*). *Imaged Words & Worded Images* (1980), as this anthology was called, was certainly a handsome presentation, in a large format on heavy paper; perhaps the principal claim I can make for it now is its presentation in several pages of John Furnival's masterpiece, *Tours de Babel Changées en Ponts* (1964). One tragedy in the history of this book is that the wall of American neglect was scarcely dented. A second misfortune was that the publisher folded soon afterwards, remaindering the unsold stock without telling me; for I would have offered to buy all of it, believing, then as now, that it is better that I store books of mine that their initial publishers no longer want, rather than allowing them to be dispersed, if only to be able to supply them later to those who desperately need my titles. (Nowadays, such eager buyers are usually scholars, or incipient scholars.)

Back in 1968, I wrote an elaborate critical-historical essay on L. Moholy-Nagy, the Hungarian polyartist who had come to America in 1938 and had lived in Chicago until his premature death at the age of 51, in 1946. This essay initially appeared in a special issue of *Salmagundi* devoted to the German refugee intellectuals. Moholy-Nagy's widow, the architectural historian Sibyl, recommended both the essay and me to Paul Cummings, a freelance art historian who had just founded a series of "Documentary Monographs in Modern Art." He contracted me to edit a book of essays by and about Moholy— to make a mosaic portrait, as well as compile an appendix of documentation. Moholy was then, and still is, one of my favorite modern artists, and the materials collected between these covers remain a continuing inspiration to me. Also, from the perspective of a decade later, it can be observed that my introduction to this book sketches in outline the kind of polyartistic career (and attitudes) that later became my own.

As my work on *Moholy-Nagy* was going well, the publisher asked me whom else I might like to document for this series. The choice of John Cage seemed obvious—he had not been honored before in this way, and his work in several areas interested me. Indeed, one theme that tied these two documentary monographs together is that their subjects were masters of several arts but slaves to none, and both books are structured to emphasize this variousness (which I would later come to call *polyartistry*). Perhaps because my *John Cage* was, until recently, the only book on this central figure of contemporary esthetics, it is the anthology of mine that both composers and visual artists tend to know best. Indeed, when someone I meet for the first time connects my name to *this* book, rather than another, I can wager securely that he or she is probably someone involved in the nonliterary arts. When the British publisher of this book decided to remainder its edition, I purchased a thousand-plus copies and upon that foundation established my not-nonprofit imprint particularly for other remaindered books of mine: RK Editions.

Once *John Cage* and *Moholy-Nagy* were delivered, the publisher asked me to do yet another book in its series of documentary monographs. I proposed devoting it to Merce Cunningham. The publisher agreed, asking me to proceed. However, I have a private rule that applies not only to the writing of essays and books but also to the making of anthologies, and that is *never do what someone else can do better.* I realized that were I to do a Merce Cunningham documentary monograph I would need to draw heavily upon the advice and research of David Vaughan, who was at the time directing Cunningham's dance school and has since become his official archivist. So I offered the project to Vaughan, who accepted my referral, met with the publisher, but never got a contract. (Perhaps I should have seized the offer myself; at least a documentary monograph on Cunningham would have appeared. For better or worse, I have never failed to fulfill an anthology contract.) A while later, I wanted to do a similar book on another polyartist who had become an enthusiasm of mine, Theo van Doesburg; but by then, this series of documentary monographs had disbanded.

Future's Fictions (1971) was edited as my substitute to *Panache* for releasing *Imaged Words & Worded Images.* My initial purpose was to expand our sense of the materials of fiction, and so I included one narrative composed entirely of numbers (my own), fictions composed entirely of line drawings (Marian Zazeela, Manfred Mohr), narratives composed entirely of sequential pictures (Jochen Gerz, John Furnival), in addition to examples of unusual prose from Dick Higgins, Madeline Gins, and Henry James Korn, among others. It was all prefaced by an essay that remains one of the most amazing I have ever written, "Twenty-Five Fictional Hypotheses." Nearly two decades later, I can hardly imagine what was in my mind when I wrote what is still such an extreme manifesto for an expanded concept of literary fiction.

Seeing through Shuck (1972) was initially meant to include some of my then-unpublished and then-bouncing manuscript on literary politics in America and thus to give it the credibility of even partial prepublication; but once my publisher turned volatile and inexplicably nasty, my own original contribution was excised and then replaced by something more modest (and innocuous). Especially since the theme of this book was the muckraking courage of a younger generation of essayists, I probably should have cancelled the project—personally either confiscated or sabotaged it—in response to such censorship; but once anyone assembles an anthology that its contributors expect will appear, his or her obligations to them, in my judgment, exceed any personal pique. Nonetheless, it pained me not that this book had a short shelf life; my principal regret was that the publisher pulped it before I was able to purchase copies. From time to time, I still get requests for this.

In Youth (1972) was another disaster for the same editor, who gave it a title that I did not see until it was too late to correct; my original title was "Writing While Young," the gerunds of one book supposedly echoing the other. Again, some of the selections in the original manuscript were not in the final copy. Again, had the book been wholly mine, I would have razed the entire publishing house without pause; but here too I felt obliged to fulfill my commitment to the surviving contributors. This book, too, disappeared quickly, alas without my retrieving the remainders.

Having liked some of my earlier anthologies, Alan Rinzler, then in his heyday at Holt, Rinehart, and Winston, asked me to do a sequel to *Future's Fictions;* and I readily agreed. However, soon after signing the contract, he succumbed to the fantasies of California. The completed manuscript I submitted to his editorial successor was deemed not just "unpublishable" but "unproducible," which apparently meant that, because of all the visual material and eccentric typographies, the publisher's production department did not know how to prepare it for the printer. So *Breakthrough Fictioneers,* as it was called, passed onto the second (after *Panache*) of my smaller publishers, whose modest staff, remarkably, did know how to produce it. (In a few can be an intelligence lost to the many.) This sequel included kinds of work represented in *Future's Fictions,* but now more abundantly, with nearly one hundred contributors. In less than a decade, I had moved at least two steps, and several light years, beyond *Twelve from the Sixties.* I am relieved, if not pleased, to observe that over a decade after its original publication, *Breakthrough Fictioneers* remains what it was meant to be at its birth: the most way-out, most advanced, most "unacceptable" fiction anthology ever published any-where, so help me God. Indicatively, few contributions to this book, in contrast to those in *Twelve from the Sixties,* were readily available elsewhere.

In the same year that it appeared, another, much larger firm issued *Innovative Fiction,* edited by Jerome Klinkowitz and John Somer. Had there been any intelligent anthology-criticism at that time, let alone a perspicacious reviewer of all kinds of new fiction, someone would have noticed that in the same year appeared two books claiming to collect the latest fiction. Both of them included writers whose names were largely unfamiliar a dozen years before, yet only one author appeared in both books, John Barth. This ideal reviewer might have then observed that my anthology included a Barth story that, unlike the one in the other book, had *not* been reprinted in Barth's own collections of his short fiction. There was obvi-ously a profound difference between us, if not a debate, as there would be when another new fiction anthology appeared with many of the Klinkowitz-Somer authors—Joe David Bella-my's *Superfiction* (1975). The dividing issue, as I see it, is that the Klinkowitz-Somer anthology, as well as the Bellamy, deal with evolutions within the history of fiction. Their books contain fictions that, in their editors' minds, go beyond the new celebrities of the 1950s and 1960s—beyond, say, Malamud, Bellow, Ellison, Barthelme, et al. Mine, on the other hand, is filled with fictions that esthetically resemble advanced contemporary art as I know it.

Klinkowitz and I once compared thoughts on the editing of anthologies. (He has been involved with several.) What we both value is a concept so strong and definite that it automatically excludes everything except what we want. In practice, we discovered, if the anthologist's definition of what he plans to collect is firm and clear, he will have no trouble fending off the designs of colleagues, friends, lovers, and others who might want to hoist their work aboard. Anything that fundamentally differs from the clear mandate of the book, we tell our supplicants, will look curious, if not suspicious; and as long as that might happen, the anthologist would, in truth, be doing his or her friend/lover/colleague a favor *not* to include it. (I once had to warn a particularly persistent supplicant that, if his inappropriate work were included, readers might conjecture me his lover or dope supplier!) Conversely, my books also include selections from people I personally dislike, even some who once did me dirty, because their work fits better than anything else.

The second truth we mutually discovered is that if the concept is strong, the anthology will almost select itself. How can that be? The key here, in my experience, as well as Klinkowitz's, is the power of literary memory. I find that once a concept is established, my memory reminds me of the strongest examples. How do I know they are strong? Because my memory automatically forgets weak ones; that is a subconscious process which I have developed from looking at lots of things—it is a critical mechanism in which I have learned to have faith. Indeed, experience with both anthologies and critical surveys tells me that my memory has surer taste than my conscious mind, because the former is not so easily deceived. No matter how hard someone tries to persuade me that his or her work is important, no matter how much I may like or dislike them personally, no matter how many reviews in praise of it I might have read or how many other people like it, if the work itself does not survive in my head, it is probably not very good; the work certainly wasn't worth remembering. I realize that this revelation may expose me to charges of solipsism; but believe me, it is the best way to work, especially in *beginning* to gather an anthology.

One more thing I have liked to do for an open-ended anthology, such as *Breakthrough Fictioneers,* is announce its purpose publicly, in media such as *Coda,* the *COSMEP Newsletter,* or even the New York *Times Book Review.* Also within the permission form that I send potential contributors is my explicit request to consider other works that fit my particular theme (which I try to define as specifically as possible). I find, on one hand, that remarkably little comes from these announcements, perhaps because any writer who has seen my anthologies knows that they are not just way-out but scrupulously principled. On the other hand, those few submissions that arrive this way are usually accepted! The paradox is that these compilations are editorially *open* within their closed conceptions.

Once *Breakthrough Fictioneers* was delivered, it seemed appropriate to do a successor for Something Else Press, an anthology applying similar avant-garde esthetic values to collecting literary and cultural exposition—stretch our sense of how *essays* could be done. Again I collected bushels of stuff that was delivered in the summer of 1973. However, by then Something Else was falling apart—it went bankrupt the following year. Fortunately, another new small press (Out of London) arose to issue *Essaying Essays,* as it was called. In part because no one else has ever produced an anthology of alternative exposition, this remains a singular book, if not the most original of my collections (with perhaps the most surprises). It

contains essays in unusual prose forms, charts, skeletal out-
lines, picture essays, innovative structures, and much else that
is different from traditional expository writing. Of my big
anthologies, it is also, in my opinion, the richest in its individual
inclusions, such as W. H. Auden's chart of romanticism, the
George Maciunas visual history of Fluxus, Moholy-Nagy's geo-
metric outline of overlapping themes in *Finnegans Wake*, and
Ihab Hassan's "Post-Modernism." Much as I believe in princi-
ple that something newer is always possible, in editing as in
art, I seriously doubt whether this, as a collection of alternative
exposition, will ever be surpassed.

Whereas my relationship to *Essaying Essays* was very close,
that to my next anthology, *Language & Structure in North
America*, was distant in more ways than one. In the summer of
1974, I was asked to guest-curate an exhibition of structurally
innovative language art. Though I had never done an exhibi-
tion before, I was seduced by the opportunity to extend my
editorial/anthological interests into another medium—in this
case, the display gallery. What I failed to anticipate were cer-
tain strategic differences: (1) Whereas contributors to an an-
thology submit sheets of paper that need not be returned,
those contributing to an exhibition send objects that they ex-
pect to get back; the clerical nuisance is thus so much greater.
(2) It follows that certain expansive principles I had developed
in editing *Breakthrough Fictioneers* or *Essaying Essays*—the inclu-
sion of as many people doing such work as possible, if only
to substantiate through large numbers the presence of my
subject—were simply hazardous in this display medium.
Whereas a book anthology can handle as many as one hundred
separate contributors, an anthological exhibition cannot feasi-
bly serve more than one-fifth that many. (3) When a gallery
reneges on its contract, as happened here when its director
resigned, the alternatives are so few that you accept the first
and only, even if it exudes suspicious odors. The next trouble
was that gallery directors can be more preemptive than book

publishers, in this case installing the show, in my absence, in ways I would have opposed, were I present, and, in the case of the accompanying catalog, choosing the illustrations without reference to what I was saying. Even though this book has my name, my ideas, my title, and my introduction, the selection of putatively supporting examples is not mine at all. Whether *Language & Structure in North America* is still my anthology is a provocative critical question. I think it is, because it reflects my ideas about language art and my critical distinctions, even if I would have chosen differently from the materials available.

As more and more of my anthologies were being published by small presses, rather than large, the differences were becoming apparent. While large presses may have dumb hierarchies, where each level panders to the stupidities and inadequacies of those above it, small presses have only a few people, if not one person; and that person's current mood can decisively affect the publication of one's book. Tom Montag commissioned *Younger Critics in North America* because he was successfully editing and publishing (and typesetting) *Margins,* the best of the small-press reviews; and he wanted to establish a book list. Since we were both passionately concerned about the survival of serious literary criticism in America, it seemed appropriate for me to do for his new imprint an anthology of the best work of emerging practitioners. However, by the time I delivered the book, Montag collapsed, perhaps of exhaustion, and moved from Milwaukee to the Wisconsin countryside, abandoning his magazine and, incidentally, many promises to his contributors. The book appeared belatedly, and it was never widely distributed.

My disappointment in its fortunes notwithstanding, one detail I like about this book is the intelligent order of the essays, as the sequence of subjects moves from traditional literature to high modern literature (Djuna Barnes, Raymond Queneau, James Joyce) to contemporary American literature to modern dance to intermedia arts to classical music to blues to rock 'n roll to film to photography to science fiction to Canadian writers to American minority writing to literary magazines to avant-garde fiction to book-art to sound poetry and, finally, to avant-garde anthologies. One test of the strength of the ordering here, in contrast to that in earlier anthologies of mine, is that each essay is in a place that it and only it can be.

A similar sense of optimal ordering informs my next anthology, *Esthetics Contemporary*, which is meant to collect the most profound essays on post-1959 art—those essays so rich with illumination about contemporary arts in general that they suggest an esthetics for our time. After my introduction, which is a critical history of American esthetics from Suzanne Langer to John Cage—from the 1940s to the 1960s—this book is divided into two major parts: essays on the arts in general, and those on specific arts. The first selection is Michael Kirby's "The Esthetics of the Avant-Garde," an inordinately illuminating essay that opens his book *The Art of Time* (1969), which has long been out of print. Then come two essays by L. Moholy-Nagy, whose last book, *Vision in Motion* (1946), survives for me as the single greatest encompassing essay on artistic modernism. The remainder of my book's first part has the following:

The Relation of Environment to Anti-Environment, by Marshall McLuhan

Apropos of "Readymades," by Marcel Duchamp

Art and Disorder, by Morse Peckham

Chance-Imagery, by George Brecht

Semi-Constructs of the Secretaire du Registre, by Carl D. Clark and Loris Essary

On Form, by Kenneth Burke

Style and Representation of Historical Time, by George Kubler

Art and Authenticity, by Nelson Goodman

Systems Esthetics, by Jack Burnham

228
Autobiographical Addenda

Aesthetics and Contemporary Arts, by Arnold Berleant

Art as Internal Technology: The Return of the Shaman—the Descent of the Goddess, by José A. Argüelles

Intermedia, by Dick Higgins

Criticism and Its Premises, by Harold Rosenberg

Anyone familiar with even a few of these essays can tell that this is a heady sequence of ideas about contemporary art, including both radicals and conservatives, both philosophers and artists, contributors born in 1946 along with those born in 1906, 1897, and 1887.

In the second part of *Esthetics Contemporary* are essays on particular arts, and again the table of contents makes its own point:

Modernist Painting; Necessity of Formalism [two essays], by Clement Greenberg

My Painting, by Jackson Pollock

"Art-as-Art," by Ad Reinhardt

The General Public is Just as Disinterested in Art as Ever, by Will Insley

Realism Now, by Linda Nochlin

10 Structurists in 20 Paragraphs, by Lucy R. Lippard

The Expanding and Disappearing Work of Art, by Lawrence Alloway

Meaningless Activity, by Walter de Maria

A Sedimentation of the Mind, by Robert Smithson

Phenomenal Art: Form, Idea, Technique, by James Seawright

De-Architecturization, by James Wines

The Composer as Specialist, by Milton Babbitt

The Future of Music, by John Cage

Music as Gradual Process, by Steve Reich

Glass and Snow, by Richard Foreman

The Impermanent Art, by Merce Cunningham

A Quasi-Survey of Some "Minimalist" Tendencies in Quantitatively Minimal Dance Activity, Midst the Plethora, by Yvonne Rainer

Words per Page, by Paul Sharits

"When the Mode of the Music Changes the Walls of the City Shake," by Allen Ginsberg

An ABC of Contemporary Reading, by Richard Kostelanetz

Pre-face, by Jerome Rothenberg

Video: The Distinctive Features of the Medium, by David Antin

The Education of the Un-Artist, III, by Allan Kaprow

Concept Art, by Henry Flynt

Paragraphs on Conceptual Art, by Sol LeWitt

A Something Else Manifesto, by Dick Higgins

In the second part of the book, to summarize, the discussion moves from painting to sculpture to artistic machines to architecture to music to dance to video to happenings theater to conceptual art to polyartistry, and as such the second part becomes a genre-centered survey that subsumes a more advanced esthetics. For the tenth anniversary revised edition, I made only a few changes in the first part of the book, while adding to the second half appropriately weighty statements about arts not covered before—photography, holography, computer-assisted image-processing, and book-art books.

My next anthology, *Visual Literature Criticism,* has a more particular subject. It began as a special issue of the literary magazine *West Coast Poetry Review;* and since I had by 1978 begun to co-edit *Precisely,* a critical journal devoted to experimental writing, it seemed appropriate to make the subject a special issue of this new magazine as well. Then, Southern Illinois University Press asked to do it as a hardback book.

Behind this project, as well as my editing of *Precisely,* stands my sense of the importance of criticism in the history of avant-garde writing. In every issue I quoted Hugh Kenner's perspicacious formulation from *The Pound Era* (1971):

There is no substitute for critical tradition: a continuum of understanding, early commenced. . . . Precisely because William Blake's contemporaries did not know what to make of him, we do not know either, though critic after critic appeases our sense of obligation to his genius by reinventing him. . . . In the 1920s, on the other hand, *something* was immediately made of *Ulysses* and *The Waste Land,* and our comfort with both works after 50 years, including our ease at allowing for their age, seems derivable from the fact that they have never been ignored.

By "Visual Literature" I mean works with language, conceived with reference to the traditions of literature, that are primarily visual in their organization and means of enhancement. Thus, David Seaman writes about French visual poetry of the Renaissance, Clive Philpott about imaginative books whose content is primarily photographs, Emma Kafelanos on Dada and Visual Poetry, Jonathan Price on the *I Ching* as a Visual Poetry, and Raymond Federman on the French novelist Maurice Roche. While scarcely the definitive work on its subject, *Visual Literature Criticism* does, I hope, lay a foundation for further critical discussion.

Its immediate sequel was a book that also began as a special issue of *Precisely. Aural Literature Criticism* (1981) contains essays on language works that must be heard to be understood, much as visual literature must be seen, because the former are enhanced primarily in terms of sound, rather than syntax or semantics. Thus, *Aural Literature Criticism* has essays about sound poetry in general, on radio literature, and on the critical methodologies relevant to intermedial literature. On the single sheet of paper announcing the project and soliciting contributions I asked for extended essays on precursors and folk analogues, such as speaking in tongues or glossolalia, but nothing on those subjects came in. One difference between compiling an anthology of previously published materials and making one up from scratch, as was done here, is that an editor necessarily depends upon his contributors; he cannot make them write what they do not know, or want to do. In this book, as in its predecessor, is a brief bibliography of "essays I would gladly have included here, had they not already been published." Always, always, should an anthology direct readers outside itself; never, never should the anthologist, particularly of criticism, assume that his book terminates the discussion.

The Yale Gertrude Stein (1980) began with a postal card to the Yale University Press, asking whether they had ever thought of issuing a one-volume selection from the eight volumes of Gertrude Stein's posthumously published books of previously unpublished writings. Those eight volumes had appeared from Yale annually from 1951 to 1958 and then were allowed to go out of print in the 1960s. (Around 1969, a publisher that reprints expensive hardbacks, mostly from libraries, reissued them at a price too high for the individual buyer—well over one hundred dollars for the set.) Yale agreed, and the anthology appeared within a year of my proposal, its pages being offset directly from the original editions. It seems odd, in retrospect, that no one had thought of prompting Yale to do this before. I guess that many people assumed that since the works in these eight volumes were all unpublished in Stein's own lifetime (and, in effect, self-published by the terms of her own will), nothing in them could be very good. Quite the contrary is true. They contain, and I reprint, all but one of Stein's most important longer poems: "Patriarchal Poetry," "Lifting Belly," and the incomparable "Stanzas in Meditation." In my introduction, I emphasize Stein's more experimental writings; for it is my considered opinion (and the point of my selection) that if you take the conventional view—that she wrote two charming books, *Three Lives* and *The Autobiography of Alice B. Toklas,* plus a lot of incomprehensible crap—then Stein is a minor writer. However, if you examine this allegedly "incomprehensible crap" closely, you will discover that Stein was a supremely experimental writer, working in a variety of unprecedented ways. Indeed, she was perhaps the single most inventive writer in the history of American letters. Incidentally, I initially wanted to call this book "Gertrude Stein at Yale," echoing *Frank Merriwell at Yale*—a series of popular boy's books from the early twentieth century—and also reminding us that not until recently were women admitted as undergraduates at Yale; but the publisher pretended to miss the joke.

Text-Sound Texts (1980) began as proposals to the Visual Arts Program of the National Endowment for the Arts. In 1976, it funded me to do a comprehensive critical survey of text-sound art (aka "sound poetry") in North America. I wanted initially to show that American work of this kind existed, even if it were less familiar than European, and that at least two dozen Americans were doing significant work. This fifty-page report was finished by the end of that year (and subsequently published, in abridged form, in *Performing Arts Journal* in 1977– 78 and unabridged in my own 1981 book, *The Old Poetries and the New*). In an appendix to this research paper I outlined a possible book of texts of the kinds of work described in the report's preceding pages. Two years later, the same NEA program gave me sufficient funds to collect these texts into a book. As before, I felt obliged to include as many people as possible. In the preface I implicitly ridiculed another kind of anthological motive. "Some anthologies are edited 'to keep people out.' This one, to be frank, was edited to put everybody in. Critical discriminations were made, to be sure, within certain kinds of work, or within an individual's work; but I have consciously endeavored to include everyone in North America doing text-sound works." So this book too had over one hundred contributors. Once I prepared a camera-ready typescript, I showed it to the trade publisher William Morrow who, to my surprise (as well as perhaps theirs), agreed to issue it in both paperback and hardback editions. Even though *Text-Sound Texts* is clearly the most avant-garde literary anthology ever published by a commercial house in this country, it was scarcely promoted and then went unadvertised and unreviewed. For better than worse, all the remaindered copies are now mine.

Scenarios (1980) likewise began with a grant, this time from the Theater Program of the New York State Council on the Arts; and Assembling Press had agreed to dollar-match the NYSCA contribution with funds from a 1979 NEA grant to the Press. Here the subject was radically alternative forms of theatrical scripting; and to make sure I would not use anything familiar, I ruled at the beginning that this book would include no scripts with dialogue—that got rid of 99 percent of all plays; no scores with specific musical notes or musical instruments—that eliminated a lot as well; no scripts for translation into media other than live performance—that eliminated radio scripts and film scripts; and no proposals for static conceptions, eliminating environmental installations. Given these rigorous exclusions, the book became a collection of monologues, visual scripts, proposals for physical activities and open-air events, texts with randomly ordered lines, and so forth. As the most radical collection of performable scripts ever published, it moves far beyond any earlier anthology of its genre. In part because I failed to keep sufficiently close track of how many contributions I was accepting, *Scenarios* is also the hugest of my collections, running over 704 pages, and likewise containing work by over a hundred people. Because the book became so big, the fee earmarked for me to edit it had to go back into the production budget; and I had to do all of the busywork myself—reading submissions, obtaining permissions, copyediting, arranging typesetting, mailing proof to the contributors, proofreading, design, paste-up, hiring the printer, and even distributing the contributors' copies. That is much too much work for one person, and never again, I swear, will I get stuck doing everything.

III

A book is a sequence of spaces. Each of these spaces is perceived at a different moment—a book is also a sequence of moments.
—Ulises Carrion, "The New Art of Making Books" (1980)

All through the 1970s I was involved with *Assembling* which, while not an anthology in the strict sense of a conscious selection of flowers, is nonetheless a compilation of the works of many people and incidentally an illustrative contrast to the traditional anthology. *Assembling* was an annual devoted to "otherwise unpublishable creative work," and what we did is this: From editing anthologies and simply reading my mail, I came to know hundreds of people who were doing imaginative work that has been otherwise unpublishable, not because it is weak, but because it is blatantly unconventional. *Assembling* invited such people to submit one thousand copies, 8½ by 11 inches, of no more than three separate sheets of whatever they want to include. Rejecting nothing from those invited, *Assembling* then collated and assembled these sheets alphabetically into a thousand books, two of which were mailed gratis to each contributor; the remainder have gone on sale to defray expenses. We have so far produced ten *Assemblings* in this way.

In 1978, Assembling Press was honored with a retrospective exhibition at the Pratt Graphics Center in New York City. For this exhibition, I edited, designed, and produced a catalog that is yet another anthology, this of history and documentation, with the same title as the exhibition, *Assembling Assembling*. In addition to my own memoir of the press, this book contains remarks by others about *Assembling* and an exhaustive bibliography of all the books of poetry, fiction, and art that it has published, in addition to the annuals, and then lists all the individuals—nearly five hundred, in sum—who have contributed to *Assembling*. The book becomes the operation's own anthology not of itself—the standard sort of celebration for a periodical—but, in an odd twist, *about itself*.

In 1979, Assembling Press received from the National Endowment for the Arts a grant to do a different kind of *Assembling*. Instead of collecting a thousand sheets from every contributor, we asked possible collaborators "to produce no more than two camera-ready pages apiece, 8½ by 11 inches, of critical commentary on radical/experimental tendencies in contemporary literature." Given the absolute contributor freedom that is the promise (and trademark) of *Assembling*, it is scarcely surprising that we received a variety of pieces, some verbal, others visual, some anti-avant-garde, most pro-, a few even criticizing me (!); and all of them were included in this 336-page book. It is possible that twenty years from now others might regard this *Ninth (Critical) Assembling* (1980) as a symposium of advanced art-literary thinking at that time.

Also in 1979, the director of the Forum Series of the Voice of America asked me to do a successor to their earlier volumes on American literature, this new book to be called *American Writing Today*. From the beginning I had doubts about working for our government propaganda agency, which obviously needed an intermediary to get contributions from writers who would instantly turn the VOA down if it approached them directly. On the other hand, I was seduced by the chance to establish for the 1980s a canon of contemporary American writing, especially for intellectuals around the world. (It is the policy of VOA to give away such books gratis, only outside the United States.) I also feared that, if I spurned the offer, the assignment would probably go to an idiot academic who would make a book that was not only unreadable but unbearable. Besides, certain earlier volumes in this Forum Series, especially Hennig Cohen's *Landmarks in American Writing*, impressed me. When I submitted a list of subjects to be covered, I calculated I would resign from the project if my selections were rejected; but since only one name was deleted (John Cage!), I went ahead, inviting writers not only to talk on radio with a VOA staffer but also to contribute an essay to the Forum book. There was, I am relieved to report, no political interference with what the writers said. The published transcript shows that Allen Ginsberg, for one, relished preaching to the world through the government's propaganda machinery.

Some problems with this book were intrinsic in the assignment. Given that the earlier VOA books on American literature were done fifteen or more years ago, my book had to have chapters on Saul Bellow, Gertrude Stein, Edmund Wilson, Kenneth Burke, and Langston Hughes, all of whom should have been treated in the earlier books, but were not. Secondly, given the assignment of making a book that would be "acceptable" now and nonetheless survive for fifteen years (and, behind that, given the current peculiarities of United States literary politics), it became difficult for me to include anyone born after 1932. Thus, those younger writers who have individual chapters in the book are there not to talk about themselves but to be experts on new developments—Samuel R. Delany (b. 1942) on science fiction, Dick Higgins (b. 1938) on alternative publishing and Sharon Spencer (b. 194?) on literary feminism. VOA proposed that I also conduct a few symposia on such general topics as short fiction and literary translation, since these make good radio; and I proposed in return adding a few additional symposia on more avant-garde developments, such as visual poetry and book-art. One way that *American Writing Today* differs from previous volumes in the VOA series is that I encouraged the contributors to be idiosyncratic. Too many other volumes in this (and similar) series give the impression that they have been written by a single machine (which is a sign of over-editing, if not more serious cultural deficiencies). Since I naturally wanted to make this anthology more substantial than previous volumes in the series, I also coauthored a concluding bibliographical essay on the major books about post-World War II American literature and culture. I was disappointed that *American Writing Today* was never reprinted in a mainland edition, for more discreditable excuses than I wish to recount, more than once from editors who insisted upon keeping the copies submitted to them, because, in truth, the books were very much worth having!

In 1979, *Poetics Today*, an Israeli magazine that is, as its title suggests, very much concerned with literary theory, asked me to coedit a special issue on "The Poetics of the New Literature," the last epithet referring to avant-garde writing of the past two decades. For this I wanted not critical surveys but theoretical interpretations and speculations, which fortunately arrived in response to my personal solicitations. This book appeared in print more than three years after it was delivered, nearly expiring even my experienced patience with smaller publishers; and to be frank, by the time I read it myself, much of it struck me as excessively academic in two currently fashionable modes, which is to say most of the contributions were either too theoretical, or not theoretical enough.

In the same year *Shantih*, a New York literary journal, asked me to edit a special issue on "New York Writing." Given my love for my hometown, that was a sympathetic suggestion. Nonetheless, I proposed, instead, devoting this book to something more specific and less familiar: The Literature of SoHo, which is to say that creative writing, done mostly in my immediate neighborhood, that differs from work done elsewhere in reflecting advanced ideas in painting, music, and the nonliterary arts—a literature of minimalism, intermedia, patterning, and radically alternative structuring. With contributions from John Cage, Rosemarie Castoro, Vito Acconci, Spalding Gray, and Richard Foreman, among others, it appeared in 1982.

My most recent anthology, *The Avant-Garde Tradition in Literature* (1982), echoes the very first in certain respects, being a collection of literary criticism; but this one is more reflective of my current interests, as well as my taste-making bias. It collects critical histories of the most experimental developments in modernist literature, such as Vladimir Markov on the Russian Futurists, Rosmarie Waldrop on concrete poetry, Michael Kirby on the new theater, and the concluding chapter of Moholy-Nagy's awesome *Vision in Motion*, along with theoretical essays by both estheticians and practitioners: Guillaume Apollinaire's "The New Spirit and the Poets," Northrop Frye's "The Archetypes of Literature," "The Pilot Plan for Concrete Poetry" by the de Campos brothers and Decio Pignatari, and so on. In addition to being a radical alternative to several available anthologies of criticism of modernist literature, this also attempts to establish, again by several hands what has not yet been done by one, what many of us consider to be the most viable current literary traditions—an extreme experimental tradition that, as we see it, survives to this day. In putting together what would not otherwise exist, as well as in other aspects, *The Avant-Garde Tradition in Literature* relates to the preceding anthologies in a continuing enterprise whose parts are elaborately interlocking. When the hardbound edition was remaindered, all these copies were purchased by RK Editions.

IV

Whoever is able to write a book and does not, it is as if he has lost a child.

—Nachman of Bratslav

Since I have done so many anthologies by now, the reader might get the false impression that publishers are begging for my proposals; quite the contrary is true. The problem is, simply, that most of my anthologies have no precedent; they are not imitations of commercially successful formulas. Nor are they designed to fit snugly into the reading lists of popular college courses. Many of them have taken several years to get into print. *Scenarios,* for instance, was first conceived in 1973, when I hit upon both the concept and the title. At the time I established a manila file in which I put either copies of works that I thought ought to be included or notes about where to find such works in my library. From time to time I proposed *Scenarios* to publishers both large and small, without any success. In 1978, Assembling Press applied for a grant to publish it, and applied again in 1979, when we were successful. The book appeared in 1980. The theme of *Esthetics Contemporary,* for another example, occurred to me in 1970, when the first outline was prepared; but not until 1976 did Prometheus Books commission it and not until 1978 did it appear. Similarly again, *The Avant-Garde Tradition in Literature* was first conceived in 1975, but not until 1981 did the same publisher contract it.

Among the anthologies I have been proposing for the past few years is a collection of critical essays on Gertrude Stein. Here I would emphasize analyses of the more experimental works, such as those favored in *The Yale Gertrude Stein;* for it is my argument, to repeat, that if you take these seriously, as I do, then Stein becomes "The Great American Person of Avant- Garde Letters." Indeed, that epithet was the title of an anthology of the more experimental Stein, selected from Stein books other than the Yale eight, that a small commercial publisher asked me to do; but it reneged on that contract. Once the *Yale Stein* has appeared, finding a publisher for this other collection, with its different introduction, becomes more problematic. That same publisher also asked me to do an anthology of previously uncollected Jack Kerouac, including his experimental masterpiece, *Old Angel Midnight;* and the manuscript for this anthology was even typeset. However, the trouble here was that the author's widow, Stella Kerouac, decided not to sign the contract that her agent had prepared for her.

From time to time I imagine that I should like to do one-person anthologies—"portables," as they are called, in one prominent line—of my very favorite authors, especially if such a collection could radically reinterpret their work, or give readers a different, fresh sense of their individual achievement. In addition to Stein and Kerouac, of course, I would like to do this for E. E. Cummings, whose more experimental writings are so rarely included in anthologies (which favor, instead, his cute lyrics); and my selections would include his *Eimi*, a spectacular prose work that has long been out of print. It might likewise be valuable to collect the most accessible Kenneth Burke into a single volume and give the selections a crystalline introduction.

Certain earlier anthologies suggest sequels that have never happened. While completing *Possibilities of Poetry*, I noticed the absence of any collections of major recent American longer poems—poems greater than, say, ten pages, but less than a book in length—even though many important native poets were working in extended forms. David Wright's anthology, *Longer Contemporary Poems* (1966), contains only poetry from the British Isles; and another way that I hoped to distinguish my proposed anthology from Wright's was by giving it a more substantial introduction, if not an extended critical essay on the post-Eliot longer poem. My theme would again be alternatives to Eliot; my title for this anthology would be "Possibilities of Longer Poetry." Among the pieces I planned to include are John Ashbery's "Europe," which I still regard as his very best poem; Allen Ginsberg's "Kaddish," which is also his very best; Jack Kerouac's "The Sea," which is his best; Kenneth Rexroth's "The Heart's Garden, the Garden's Heart," his best; and Jerome Rothenberg's "The Cokboy," ditto. From time to time publishers express interest in this proposal; as recently as

1979, one spent a full year purportedly thinking about it. I mentioned before my assumption that everything I want to do will eventually happen; and even though this proposal has been traveling for over a dozen years now, I read, think, and take notes as though it will occur.

Since the beginning of the 1970s, I have from time to time proposed an anthology of avant-garde poetry that would be comparable to those I had already done on fiction, essays, and theatrical scripts. I expected it to get contracted long ago, especially since I promised that it could do for poetry now what Donald Allen's 1960 anthology, *New American Poets*, did for the 1960s and 1970s. Since Allen's anthology had at last count gone through nearly twenty printings, I confidently calculated that my own might do at least half as well. However, no publisher has ever believed me about this, and so this book does not exist either, its potential cultural impact lost. By now the kinds of poetry I would have included—visual poetry, sound poetry, language-centered poetry, minimal poetry, etc.—have become more familiar, at least in sophisticated circles. Since such an anthology would have lost its cutting edge by the 1980s, perhaps it would be better now to present fuller selections of the very best new poets. My current scheme involves having eight poets with forty-eight pages apiece—eight retrospectives the length of a normal poetry collection—all within a single volume whose tentative title would be "Eight for the Eighties."

In 1981 I returned from several months in Germany—my first extended trip abroad in sixteen years—with a new interest in radio drama: not the conventional radio plays with their emphatic voices and sound effects but something else. The German term *Neue Hörspiel* refers to ear-plays that neither adapt live theater nor create the illusion of it but, instead, exploit the unique possibilities of radio (audio) to create something that can exist only in sound. The pioneering anthology of such texts is Klaus Schöning's *Neues Hörspiel* (1969). It includes Max Bense and Ludwig Harig's *Der Monolog der Terry Jo,* which presents only the thoughts within the mind of a hospitalized woman whose recovery of consciousness is portrayed in her progressing from nonsensical oral sounds to articulate speech; and Ernst Jandl and Friederike Mayrocker's *Funf Mann Menschen,* which compresses fourteen stages of a man's life into fourteen vignettes, each dominated by a characteristic spoken sound. Once I saw that no Americans were included in Schöning's book, I realized that someone ought to do a book of comparably advanced American radio texts and then that that someone would, alas, be me. It would incidentally be the first book of American radio plays in nearly four decades. The purposes of this project have been announced; submissions have come in. As I write, the project needs only sufficient support to get into production.

In the course of writing my experimental *Autobiographies,* I became interested in the question of alternative forms of self-history; and since most of those departures that I liked are American in authorship (and since I am at heart culturally a patriot), it seemed appropriate to propose a collection that would include Buckminster Fuller's "Chronofile," James Agee's "Plans for Work 1937," and Robert Lowell's "92 Revere Street." My suspicion now is that this project needs further research to discover more examples and that this next stage will not happen until the project is contractually commissioned.

Most of my proposals, like most of my anthologies, chart virgin territory. From time to time I also get ideas for radically reinterpreting a familiar subject. Even if Jerome Rothenberg is usually a good anthologist (and along with Eric Bentley, the only other American I call *peer*), he did one collection that strikes me as deficient—*America, a Prophecy* (1973). It is not as tightly structured as his other anthologies, in part because of an unfortunate editorial collaboration; and his notion of prophecy as the center of American poetry is, in my judgment, all wrong. Reading his book closely led me to posit a radical alternative: The American tradition in poetry, as in music and in painting, is one of formal inventions in the machinery of the art—a tradition of doing technically what has not been done before, either in Europe or here. Therefore, my anthology, to be titled "The American Tradition in Poetry," would include the more inventive poems of John Wilson, John Fiske, Edgar Allen Poe, Walt Whitman, Gertrude Stein, Vachel Lindsay, E. E. Cummings, Langston Hughes, Eugene Jolas, Melvin Tolson, Bob Brown, Charles Olson, Jack Kerouac, John Ashbery, John Cage, Jackson Mac Low, as well as those contemporaries extending this indigenous tradition. Since the subject and authors here are already so familiar, my aim would be to publish a succession of selections that would, like innovative art itself, surprise as it persuades. Even though my proposal for this is a few years old by now, while my thinking about it is nearly a decade old, I expect that, as long as I do not forget about it, this anthology too will eventually appear.

Among other anthologies I would like to do would be an appropriate sequel to *Text-Sound Texts,* which should be a "Text-Sound Tapes," that would, on either a pair of cassettes or a pair of long-playing records, collect the best text-sound art ever done in America; for it is my working belief, here and elsewhere, that it is only by the very best work that any new art should be judged and that, by extension, unless the best of the new is gathered together in a single place, the entire development can easily become lost from public view. My most detailed proposal for this "Text-Sound Tapes" appeared at the end of my contribution to *Aural Literature Criticism;* I have done shorter versions of the project within radio features prepared for Australian and German radio.

At any time in the past decade, an adventurous publisher could have asked me to do a selection of advanced creative writings, and the title I had in mind, along with a file of possible selections, is "New Writing Now." Unfortunately, no one asked; or perhaps I should be grateful for little favors—I already had enough else to do. Someday I would also like to put together an anthology of my own work, "A Richard Kostelanetz Reader," so to speak, not only because the subject has long been familiar to me, but because I have had a lot of experience doing such selections. My suspicion is that the contract for this, tentatively titled "All Along the Edge," will come from a European publisher before it comes from an American one.

From time to time I have heard others warn me against making public my plans for books, on the grounds that someone might pilfer them. However, my ideas for anthologies, as well as art, are usually too idiosyncratic for anyone else to want them, and mostly too noncommercial as well, which is to say that in economic terms they simply are not worth stealing. It is also true that if someone else produced a persuasive selection of, say, avant-garde American poetries today, there would be one less task for me, and that would be good, as I tend to have much too much work to do. As far as I am concerned, it is better that this child be borne by someone else (and better as well if borne by someone else than not be borne at all). Besides, by this point in time, doing or not doing another anthology will scarcely add or subtract from my reputation (or achievement) as an anthologist. Since another book no longer matters, either to others or to me (even if I wished that it might), I am now essentially free to do, or not do, what I want. All this explains why there have been no new anthologies from me in the past four years and yet why there may still be more, as well as a library exhibition with a catalog based on this essay.

There are certain variations on the *Assemblings* that I wanted to generate. One, "American Writing in 198X," would be a fifteen hundred-page book for which I would request one page, camera-ready, from every familiar American literary writer, however they wished to represent themselves within a single page in an alphabetical inventory of literature in

America today. Between a single set of covers, I figured, we could represent the totality of what is really happening in American writing today. Three times this was proposed to the NEA, and three times it was rejected. Three times Assembling Press proposed as well, to both NYSCA and the NEA, to do a comparable project for American photography—one black-white photograph apiece from four hundred American photographers; and six times we wasted our effort. At least once we made a similar proposal to represent "American Art in 198X." The quality of our effort and intention notwithstanding, we were never able to advance our principle to a higher, more comprehensive, more generously serving form; what remains in my mind as conceptually the best "Assembling"—certainly the most complete "Assembling"—never appeared.

In 1982, *Assembling* received a grant to devote our eleventh number to *Proposals*. Scores of artists and writers were asked the following question: "If you could apply for a grant of $500,000, what precisely would you propose to do?" Their one-page camera-ready replies were published in alphabetical order, making a marvelous collection of fantasies, cultural jokes, and feasible projects, all adding to our sense of what might be possible in contemporary art.

And that, in a fundamental sense, is perhaps what my anthologies in sum are all about: What is possible in contemporary art and thought.

Teaching and the
"Nonstandard" Writer (1990)

People talk about criminals being the results of their environment,
but they seldom speak about artists being victims of *their*
environment, though in fact they are.
　　　　　　　—Philip Glass, *Music by Philip Glass* (1987)

UNIVERSITY TEACHING IS, for better as well as
worse, what most American literary writers do for a
living nowadays, and this fact makes our literary culture, as
well as the preconditions of our literary production, different
from everywhere else in the world (to a degree that few dare
discuss). Teaching can provide a good living if you can get a
professorship and tenure, but only a marginal living if you
cannot. Determined from the beginning to be a full-time
writer (in part because such professional heroes as Edmund
Wilson and Ezra Pound were), I've almost entirely avoided
teaching; but after living marginally for over two decades now,
I have a need to consider it.

People who have regular paychecks tell me that they are
very much worth having; I wouldn't know. When the twenty-
fifth reunion committee of my college class asked for a superla-
tive that would characterize my life, I replied, "longest unem-
ployed—24⅔rds years." One truth I do know was articulated
by Delmore Schwartz, in a 1954 letter to Karl Shapiro: "The
trouble with everything but teaching is that one spends so
much time thinking of making money . . . that one is more
distracted than ever." By this time my principal administrative/
financial skill is running a low-budget business that is me,
which is to say that I'm the boss who also sweeps the place.

Though there is, thankfully, neither a family nor a car to support, I do waste too much time thinking about making money.

Having learned to live on little income, I find myself envying less the money than certain perks that most academics take for granted—comprehensive health insurance, long-distance telephoning, free photocopying and typing, factotums who collect mail and messages during personal absences, travel reimbursements, the power to dispense beneficence to people (especially fellow academics) who would then be predisposed to grant favors in return, and a circumscribed hierarchy of bosses. Academics have no idea of what it is like to work for a large number of benefactors, most of whom would like you to believe that your relationship with them can affect your career and livelihood (over two dozen for me last year, none of them providing more than 10 percent of my income)—there is a level of vulnerability and struggle that, if mastered, can make other kinds of survival, and negotiation, child's play.

Remembering Milton Friedman's dictum about the nonexistence of a free lunch, I'm sure that a teaching position extracts a price, not only in time available for one's own work but in less obvious effects. I know well the psychological costs of independence, having lived that life. As you confront the world with much less money than people of similar age and education, you are likely to avoid social situations that you cannot afford; you dress badly, not only because you cannot afford to dress well but because you don't want anyone to think you can.

More seriously, you meet the world without any tag attached to your name, which means people whose own professional lives depend upon titles are likely to think you suspect, if they acknowledge you at all. (I'm reluctant to write references for academic positions, because I sense that on university hiring committees only the letterhead is read; I have none.) Worse, if people don't know what you've done from your name alone, you sometimes have reason to remind them, meanwhile falling into the uncomfortable posture of unnecessary boastfulness. (As Kenneth Rexroth and Robert Duncan, for two examples, were unable to identify themselves as professors of English, both wasted a lot of energy and no doubt time demonstrating that they knew as much literature as any professor of English.)

As you get paid mostly in small checks, you work like a cab driver, always looking for ways to pick up an extra nickel or dime. You waste a lot of energy and attention trying to find an edge in your dealings with paying customers or, simply, another fare, which is to say an opportunity that did not exist before. Grub Street means grubbing, often to the embarrassment not only of one's better-heeled associates but to yourself. Whereas professors think like other salaried employees, independent writers and artists tend to think like small businessmen, petit bourgeois, which, you can't forget, is what in fact they are.

Since creative academics I know are reluctant to discuss what effects teaching might have upon their own psyches, I have made a few observations of my own. One peril endemic to academic artists, to be frank, is expecting that the respect they receive at home should necessarily be extended to the larger world; so that the more success that middling artists have on their own campuses, in terms of promotions and accompanying emoluments, the greater their frustrations and thus their alienation from a professional world outside the academy. That accounts for their tendency to let their cultural presence depend upon their position and their license-credentials, rather than knowledge or achievements. Second, since their salaries are guaranteed, academics get as hysterical about losing perks as independents do about being short-changed. Third, if you spend much of your life talking to people who don't know much, over whose fortunes you have some authority, you come to think you can get away with a lot of cultural garbage. At a recent professional conference dominated by academics, I heard ignorance and fakery that would be unacceptable among professionals who had to worry about the deleterious effects of seeming foolish. Reminded of George Orwell's dictum about only intellectuals believing certain nonsense, I thought that only tenured professors could think they could get away with so much intellectual flaccidity. Another indulgence available to academics is far more arrogance and nastiness in dealing with their professional colleagues, simply because, thanks to tenure, academia rivals the U.S. Post Office as the last refuges for the sorts of "difficult personality" that could not possibly survive unaffiliated. Independents and academics tend to regard each other as suspect, professors thinking the untitled are academically unqualified, independents thinking that academics are the second- raters who could not survive, either economically or psychologically, without such a job. (And neither is entirely wrong.)

Perhaps because the worlds are so different, it seems that few middle-aged independents make the transition into the academy without incurring serious loss that is reflected in their work. The examples most vividly in my mind are the filmmaker Stan VanDerBeek and the poet Galway Kinnell, both of whom did masterpieces before entering the academy and nothing remotely comparable afterwards. (Indeed, I've also noticed that, even if they can compensate for financial losses, few have gone from academia to independence without similar loss of quality. It would seem, in general, that once you commit yourself to one ship or the other, it would be wise not to jump.)

Another reason for my reluctance to teach writing is that my own recollection of creative writing courses is not favorable. At the Ivy League college I attended, one guy taught only what he did, with reference only to select enthusiasms for work similar to his own, scarcely caring about other kinds of writing; a colleague of his seemed to take pride in being pompously unhelpful. In a memoir recently published, the latter speaks proudly of other writers he invited to teach at this university, but makes no mention of any students, past or present—none at all (raising the question of who is paying whom for what). My suspicion, now that I've been around longer, is that these two professors regarded the literary world as a highly competitive place, which indeed it is, and thus it would be "smart" for them not to prepare anyone to advance in the competition. That perhaps accounts for why of the dozen or so college contemporaries of mine who became visible writers, none, as far as I can tell, majored in creative writing! (Maybe the failure to produce professionals was scarcely limited to the writing program, as only one of the alumni who are now visual artists majored in art, while the famous composer, Wendy [né Walter] Carlos, majored in physics!)

I had the good fortune of having another writing teacher, S. Foster Damon, a poet better known for his pioneering scholarship on William Blake. In regular dinners, in addition to courses, Damon taught me, simply, not "how to write" (or how he wrote) but how to be a writer, which is to say how to do one's own work. Thanks to my contact with him, I've always thought, works of mine began to appear in print soon after my graduation from college.

II

Universities in a democracy must remain universities, and that means academic freedom, the unrestricted pursuit of undiscovered truth, and not the repeating of the truths that the different pressure groups in society think they already have. All pressure groups in society are anti-educational, no matter what they are pressing for.
—Northrop Frye, "The Writer and the University" (1957)

My hesitancy over university teaching also comes from the sense that, in the recent explosion of the creative writing biz, I don't fit. I don't have an M.F.A., which seems to be required now, and I didn't arrive in academia early enough to get tenure in a department that could then "lend" me to a creative writing program. Whereas most writing programs nowadays are divided into poetry and fiction (and would prefer that people hired by them be distinguished in only one or the other), I have published poetry, fiction, and experimental prose, in addition to criticism and journalism, and then done visual art, music, and holography that has won some recognition. Also even the poetry and fiction I do is so different from common M.F.A. produce that, to my count, nobody committed to doing similarly innovative work teaches writing in American universities—no one.

My own reason for not teaching poetry writing or fiction writing is based upon a professional rule I've evolved over the years as an independent writer: Never do anything, even the smallest thing, that someone else could do better. This rule was designed to keep me honest, as insurance against receiving any spoils or privilege that might cause inferior work; it also deflects resentment over unwarranted rewards. Not only could many others teach just poetry and just fiction better than I, but one sure way not to write like everyone else is not to teach what others teach. Since that first principle is important to me, I would rather not have cause to compromise it. So the two times I have been asked to teach, initially for a week-long conference at Indiana University in July 1976 and then for a semester at the University of Texas at Austin (accounting for that aberrant one-third year), I agreed only on the condition that my course be called "Experimental Writing."

At Indiana, that title appeared in a program that otherwise included the standard fare of fiction, poetry, nonfiction, and drama. While the other workshops in the summer session were filled to the brim with twenty students each, mine had only seven customers, which meant that it did not pay for itself (and was not renewed). After a week of daily meetings with our classes, the faculty gathered to share experiences. All the other instructors commented, as I remember them, that none of their students did publishable work—absolutely none; my response was that three of mine would be publishing (and are still publishing, over a decade later). One of the other instructors replied, after shock passed from his face, "With a course title like yours, Richard, you're going to get only the best students." I should add that many years later I was once approached about heading a similar summer conference at a school customarily regarded as "progressive." The key question in the preliminary telephone discussion was which celebrities I could get to visit the conference cheap. I withdrew, not wishing to exploit my friends in that way. The only business I ever want to run is my own, thanks; university teaching should be about something else.

At the University of Texas, my sponsor was not the Department of English or Creative Writing but "American Studies." As we had seventeen weeks, I opened the course by showing my own work, as well as my more adventurous anthologies, partly to introduce my esthetics to an unfamiliar audience. The requirement for the course, I told them, was to produce something "radically unlike anything any of us has ever seen before, with some reference to literature." At the time I remember seeing dejected expressions, as a few students realized that they could not submit manuscripts already in progress. I added, "I'm not sure I can evaluate the quality of what you do, but I can judge effort." (Actually, I wanted them to evaluate one another's performance at the end, as it was fairly obvious to everyone concerned how much effort each student had expended; but my chairman discouraged that.) What came from this provocative assignment was a variety of works, some of them in media other than typed pages. Two students in particular took off, writing fictions whose sentences did not relate to one another, each trying to outdo the other in approaching abstractness (and both of them have since published both fiction and criticism). At our last class, I said, "Whether or not you continue working as you have done here is your business, but I think all of you have done something you did not think you would or could do when you began this course. For that alone, it has been a success." Nonetheless, "experimental writing" has not been given again, at least by me.

III

He who can does. He who cannot, teaches.
—George Bernard Shaw, *Maxims for Revolutionists* (1903)

Now that I've reached mid-career, with greater visible recognition in the face of declining income, there is cause for me to think again about university teaching. Though I earned two decades ago an "advanced" degree in American history, I could not possibly teach it now (and would not want to, given my rule about not doing what others could do better). Like all independent writers, I've known what I've written about; but having already put it into print, I would be reluctant to repeat it aloud. (Conversely, when I was recently asked to revise my M.A. thesis for book publication I found myself unable to revise as much as I planned, because, unlike an academic, I have had no occasion to teach the material in the intervening twenty-five years.) I suppose I could base a course upon one or another work in progress, but am unsure about the value of that, or in what academic context it would fit. (One scholarly course I'd like to teach, if only as an experiment, would deal with my own work; but how could this be titled without causing offense?)

A few years ago I heard about a position that was conceptually attractive: running a criticism program in an arts college, if only because I could thus expand it to include imaginative writing that resembles contemporary art (rather than "poetry" and "fiction"), as well as writing directly for media such as video and holography and, finally, the Write of Arting, or expositions of one's purposes as an artist, all of which interest me. However, this criticism position was designed by the college's painting professors to reward a critic who had written about them, wishing to use local power for larger worldly ends (a sin stemming from the frustrations mentioned before). Once the favored critic was elected, the administration intervened, cancelling the position (that still doesn't exist at this college).

Recently encouraged to think again about teaching, this time at a small liberal arts college with a "progressive" reputation (and no current "creative writing" program to defend, thankfully), I proposed the following courses, not because they are already given, but because they aren't, at least not in any place known to me:

(1) A year-long workshop in the production of a book, which would include not only the writing (or equivalent production) of a book-length manuscript but the necessary follow-up of copyediting, design, and production, by any means available, of a camera-ready dummy. Since I believe that, once you think in terms of doing a book, certain problems are common, this course would be open to those wishing to produce book-length manuscripts of poetry as well as fiction, visual books (of photographs, say, or related drawings) as well as exposition. Participants would be required to make copies of works in progress available to one another for criticism and comment throughout the course of the year. (Now that I've produced some books myself, I wish I'd taken such a course as an undergraduate.)

(2) A year-long workshop in the production of major art projects, open to practitioners of all arts, where the requirement is simply the creation from scratch of major art work, representing the sum of all the student has learned, plus inten-

sive labor. The emphasis would be on learning how to think like a professional artist, rather than mastering the mechanics of a discipline. I believe that though the techniques of the various arts may differ, the production of it involves common problems and that working alongside people in arts other than your own has two advantages—an increase in general intelligence about art and a decrease in feelings of specific competition. As I had never regarded my activity as existing in a universe of limited success, there is space for others and opportunities to share.

(3) A one-semester workshop in experimental art, where the requirement is simply to create something radically unlike anything seen before, likewise open to aspirants in all arts. This course, whose theme is stretching the imagination, would best be given in the fall semester.

(4) A one-semester workshop in the writing of arts criticism, with an emphasis upon *writing* and thus open to critical aspirants in every art. (Once you know your art, I find, the problems of writing criticism of any length and focus are fairly similar.) This course, which would consist of exercises with various forms, would best be given in the spring.

(5) A one-semester seminar in the Write of Arting, open to practitioners of all arts, requiring self-definition through the writing of manifestos, program notes, autobiographical summaries, proposals, etc.

Even though this last university position may not come to me, the idea of it has given me the opportunity to imagine "nonstandard" writing courses that might be unique to me and perhaps valuable to others. If it is indeed offered to me, may I please, Lord God, have enough self-consciousness to avoid those predicaments that, from the outside, I have come to associate with other literary professors (and perhaps enough courage to record sometime in print how others will come to regard me differently once I have a tag after my name!).

Appendix A
Appendix B
Index

Appendix A
Catalog of Taped
Audio-Musical Works

At the present time, however, and throughout the world, not only most popular music but much so-called serious music is produced without recourse to notations. This is in large part the effect of a change from print to electronic technology.

—John Cage, flyleaf to *Notations* (1969)

THESE ARE AVAILABLE for broadcast or concert performance on reel-to-reel audiotapes, audiocassettes (with Dolby B or C, or DBX), or PCM or HiFi VHS cassettes, all stereo (unless otherwise noted). Though all are based upon texts, none are simple reproductions of live readings; indeed, none of the texts can be performed live as they are heard here. Where a visual component exists, it is described. As the works are published by Wordsand Music, ASCAP, which also issues annual Standard Awards to their composers, all public performances should be reported to ASCAP or its European affiliates.

Invocations (1981; revised, 1984) incorporates prayers spoken by over four dozen ministers, in over two dozen languages, into duets, quintets, choruses, and successive solos that are ultimately about the sound of the language of prayer. Recorded in West Berlin, this was mixed at the Electronic Music Studio of Stockholm and subsequently acknowledged in Thomas B. Holmes's *Electronic and Experimental Music* (1985) and the third edition of Eric Salzman's *Twentieth Century Music: An Introduction* (1988), among other books. There are six versions that are identical for fifty-eight minutes but have different openings that are between two and three minutes long: (1) Hebrew-Assyriac, (2) English, (3) Swedish-Danish-English, (4) Latin, (5) German, (6) Mediterranean languages. The first is available on Folkways (FRS 37092).

Americas' Game: Baseball (1988) is an extended composition of and about sounds unique to the most popular game in North and Central America, in two parts, respectively 29:40 and 29:55 in length.

New York City (1983–84) is three compositions of and about sounds particular to my hometown, initially commissioned by Westdeutscher Rundfunk for a series of programs about the world's great metropolises, which can be accompanied by thousands of slides of images likewise unique to New York, in either a concert or continuous installation—one composition initially 60:00 for international broadcast, another 87:00 that is probably the best, and a third version 140:00 primarily for American audiences.

The Gospels (1982) is a continuous fugue of the opening four books of the New Testament that are here heard, since they tell the same story, simultaneously—an exhausting piece that, in my considered opinion, is nonetheless filled with luminous passages, 120:00. *The Gospels Abridged* attempts to isolated choice passages from the longer work, 61:00. *Die Evangelien* (1982) is the same sort of fugue, but in German and also considerably abridged, 60:00.

Kaddish (1990) exposes the sound of the Jewish Diaspora through a wide variety of declamations of the Jewish prayer for the dead, mixed on a Lexicon Opus Digital Production system with Frank Cunningham, 23:22

Excelsior (1975) swiftly portrays a seduction in single-word paragraphs, spoken in stereo by two voices, which sound as though they may be the same voice, 1:20.

Plateaux (1975) has a solo voice reciting a text about a love affair to the background of a synthesizer that is steadily declining in pitch, 2:50.

Milestones in a Life (1976) tells, amidst changing reverberation, of seventy-seven years of a bourgeois life in terms of the single most important event (milestone) to happen in each year, 3:55.

This Is My Poem (1977) is a series in which the root four-word phrase of the title is subjected to several kinds of tape-delay, each of which accents different parts of the phrase. They too can be broadcast individually, in immediate succession, or between other works, 0:55, 0:54, 0:42, 2:10.

Declaration of Independence (1975) is based upon a text written for the American bicentennial, in which the familiar words of the historic American document are read backwards word by word, in this case by a chorus of male voices, each one trying to be in unison with the others, but ultimately failing. One version of this work, perhaps more suitable for popular radio broadcast, incorporates into the course of the piece three sets of explanatory voice-over remarks, 10:01.

Foreshortenings (1976) has eighty-four sentences that are rearranged in several systematic ways to suggest alternative stories. Here they are read in one version by the author in dialogues with a quartet of himself (26:00) and in another version by the author in a duet with John Morgan (23:00).

Seductions (1981) contains sixteen seduction stories told by sixteen different amplifications of the author's voice and interwoven one sentence at a time into a continuous, albeit spatial, narrative, 24:46.

Relationships (1983) is an extended recital of a man's recollections of why he slept with certain women, as well as his conjectures of why they slept with him, all elaborately processed electronically, and, in truth, not recommended for immature audiences, 31:10.

Conversations (1983) is a sequence of twenty-seven pieces, various in length, in which three German words—Jah, Nein, Doch—are exchanged in various, infinitely suggestive ways. This was composed on a Fairlight CMI during a residency at PASS in New York City, 0:32, 1:25, 0:24, 1:30, 0:15, 0:57, 0:21, 1:22, 5:49, 0:18, 0:40, 1:06, 5:00, 1:46, 1:55, 0:27, 1:35, 2:13, 0:24, 2:15, 0:46, 0:17, 0:42, 0:17, 4:29, 2:51, 0:52. Like other multi-part sets of mine, these pieces may be played individually, in continuous sequence, or interspersed between other pieces.

Dialogues (1975) are skeletal, implicitly erotic conversations between two voices—one male, the other female—speaking only two words, "yes" and "no," 0:35, 0:30, 0:35. A later version was done in German (1983), with the addition of a third word ("doch" for *sure*), all processed on a Fairlight CMI (Computer Music Instrument), 0:40, 0:30, 0:18, 0:12, 0:09, 0:07, 0:045, 0:03, 1:00, 2:00, 3:00, 0:03. Individual sections of both versions may be played/broadcast individually, in immediate succession, or apart from each other, say, between other pieces in the course of a concert/program.

Richard Kostelanetz Mantra (1977) sounds as though I am repeating the trochaic rhythms of my name without taking a breath, as its volume runs down into silence. It is the most appropriate coda to any concert of my work, 1:40.

What's in a Name (1983) explores, in six movements, the trochaic rhythms of my name with various superhuman enhancements (mostly from a Fairlight CMI), 7:25.

Resumé (1986), with me reading about me, with linear disintegration and variable disintegration, both processed by Skip Brunner at the Conservatory of Music, Brooklyn College, each 37:20.

Turfs/Arenas/Pitches/Fields (1980) are four-word poems—one hundred in English, eleven in French—spoken in unison by a chorus of four, processed in various ways at EMS, 21:26. *Grounds, etc.* is a sequel with sets of eight related words spoken in unison by a chorus of eight, 10:28.

Carnival of the Animals/Karneval der Tiere (1988), a poem of animal names, produced with a sampler and synthesizer, read by the author in English, and in acoustic German translations by Tilman Reitzle, each 14:03.

Onomatopoeia (1988), produced with similar equipment, in two versions, one heavily processed, the other not, both read by the author, each 10:42.

The Drunken Boat/Le Bateau Ivre (1986), a binaural reading, with the French original on one side and English translations on the other, one by Jonathan Cott read by Janet Cannon (and processed by Skip Brunner), the other by Charles Doria, each, 5:38

Praying to the Lord (1977, 1981) has two sacred texts, the Lord's Prayer in English and a comparable Hebrew prayer, which are successively and progressively multiplied into fugues of eight voices, 64 voices, and 512 voices, 5:40.

The Eight Nights of Hanukah (1983) is the familiar prayer for lighting the candles, here read by two dozen laymen of diverse ages speaking Hebrew with a variety of accents, in various styles, mixed with one another into eight separate fugues of successively increasing numbers of voices, 5:20.

Asdescent/Anacatabasis (1978) are electronically processed readings of two related pieces that draw upon the texts of my reworkings of sentences from the 1 Cor. 13. Each is 23:00, mono, and, in truth, more difficult as a listening experience than other works.

Epiphanies (1982–) is a large number of single-sentence stories that are given individual settings. About 180 minutes have been finished, as of this writing; the work is meant to be at least 240 minutes. German translations of selected stories, with sixteen readers, are available in two sets of mono tapes, one with two sections, the other with six sections: 26:15 and 27:00; 9:30, 9:07, 9:25, 8:53, 8:30, and 10:31. Chinese translations, with six readers, both native Chinese and Americans, 6:00.

Audio Writing (1984) is a 92-minute sampler of excerpts from many pre-1985 works, with my accompanying narration.

Appendix B
Catalog of Taped
Audio-Video Works

One may nowadays repeat music not only by means of printed notes but by means of sound recordings, disc or tape. One may also compose new music by these same recording means, and by other means: the activation of electric and electronic sound-systems, the programming of computer output of actual sounds, etc.

—John Cage, flyleaf, *Notations* (1969)

THESE ARE AVAILABLE for broadcast or exhibition on NTSC 3/4-inch U-Matic or NTSC VHS 1/2-inch videotape cassettes. All are in color, unless otherwise noted. All public performances should be reported to ASCAP (with Wordsand Music as the audio publisher) or its European affiliates. A single asterisk identifies tapes that have a hi-fi stereo sound track; those with a double asterisk would benefit from large-screen projection TV; those with a triple asterisk are also available in the historic 1/2-inch reel-to-reel. The works fall into distinct groups:

1. Tapes whose screen content is exclusively linguistic:

Kinetic Writings (1989, 22:00) consists of mute language realizations, of both poems and fictions, that exploit capabilities unique to video.

Video Strings (*, 1989, 29:42) offers seemingly endless streams of overlapping words, enhanced in different ways, with one example in German.

Stringsieben (1989, 12:00) has a different, more spectacular continuous realization of the complete, similarly overlapping German text.

Turfs/Grounds/Lawns (*, 1989, 23:00) has successions of four-word poems, eight-word poems, and sixteen-word poems appearing on screen, the first two groups sometimes accompanied by aural realizations of the same texts.

Partitions (1986, 27:40) offers long words in which shorter words are embedded, in increasingly complex configurations.

"Video Poems," "Video Fictions," in progress, each to be sixty minutes long.

2. Video fantasias to audio tracks produced at sophisticated electronic music studios:

Invocations (**, 1988, 61:00), of and about the sound of the language of prayer. [This is available with six different openings: (1) English, (2) Latin, (3) German, (4) Hebrew-Assyriac, (5) Italian-Yugoslav-Greek, (6) Swedish-Danish.]

The Gospels (**, 1989, 120:00) has parts of the four opening books of the New Testament heard as a continuous fugue. *The Gospels Abridged* (**, 1988, 61:00) has continuous imagery accompanying an acoustic abridgement. *Die Evangelien* (**, 1989, 60:00) is visually similar, now to a preabridged text.

Seductions (**, 1988, 25:30) has sixteen complimentary stories, interwoven one sentence at a time, all spoken by RK, his voice amplified in various ways. *Relationships* (**, 1988, 31:45) is an elaborate intimate memoir.

Two Erotic Videotapes (**, 1988, 56:10) offers different video syntheses of the two preceding audiotapes.

Two Sacred Texts (**, 1988, 12:00) has differing video accompaniments to two audiotapes: *Praying to the Lord* and *The Eight Nights of Hanukah*. Eight different realizations to the former alone (*) are also available towards an eight-monitor installation.

3. Recent departures:

Home Movies Reconsidered: My First Twenty-Seven Years (1987, 46:00) is an edited critical interpretaton of eight-millimeter family film taken between 1937 and 1967. (Presently silent, it functions best as the basis of a live performance.)

Americas' Game (1988, 60:00) shows a well-illuminated baseball to accompany a busy soundtrack of and about sounds, including language, unique to baseball; it differs from the other videotapes in having imagery shot through a video camera.

4. Early works, mostly audio-video settings to texts that preceded involvement with video:

Three Prose Pieces (***, 1975, 20:00) has imagery indigenous to video, as produced during a residency at Synapse, Syracuse University: (1) *Excelsior* (1975, 1:05) switches rapidly between two voices and two shapes seducing each other, the spoken words eroticizing the abstract imagery. (2) *Plateaux* (1975, 3:55) relates the stages of a love affair in one-word paragraphs, the screen showing an evolving moiré pattern whose languid circularity complements the circularity of the verbal narrative. (3) *Recyclings* (1975, 14:05) is an incremental sequence of nonsyntactic prose texts (drawn from a 1974 RK book of that title, reissued in 1984) that are read by several nonsynchronous, identical voices (all RK's). The image consists only of pairs of lips (likewise RK's), moving synchronously with audible speech, the differences in hue indicating the age of the image. The first section has one voice and one pair of lips; the last (and sixth) section has six voices and six pairs of lips, each generation of lips-voices reading the same nonsyntactic text nonsynchronously.

Openings & Closings (***, 1975, 56:10), also produced during the Synapse residency, draws upon a book of that title, published in the same year, in which single-sentence stories are alternately the openings and the closings of hypothetical longer fictions. The author is seated in a chair reading the openings in color and the closings in black-white, with each new image as different as can be from the one(s) before, ideally realizing visually the leaps in time and space that characterize the book's text.

Literary Video (1977) has four bits of alternative literary recital: (1) A bearded mouth reading the title piece, a 1976 manifesto about video as a propitious medium for literary ideas (b/w, 5:45). (2) *Milestones in a Life* (1977) with dark male eyes that hardly blink, while the sound track broadcasts a story about a bourgeois life that is told exclusively in terms of numbers followed by single-word paragraphs (b/w, 4:10).

(3) *Dialogues* (1977) with three dramatically different exchanges of the words Yes and No, in which only a hirsute Adam's apple is visible (b/w, 0:30, 0:35, 0:40). (4) *Plateaux* (1977) with only the side of a face that is reciting a story whose single-word paragraphs relate the evolution of an affair (b/w, 3:32).

Declaration of Independence (1979, 9:20) has four pairs of superimposed bearded lips, each visibly different in size, reading RK's contemporary "Declaration of Independence," roughly simultaneously, from beginning to end. From time to time an explanatory gloss, in capital letters larger than those of televised movie subtitles, crawls along the bottom of the screen.

Epiphanies (1980, 31:00, b/w) has single-sentence stories, produced entirely on a character-generator, that are the epiphanies, which is to say resonant moments that illuminate the entire (but here nonexistent) story.

Early Literary Videotapes is a single 120:00 NTSC VHS with copies of *Literary Video, Three Prose Pieces, Openings & Closings, Declaration of Independence* and *Epiphanies*.

Video Writing (1987, 53:40) is an informal retrospective about this early work and the environment behind its production, narrated by RK and directed by Robert Boynton Weyr.

Also available are videotape copies of RK works originally produced in other media:

Epiphanies (1980, 44:20) documents the initial performance of the theatrical version of the single-sentence texts mentioned before, now directed by Suzanne Bennett with four readers at the University of North Dakota, March, 1980.

Epiphanies (1981, 48:45) documents a different performance, this with several readers declaiming perhaps three times as many stories, directed by E. St. John Villard at Vassar College, October, 1981.

Epiphanies (1982, 29:35) copies a film whose visual track contains clips of various lengths that have this same epiphany quality. On the sound track are voices reading stories that, typically, have no connection, other than similar form, to the visual track.

Epiphanies (1983, 19:50) copies a film that no longer exists, broadcast over German television, with a wholly German sound track and sections different from those in the English film noted above. Broadcast rights for German-language television must be obtained from SFB.

Five Versions of Epiphanies (1988, 32:00) has excerpts from the four previous tapes, as well as the video version, mentioned before, for character-generator.

Ein Verlorenes Berlin (1983, 21:00) copies an imaginative film documentary about Berlin's great Jewish cemetery as the principal surviving relic of "A Lost Berlin." The visual track has current scenes from the cemetery; the sound track has the voices of Berliners remembering, in German, the cemetery and its relation to the Berlin they knew. *A Berlin Lost* (1985), which won a prize at the Ann Arbor Film Festival (and later toured with it), has the same footage, to the same length, now with ex-Berliners speaking English with different testimony. *Ett Forlorat Berlin* (1984) has a sound track of Swedish-speaking Berliners with yet other testimony. *Berlin Perdu* (1986) is the same footage with a fresh French sound track. *El Berlin Perdido* (1987) is Spanish; *Berlin Sche-Einera Jother* (1988) is Hebrew. Various combinations of two Berlin films on 3/4-inch tape, or even more films on 1/2-inch VHS tape, can be made for appropriate reasons.

Constructivist Fictions/Openings & Closings (1984) copies two early b/w films of texts of RK books with the same titles.

Index

Acconci, Vito, 237
Agee, James, 242
Allen, Donald, 217, 241
Allen, Steve, 50
Allen, Woody, 9
Amachai, Yehuda, 45
American Academy and
  National Institute of Arts and
  Letters, 53, 59
American Poetry Archive, 44
American text-sound art, 24
Amirkhanian, Charles, 19, 20,
  23, 24, 25, 29, 148
Ammons, A, R., 145
Anderson, Beth, 19, 20
Antin, David, 146
Antonelli, John: *Kerouac*, 50
Apollinaire, Guillaume, 125,
  181, 238
Arias-Misson, Alain, 146
Arrowsmith, William 104
Artforum, 15
Ashbery, John, 10, 45, 145,
  216, 240, 243
Ashley, Robert, 20
Assembling Press, 233, 235,
  239, 245

Atlas, James, 147
Auden, W. H., 65, 156, 225
Audio artists, 181

Babbitt, Milton, 6, 32–37, 104;
  Philomel, 32, 34; *Phonemena*,
  32, 35; *Vision and Prayer*, 32
Bach, J. S., 164, 189
Baldwin, James, 145
Baraka, Amiri, 46
Barnes, Djuna, 54, 226
Barth, John, 143, 214, 222
Barthelme, Donald, 143, 223
Barthes, Roland, 51, 211
Bate, Walter Jackson, 95
Batterham, Elizabeth (Libbie),
  55, 58
Batterham, Lily, 55
Beardslee, Bethany, 33
Bellow, Saul, 144, 223, 236
Bely, Andrei: *Kotik Lateav*, 128;
  St. Petersburg, 128
Bense, Max, 242
Bentley, Eric, 134, 147, 242
Berg, Stephen, 138–41, 147;
  Singular Voices, 138, 140
Berlin, Isaiah, 157

269

RICHARD KOSTELANETZ is commonly ranked among America's most distinguished independent artists/intellectuals. Born in New York, New York, in 1940, he took his A.B. with honors in American civilization from Brown University in 1962 and his M.A. in American history from Columbia University in 1966. For this graduate work he received Woodrow Wilson, New York State Regents, and International fellowships. In 1964–65, he was a Fulbright Scholar at King's College, University of London. He has since published numerous books of poetry, fiction, criticism, and cultural history, in addition to editing more than two dozen anthologies of literature, art, and criticism. His poems, stories, and essays have appeared in countless periodicals, both large and small, here and abroad, and he has been a guest lecturer all over the United States. His language-based visual art, audiotapes, videotapes, films, and holograms have been exhibited and broadcast around the world. For his independent work he has received personal grants from the Guggenheim Foundation, the National Endowment for the Arts, the American Public Radio Program Fund, the Fund for Investigative Journalism, the Ludwig Vogelstein Foundation, the Coordinating Council of Literary Magazines, ASCAP, and the DAAD Berliner Kunstlerprogramm. Among his current criticism projects are books about the art of radio in North America, "An ABC of Contemporary Reading," "The Maturity of American Thought, 1945–67," and "Unfinished Business," which collects his unfunded proposals—what he calls "my intellectual nonhistory." He continues to live unaffiliated, as well as unclassifiable, in New York.